GRAY DAWN

Also by Peter G. Peterson

Will America Grow Up Before It Grows Old?

Facing Up

On Borrowed Time

PETER G. PETERSON

GRAY DAWN

How the Coming Age Wave Will Transform America— and the World

There's an iceberg dead ahead. It's called global aging, and it threatens to bankrupt the great powers. As the populations of the world's leading economies age and shrink, we will face unprecedented political, economic, and moral challenges. But we are woefully unprepared. Now is the time to ring the alarm bell . . .

TIMES BOOKS

RANDOM HOUSE

Peterson, Peter G.
　Gray dawn: How the coming age wave will transform
　　America—and the world / Peter G. Peterson.—1st ed.
　　　p.　　cm.
　ISBN 0-8129-3195-5
　　1. Aging—Government policy.　2. Aging—Economic aspects.
　3. Aging—Social aspects.　4. Age distribution (Demography)
　5. Economic policy.　6. Social policy.　I. Title.
　HQ1061.P388　1999
　305.26—dc21　　　　　　　　　　　　　　　　98-47749

Random House website address: www.atrandom.com
Printed in the United States of America on acid-free paper

9876543

SPECIAL SALES

Times Books are available at special discounts for bulk purchases for sales promotions or premiums. Special editions, including personalized covers, excerpts of existing books, and corporate imprints, can be created in large quantities for special needs. For more information, write to Special Markets, Times Books, 201 East 50th Street, New York, New York 10022, or call 800-800-3246.

For my five grandchildren,
Alexandra, Peter Cary, Steven, Chloe, and Jack

Contents

GRAY DAWN

1

Gray Dawn

"By the way, Sam, as someday you'll be paying for my entitlements, I'd like to thank you in advance."

THE CHALLENGE OF GLOBAL AGING, LIKE A MASSIVE ICEBERG, looms ahead in the future of the largest and most affluent economies of the world. Visible above the waterline are the unprecedented growth in the number of elderly and the unprecedented decline in the number of youth over the next several decades. Lurking beneath the waves, and not yet widely understood, are the wrenching economic and social costs that will accompany this demographic transformation—costs that threaten to bankrupt even the greatest of powers, the United States included, unless they take action in time. Those who are most aware of the implications of this extraordinary demographic shift will best be able to prepare themselves for it, and even profit from the many opportunities it will leave in its wake.

The list of great hazards in the next century is long and generally familiar. It includes proliferation of nuclear, chemical, and biological weapons; high-tech terrorism; deadly superviruses; extreme climate change; the financial, economic, and political aftershocks of globalization; and the ethnic and military explosions waiting to be detonated by today's unsteady new democracies. Yet there is a less-understood challenge—the graying of the developed world's population—that may actually do more to reshape our collective future than any of the above.

This demographic shift cannot be avoided. It is inevitable. The timing and magnitude of the coming transformation is virtually locked in. The elderly of the first half of the next century have already been born and can be counted—and the retirement benefit systems on which they will depend are already in place. The future costs can therefore be projected with a fair degree of certainty. Unlike global warming, for example, there can be little theoretical debate over whether global aging will manifest itself—or when. And unlike other challenges, such as financial support for new democracies, the cost of global aging will be far beyond our means—even the collective means of all the world's wealthy nations. How we confront global aging will have direct economic implications—measurable, over the next century, in the quadrillions of dollars—that will likely dwarf the other challenges. Indeed, it will greatly influence how the other challenges ultimately play out.

Societies in the developed world—by which I mean primarily the countries of North America, Western Europe, Japan, and Australia—are aging for three major reasons:

- Medical advances, along with increased affluence and improvement in public health, nutrition, and safety, are raising average life expectancy dramatically.
- A huge outsized baby boom generation in the United States and several other countries is now making its way through middle age.
- Fertility rates have fallen, and in Japan and a number of European countries are now running far beneath the "replacement rate" necessary to replace today's population. The impact of so few young people entering tomorrow's tax-paying workforce, while so many are entering benefit-receiving elderhood, is of profound consequence.

As a result, I believe that global aging will become the transcendent political and economic issue of the twenty-first century. I will argue that—like it or not, and there's every reason to believe we won't like it—renegotiating the established social contract in response to global aging will soon dominate and daunt the public policy agendas of all the developed countries.

By the 2030s, these countries will be much older than they are today. Some of them may exceed a median age of 55, twenty years older than the oldest median age (35) of *any* country on earth as recently as 1970. Over half of the adult population of today's developed countries and perhaps two-thirds of their voters will be near or beyond today's eligibility age for publicly financed retirement. So we have to ask: When that time comes, who will be doing the work, paying the taxes, saving for the future, and raising the next generation? Can even the wealthiest of nations afford to pay for such a vast number of senior citizens living a third or more of their adult lives in what are now commonly thought of as the retirement years? Or will many of those future elderly have to do without the retirement benefits they are now promised? And what happens then?

This is not the first time I have spoken out on demographic trends and the clash between popular expectations and fiscal realities. In 1982, I began writing on the long-term challenges facing the U.S. Social Security system—a concern that is now, at last, moving onto the center stage of national discussion where it should have been long ago. After studying the early Reagan budgets, I spoke out against the danger of ballooning federal budget deficits, and began organizing national bipartisan efforts to control and reduce them. In the 1980s, five former Secretaries of Treasury and I founded the Bi-Partisan Budget Appeal, made up of 500 former public officials and business CEOs. In 1992, with Senators Warren Rudman and Paul Tsongas, I cofounded The Concord Coalition. This organization was devoted originally to balancing the budget. With the short-term budget outlook improving, it is now focusing on the long-term impact of ballooning spending on federal entitlement programs, which threatens to unbalance the budget again early in the next century, and on the great advantage of acting to reform them sooner rather than later. (It was in that context that the White House asked The Concord Coalition in 1998 to cohost a series of televised national conferences on the future of Social Security with an unlikely bedfellow, the American Association of Retired Persons.)

In 1996, I presented my views about the aging of America and the impending crisis in U.S. retirement programs in my book, *Will America Grow Up Before It Grows Old?* So, one might ask, why write another book on what sounds like the same subject? The answer is, it's not the same subject. My last book focused on America's own *domestic* problem. But while writing that book, I became aware that, imposing as the challenge of an aging society is in the United States, it is even more serious in Japan and much of Europe. In most of the other developed countries, populations are aging faster, birthrates are lower, the influx of younger immigrants from developing countries is smaller, public pension benefits for senior citizens are more generous, and private pension systems are weaker. Most of the other leading economies therefore face far worse fiscal fundamentals than we do. Even some major developing countries—China, for example—face serious aging challenges in the next century.

Given the instant and sometimes painful interactions within global capital markets and the likelihood of varying national responses to the coming fiscal challenge, I can easily envision that sometime in the next decade or two demographic aging will trigger unprecedented financial pressures, both on fragile regional economic arrangements such as the European Economic and Monetary Union and on the world economy as a whole. The economic and political outcome could make today's Asian or Russian crisis look like child's play.

Demographic aging is, at bottom, a global challenge that cries out for a global solution. That is why I have written this book.

WHOSE WATCH IS IT, ANYWAY?

The leaders of the developed world all know what is coming. In private discussions I have had in recent years with President Clinton, Prime Minister Hashimoto, Prime Minister Thatcher, and other leaders of major economies, I learned that they were all fully briefed on the stunning demographic trends that lie ahead. But so far, despite the magnitude of the challenge, the political response has been paralysis rather than action, fear not commitment. Hardly any country is doing what it should to prepare. Hardly any country is doing much at all. Yet year after year the crisis approaches with the measurable certainty of an advancing tidal wave.

In 1994 I served on the Kerrey-Danforth Commission on Entitlement and Tax Reform, established by President Clinton. After studying demographic projections and their cost implications, we issued a report that was endorsed unanimously by the Commission's 20 Democratic and Republican congressional members and by 30 of its 31 total members. (The sole exception was the President of the United Mine Workers.) The report demonstrated beyond question that if we do not reform tax and spending policies, the benefit outlays for just five programs—Social Security, Medicare, Medicaid, and federal civilian and military pensions—will exceed total federal revenues by the year 2030. This would leave zero tax revenue for any other purpose—not even for interest payments, nor for national defense, nor for education, nor for child health, nor for the federal payroll. *Not a penny available for anything else.*

The report was the clearest official description to date of the staggering fiscal challenges posed by America's demographic aging. Both Democrats and Republicans on the Commission, compelled by hard facts, for the first time agreed on the scope of the crisis.

America's political leadership thanked us for the report, shook our hands, and walked away. After that, silence. Soon, after the 1994 congressional elections, the White House and congressional leaders decided that the Commission was politically toxic since its conclusions pointed so inescapably toward Social Security and Medicare reform. In the end the Commission expired without agreeing on a single concrete proposal to reform a system it had in its own report called "unsustainable."

The possibility of reform had run aground on a familiar obstacle: the growing disjuncture between what leaders know must be done and what policy changes they are willing to take to the voters. Something similar happened in 1996. Months after both parties in Congress agreed to appoint a commission to avert Medicare's imminent bankruptcy, the Democratic party ran an aggressive, demagogic, and successful "Mediscare" campaign to vilify any candidate who proposed "cutting" Medicare's rate of cost growth—a rate that everyone agreed would spend the program dry. And it happened again in 1998, when President Clinton in his State of the Union address proposed a commendable "dialogue" on the future of Social Security. The dialogue has begun, but leaders of both parties have thus far carefully avoided endorsing any specific reforms.

Denial is not a peculiarly American response. The flight from reality is re-enacted daily from Rome to Paris to Bonn to Tokyo. Like the United States, the other developed countries acknowledge the problem but refuse to deal with it.

A wise man once said that the real tragedy of life is that everyone has his reasons. Politicians are no exception. All over the world, they fear backing proposals that will cut or change retirement benefits because they think they'll lose their jobs if they do, as others have. In 1995, Silvio Berlusconi's Forza Italia government was buffeted by a number of political storms, all of which were arguably survivable—except for the gridlock over pension reform, which shattered his coalition. That same year, the Dutch Parliament was forced to repeal a recently enacted cut in retirement benefits after a strong Pension Party, backed by the elderly, emerged from nowhere to punish the reformers. In 1996, the French government's modest proposal to trim pensions triggered strikes and even riots. A year later the Socialists overturned the ruling government at the polls.

Rarely have so many official multilateral bodies—such as the International Monetary Fund (IMF), the World Bank, and the Organization for Economic Cooperation and Development (OECD)—agreed with such unanimity on the dimensions of a problem. Margaret Thatcher told me that she repeatedly tried to raise this issue at G-7 summit meetings. Yet the answer from her fellow leaders was, in effect, "Of course aging is a profound challenge, but it doesn't hit until early in the next century. That means it won't hit on my watch."

LIVING HAND TO MOUTH

Before they can grapple with the needed reforms, leaders of the developed world will have to speak out about the real truths and face up to the real choices. In particular, they will have to acknowledge that it may be impossible to reconcile rapid demographic aging with today's generous "pay-as-you-go" retirement systems—a misleadingly cheerful phrase that really means "hand-to-mouth" financing, in which a static or shrinking working-age population supports a rapidly growing retired population. Direct cash transfers from the working young to the nonworking old are now the norm throughout the developed world. But how does a politician inform voters that the benefits being paid to today's retirees cannot be sustained for tomorrow's? Telling the public that the unfunded benefits they are counting on may not be forthcoming is like admitting that a bank with everyone's life savings in deposit has just disappeared. The response is almost certain to follow the typical pattern, from disbelief to denial to outrage. No wonder politicians choose not to deliver such awful news.

The politicians are hardly the only culprits in this denial game. The public is often a willing accomplice. Voters have become habituated to a pay-as-you-go system that banks every generation's future retirement on the next generation's resources rather like a giant Ponzi scheme. But try telling people that a system that worked just wonderfully for their parents (who signed up early) won't do nearly so well for their kids (who are signing up late). You might as well tell an addict to end his dependency because the supply of drugs is running low.

Each country's resistance is colored by its political and cultural institutions. In Europe, where the "welfare state" is more expansive, the public can hardly imagine that the promises made by previous generations of politicians can no longer be kept. They therefore support leaders, unions, and party coalitions that make generous unfunded pensions the very cornerstone of social democracy. In the United States, the problem is not so much a habit of welfare-state dependence as the peculiar American notion that every citizen has personally earned and therefore is "entitled" to whatever benefits government happens to have promised. Over the past fifty years, as this notion of "earned benefits" has expanded,

America's personal savings rate has fallen from near the top to the very bottom among developed nations. From a society that once felt obliged to endow future generations, we have become a society that feels entitled to support from our children. Unless this mindset changes, Americans may one day find that all they really are "entitled to" is a piece of the national debt.

OVERPOPULATION OR SHRINKING POPULATION?

Let's be frank: One reason many people are reluctant to focus on global aging is that, in the past, demographers have sometimes erred badly in their forecasts. Only yesterday, it seems like they were all talking about worldwide overpopulation. So why trust what demographers are saying now?

Let me explain why. Human fertility, the variable demographers find hardest to predict, doesn't influence the fiscal projections I use in this book *at all* over the next twenty years (the time span needed for a newborn to grow up to be a taxpayer) and very little over the next thirty years. In the near and medium term, therefore, the aging scenario I describe is virtually locked in. Beyond that, fertility does play a growing role in fiscal projections and, admittedly, demographers have often been wrong on this question. What is less well known is that almost all such errors have been *overestimates*. Projections of population aging, therefore, have almost always been *underestimates*. A very long-term trend is at work here. Over the last century and a half, fertility in the world's most affluent nations has been in almost steady decline. This decline has repeatedly surprised experts who assumed it couldn't continue.

The single major exception was the post-World War II baby boom in a number of large developed countries, notably the United States. It was this boom that triggered the "overpopulation" anxieties of the early postwar era and led, by the 1960s, to newspaper headlines about the "population bomb" and anti-birth movements like ZPG (Zero Population

Growth). It also spawned an entire industry of birth control experts and advocates who galvanized elite opinion and spurred multilateral agencies to take action. But, as it turned out, this postwar birth boom quickly subsided. By the 1970s, the fertility rate in the developed world was again falling to unprecedented lows. And it has continued to fall ever since, thanks to such long-term drivers of lower fertility as growing affluence, increased female employment, later marriage, and widening access to birth control and abortion. In hindsight, it is clear that the postwar birth boom was a historical anomaly, though one whose full impact has yet to be felt. To date, it has *slowed* the pace of aging in the United States and a few other countries—but in the future it will *accelerate* the pace of aging when this huge generation of baby boomers becomes senior boomers.

It is possible that social and cultural changes might alter today's demographic projections. Over the long run, aging in the developed world could be slower than the official forecasts now indicate, although I believe it is *much more likely to be faster*. But it would be folly to reject rational deliberation simply because experts have sometimes been wrong. Back in the 1970s, many climatologists warned of a coming global ice age, but this does not deter us from giving a fair hearing to the evidence offered by experts who today warn of global warming.

GRAY DAWN

A gray dawn is fast approaching. The more we know about this historic demographic transformation, the better prepared we will be. In Chapter 2, I provide an overview of its magnitude and consequences. Let me preview the main findings:

- *Global aging will transform the world into societies that are much older than any we have ever known or imagined.* Until the industrial revolution, the odds of encountering an elderly person (age 65 or older) in an

Just thirty years from now, one in four people in the developed world* will be aged 65 or older, up from one in seven today.

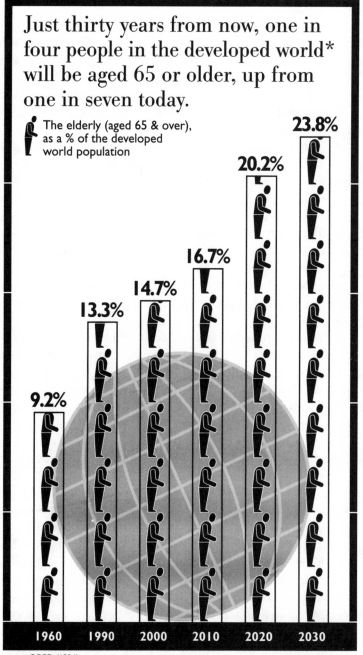

The elderly (aged 65 & over), as a % of the developed world population

9.2% — 1960
13.3% — 1990
14.7% — 2000
16.7% — 2010
20.2% — 2020
23.8% — 2030

SOURCE: OECD (1996)
*Here and throughout, "developed world" refers to the 23 nations listed in note 2, chapter 2.

affluent nation was about 1 in 40. By 1990 it was about 1 in 10. In a few decades, it will be 1 in 4—and in the fastest-aging countries, 1 in 3 or even higher. By 2015, most developed countries will have more elders as a share of their population than the state of Florida has today.

• *As the number of elderly explodes, global aging will place an unprecedented economic burden on working-age people.* Today the ratio of working taxpayers to nonworking pensioners in the developed world is around 3 to 1. By 2030, absent reform, this ratio will fall to 1.5 to 1—and in some countries, such as Germany and Italy, it will drop all the way down to 1 to 1 or even lower. Thus, in the year 2030, the typical working couple will be required to fund the full cash pension and health-care needs of at least one anonymous retiree.

• *Global aging is what happens when people start living much longer.* Global life expectancies have grown more over the last fifty years than over the previous five thousand. Perhaps two-thirds of all the people who have ever lived to the age of 65 are alive today. Over the next thirty years, global life expectancy is projected to rise by another seven or eight years. This advance alone will raise the number of elderly by roughly one-third.

• *Even among the elderly, the number of "old old" (aged 85 and over) is growing much faster than the number of "young old"—a phenomenon demographers call "the aging of the aged."* Over the next fifty years, while the number of people aged 65 to 84 is projected to triple, the number of those aged 85 and over is projected to grow sixfold. In the United States, these old old consume twice as much hospital care per capita—and over twenty times as much nursing-home care—as elders between ages 65 and 74.

• *Global aging is also what happens when people start having fewer babies.* Thirty years ago, the typical woman worldwide had 5.0 children over her lifetime. Today that figure is 2.7. Meanwhile, the "total fertility rate" in the developed countries has fallen all the way to 1.6—which is already 25 percent beneath the rate necessary to replace the population generation to generation.

• *Global aging is pushing the developed world—and perhaps even the entire world—toward eventual population decline.* By the 2020s, working-age populations will be declining in virtually every developed country. By the year 2050, all the developed countries will likely shrink from 15 to 10 percent of the world population—while the Mideast, Central Asia, Africa, and Latin America will climb from 48 to 60 percent. Absent sizable immigration—and unless their fertility rates rise again—Western Europe and Japan will shrink to about one-half of their current population before the end of the twenty-first century.

• *Global aging will revolutionize the family, by drastically narrowing and lengthening its shape.* While the family tree narrows—and the number of a typical person's siblings, cousins, and children enters a steep decline—the surge in life expectancy will make the tree taller. Early in the next century, many developed countries will have more grandparents than grandchildren.

• *The official projections may err on the side of optimism, since they assume that the underlying causes of global aging will weaken over time.* In the United States, for example, life expectancy is officially forecast to rise no higher by the year 2050 than it already is in Japan today. Yet some experts believe that scientific advances will greatly increase longevity—even to 100 years or more. As for fertility, most official forecasts assume that women will have as many or more children in the future—not fewer—than they are having today.

UNPRECEDENTED QUESTIONS

In an aging world, every sphere of social life will experience profound changes and grapple with unprecedented questions. In Chapter 6, I suggest some of the ways demographic aging may reshape the political, economic, and cultural agendas of the world:

- *In economics and business:* As populations shrink, will economies shrink as well? What business sectors will be most affected? Does aging mean declining savings and sluggish productivity? Will the exploding cost of retirement benefits trigger massive budget deficits and overwhelm global capital markets? With what negative effects?
- *In ethics:* What happens as medical progress inevitably confronts increasingly scarce public resources? How will we decide whether to spend an extra dollar on the latest high-tech treatment for the old or on education and training for the young? How will all this reshape the ethics of life and death? Who lives? Who dies? Who decides?
- *In politics:* As the number of elderly swells, will the senior benefit lobbies become ever-more powerful and lay claim to an ever-larger share of public budgets? Will young people remain apathetic, even in the face of the unthinkable tax bills they will soon be paying? Or does generational war loom?
- *In culture:* How will global aging change people's outlook on life? Think of marketing. For many decades, the most targeted "demographic" among advertisers and media executives was the 18- to 49-year-old age group. That's because it was big, and its members spent. But already today, the most densely populated age bracket is getting older—and so the targeted demographic is getting older with it. What's sold to them, and how it's

sold, is changing and will continue to change. What will TV be like when the median viewer is aged 40? And what will automobiles be like when the median driver is aged 50? What about Hollywood? Or Broadway? Or Madison Avenue? How will aging affect society's power to innovate and to imagine and create a new future?

• *In world affairs:* In an increasingly volatile world, will metastasizing public retirement spending choke off resources available for vital defense and multinational priorities? With youth so scarce, will sending large combat forces in harm's way become politically unacceptable? If older developed countries try to depend on the savings of younger developing countries, how will this change the global balance of power?

GRAYING MEANS PAYING:
THE "$64 TRILLION QUESTION"

I do not subscribe to a lugubrious view of demographic aging. In many respects, population aging is a highly positive transformation, a triumph of modern science. A great number of today's elders are energetic and talented, with serious contributions to make. They can teach younger people the wisdom that comes only from experience. They can provide leadership and guidance—comfort, too. This potential is eloquently described in a number of recent books, most notably President Jimmy Carter's *Virtues of Aging*. It's good that more grandchildren will know, really know, their grandparents and great-grandparents. (Perhaps this will help heal the strains the nuclear family has undergone in recent years.) There may be less crime as the population ages, since crime, especially violent crime, is a young man's game. The old are often more religious than the young, and here too they have much to teach.

So there is much good that can come from longer lifespans. But along with the good is the inescapable fact that graying means paying—paying for pensions, for hospitals, for doctors and nurses, for nursing homes and related social services.

Within the next thirty years, the official projections suggest that governments in most developed countries will have to spend at least an extra 9 to 16 percent of GDP annually simply to meet their old-age benefit promises. To pay these costs through increased taxation would raise the total tax burden by an unthinkable extra 25 to 40 percent of every worker's taxable wages—in countries where total payroll tax rates often already exceed 40 percent. Or, if we resort to deficit spending, we would have to consume all the savings and more of the entire developed world.

For the developed countries, the unfunded liabilities for pensions alone are about $35 trillion. Including healthcare, the figure is at least twice as much. To paraphrase the old quiz show, this makes the global issue at least a "$64 trillion question." Should we continue to ignore this problem, personal living standards will stagnate or decline and all other public spending priorities—whether basic research or the environment or education or defense—will be crowded out of public budgets. Our economies, our governments, and our democracies may find it hard to bear this enormous pressure. Furthermore, the official projections may be a best-case scenario, since they ignore the negative feedback effects of the mounting fiscal burden on the economy—through more borrowing, higher interest rates, more taxes, less savings, and lower rates of productivity and wage growth.

If we don't prepare for this challenge, much of what is good about an aging society could turn sour. After all, how will young and old live happily together if they see themselves as competitors for scarce resources? And, if this comes to pass, what wisdom will the old have after all to offer the young? And who among the young will listen? I very much respect the gifts that aging individuals can give to our communities and culture: But will the aged be praised for increasing the quality of life if they are deemed responsible for bankrupting the global economy?

VISIONARIES DON'T ALWAYS SEE CLEARLY

What lightens the burdens of civilization is the hope of progress over time, of optimism about the future. But to insist that everything will surely be better down the road is, I believe, unwise and intemperate. Progress doesn't just happen. It is created by facing the future with open eyes.

Global aging in itself doesn't make progress impossible, but it raises challenges that many of today's fashionable visionaries—those who speak passionately about a "new economy" or even a "new world order"—have yet to acknowledge.

Take the visionary talk of the "new economy." It is said that massive investments in technology, globalized capital markets, and entrepreneurial risk taking will turn the developed economies into dynamos of growth—enough growth to cover the additional fiscal costs of global aging. This is a welcome scenario, to be sure. But more investment normally requires more saving and less consumption, which in an aging world is precisely the problem. As people get old, they tend to save less and spend more. And as societies themselves age, their governments tend to run ever-larger deficits, further depleting savings. Unless the developed world changes its policies, demographic aging will so forcefully suppress both private and public savings that today's biggest economies may actually begin running *negative national savings rates* sometime in the 2020s. Some talk grandly about a dawning "golden age of capitalism." But unless the major developed nations confront their own aging, the "capital" in question will have to be imported massively from abroad. And if it is imported, from whom?

As for risk taking, tomorrow's workers and managers may yet become the lean, mobile, and ultra-flexible cyberforce depicted in today's futurology texts. But more and more of them will be graying, homeowning careerists with families, looking forward to their pensions. As recently as 1980, twentysomethings outnumbered fiftysomethings two-to-one in the developed world. By 2030, the two groups will be roughly the same size. The risk-averse middle-aged are on track to dominate the commercial, political, and cultural institutions of the cyberage.

Other visionaries say that the world is entering an era of smaller government and limited national authority. Growing voter distrust of public institutions, they predict, will soon produce governments that spend less, tax less, and regulate less—freeing individuals to identify with communities and regions in which national boundaries don't matter as much. But think again. For better or worse, the nation-state is hardly going to become less important to anyone who pays taxes, gets sick, or retires over the next half century. In fact, the doubling or tripling of the ratio of pensioners to workers ensures that the size of public budgets relative to the economy (and the importance of fiscal politics to the typical household) will expand dramatically. Tomorrow's "virtual state" is scheduled to bring with it a crushing and all-too-real tax load—either that, or yawning deficits and disappointed retirees. And, ironically, those who distrust government the very most may be the very first to demand their benefits. Political battles over declining returns on pay-as-you-go chain letters are likely to rage at the very center of national life.

Still another school of visionaries talks about hopes for the next century's "new world order," in which today's great powers orchestrate an era of stable and peaceful geopolitics. I share these hopes. But here again, global aging poses some real challenges. Within the next twenty-five years, the population of the developed countries is projected to peak and then decline. In Japan and many European nations, this decline may be so rapid that real GDP will start trending downward as well. With defense and foreign affairs spending crowded out by the growing cost of retirement benefits, the developed countries will be under constant pressure to roll back their international presence.

Can the older countries retain their leadership role in a world in which younger countries, which may not face the same fiscal constraints, are still growing? Will the world be more safe—or less—if the more stable democracies lose their grip on global affairs? I believe less. Consider, in particular, how the tables may turn if countries like Japan or Germany or the United States eventually find themselves mortgaged to today's developing debtor countries—some of which have been growing so fast that they are likely to become tomorrow's global creditors.

My purpose here is not to criticize the visionaries, but to ask how, in an aging world, can salvage a future in which progress is still possible. After the French philosopher Blaise Pascal experienced a religious conversion, he said to his friends who were atheists, "Wager that there is a God, and live your life as if He exists. If it turns out you are right, and there is a God, when you die you will go to heaven. If it turns out you're wrong, no harm will have been done, and you will probably have lived a better life." Either way, you win.

In the same vein I would say: Let us arrange our affairs as if the coming age wave is a profound challenge. If we are right, we will have averted a catastrophe. If we are wrong—which I consider most unlikely—no great harm will have been done, and we will probably leave behind a better world for posterity.

STRATEGIES FOR AN AGING WORLD

So how, exactly, should we arrange our affairs? It is wrong to suppose that the solution is simply a combination of across-the-board tax hikes and benefit cuts. With most younger workers already hard-pressed by taxes—and with most older workers already unprepared financially for retirement—this is not a solution at all. It is merely a restatement of the problem. Instead, we should attempt to create a new paradigm of aging, one as revolutionary as the demographic transformation we are entering. This new paradigm can best be defined by its objective: We must make aging both more secure for older generations and less burdensome for younger generations.

In Chapter 5, I describe six possible strategies. While all of them promise huge fiscal and economic payoffs, all of them will be difficult—even very difficult—to implement. Some, like later retirement or adjusting benefits according to need, will challenge settled popular expectations—in this case, that government should subsidize early retirement for *all* households. Some, like pronatal policies and stepped-up immigration, will trigger cultural and social controversy. Some, like investing more in children, may require more patience and (perhaps) more wisdom than most governments now possess. And practically all of them will be more acceptable in some countries than in others. Stressing filial piety, for example, will be easier in Asia than in North America, while mandatory savings accounts will appeal more to North Americans than to continental Europeans.

It remains to be seen which of all these strategies will prove most popular and effective. But of one thing I am certain: As the pay-as-you-go era ends, every country, rich or poor, must ultimately assemble a new paradigm of aging from building blocks such as these if it is to thrive in the next century.

WILL IT TAKE ANOTHER PEARL HARBOR?

Can the world's great powers respond to a silent and slow-motion crisis that will, for all of its vast scale, take decades to engulf us? Global aging will be a test. It has been said that all democracies suffer from a fundamental problem: It is easier for them to mobilize opinion and resources against a current emergency than to act in advance to avert a future emergency. In American circles, some call this the "Pearl Harbor" syndrome. I like to draw the frog analogy. When a frog falls into boiling water, it jumps out. But when a frog falls into cold water that is then slowly heated, it swims around calmly until it cooks.

We're swimming right now ourselves. Is the temperature rising too slowly for anyone to notice?

Some pessimists say yes. Popular democracies with short-term electoral cycles, they say, cannot focus on long-term choices. But I disagree. Democracies don't get much more popular than the United States, which focused just fine when it came time to pay for the Marshall Plan in the 1950s or remedy civil rights injustices in the 1960s or invest in a cleaner environment in the 1970s. I see no reason why such past successes cannot be repeated. Though the public in developed countries may not yet be ready to act, it is very much aware that global aging poses urgent choices. Over 90 percent of all U.S. voters say that Social Security will require "major change," and 65 percent agree that it "is in need of major reform now."

A better explanation for political gridlock on global aging is declining confidence in government. People know something has to be done, but they don't trust their politicians to act honestly in their long-term interest or to distribute the short-term sacrifices fairly. Without that trust, voters cling with white-knuckled anxiety to the retirement status quo, however unsustainable.

Fruitless partisanship feeds voter apathy. For the sake of effective action, the developed world must transcend ideology and engage the practical realities of the aging challenge. The left will have to stop defending the expansion of retirement benefits as the cornerstone of progressive government, and realize that they are fast pushing all future-oriented spending out of public budgets. The right will have to move beyond a program of mere fiscal restraint, and offer a coherent blueprint for how society intends to care for tomorrow's vast number of elder dependents. Both sides will have to resist the powerful political influence of the organized elderly who favor the status quo over what most senior citizens personally care about—their children and their grandchildren's future. Otherwise, we face the very real possibility of a socially destructive "war between generations" over the use of public resources.

Amid all the partisan crossfire, people can easily forget that they share a common future. If timely political action is to take place, every special interest must become part of a new coalition, a "special interest" in behalf of the general interest. If they don't, their own narrow agendas will ultimately suffer as well.

Aging presents a global challenge that requires a global solution. In Chapter 7, with this in mind, I call for a global summit on aging. The summit would include leaders of developed and developing countries and would establish an Agency on Global Aging to keep this issue in sharp focus.

CONFESSIONS OF A GEEZER

Sheer luck is a force in life, and at age 72, I've been lucky to live longer than "three score years and ten" in mostly excellent health. But it was more than luck. I have benefited from the extraordinary advances in medicine and technology that have helped people like me not only continue living but continue loving it. I have a gifted and hard-working wife, and she keeps me young. When I'm with my children and grandchildren, I find their energy contagious. I work full time and can't imagine stopping. I like what I do.

I expect to be a personal beneficiary of the longevity revolution—and live, work, and opine well into the next century! My purpose in this book is to raise some of the right questions and provide at least a few of the answers that can help us to create genuine retirement security for future generations when they reach my age, not the false security of empty promises about empty trust funds.

I find most senior citizens to be far less selfish personally than the positions taken by their so-called advocacy groups. Most understand the moral imperative so clearly stated by

Dietrich Bonhoeffer: "The ultimate test of a moral society is the kind of world it leaves to its children." Most seniors I know want a chance to contribute and a chance to make things better for their children and grandchildren. They are not opposed to sacrifice, but they want to know that any sacrifice they are asked to make is effective and fair.

Like many other seniors in my generation, I was schooled in the American Dream by my parents, immigrants who worked and saved and worked and saved so their children could get "the best education money can buy" and go on to "do better." That was what my father always said: Do better.

So I confess, what really makes me lucky are all the unforgettable sacrifices that I—and indeed most of my generation—received from the generation of our mothers and fathers. As parents, they spent time on us. As savers, they invested for us. As voters, they taxed themselves for us. And as citizen-soldiers, they bled for us. But will my children and grandchildren be as lucky? And will yours? Will they be able to "do better" and enjoy a life of material and moral progress in a world in which a vast share of their paychecks is earmarked for my generation? Shouldn't that money go, really, to their own children? And be invested in their future?

That's why my highest loyalty isn't to the AARP—or any other group of like-minded senior citizens. It's to junior citizens like my kids and yours. It's to the future. It's to fairness, too.

I want life to be fair for them. And so I've written this book that says, essentially, "Iceberg dead ahead." The crucial moment is upon us. If we seize the wheel of the ship—which is admittedly big and heavy—and turn it now, there is still time to avert the coming collision. If we stand on deck and debate too long about whether it is or isn't an iceberg out there, valuable time will be lost. Worse yet, in our hubris, we might ignore the warnings altogether and make our way to the deck for a last dance as the ship's orchestra strikes up another jaunty tune. After all, some will say, our economy is far too modern and sophisticated—too unsinkable, in fact—to be troubled by a mere shadow on the horizon.

This book asks you to take the warning seriously and to join in turning the wheel. If we begin now, together, the needed reforms can be gradual, compassionate, and effective. If we wait, if we dither and debate, if we talk endlessly about how to turn the wheel but never quite get to turning it—then the sharp turn will be sudden and destructive. Maybe even catastrophic.

We know the challenge is real. Unlike so much of what gets written about the future, this iceberg is a certainty. The only open question is whether or not posterity will thank us for doing what's necessary and doing it in time. Global aging will not adjust to our visions. We will have to adjust to it.

2

Is Demography Destiny?

"Do you have a minute to talk about your retirement years?"

THIRTY YEARS AGO, UNCONTROLLABLE POPULATION GROWTH seemed to be a major threat to the world's long-term future. Paul Erlich's worldwide best seller *The Population Bomb* predicted a teeming and youthful humanity falling off the edges of all seven continents. More recently, in a little-noticed shift of expert opinion, demographers now project a dramatic deceleration in global population growth and an equally dramatic aging of societies worldwide. Thirty years ago, the future was crowded with babies. Today, it's crowded with elders.

THE SHAPE OF THINGS TO COME

Most young people have difficulty contemplating their own old age, much less preparing for the discomfort and dependency that often accompany it. Likewise, the world today finds it hard to confront its collective aging, much less the difficult political and economic choices that aging societies will have to make. Yet we can no longer afford denial. The accumulating evidence is now overwhelming: The world stands on the threshold of a social transformation—even a revolution—with few parallels in humanity's past. Indeed, this revolution has already begun. Perhaps two-thirds of all the people who have ever lived to the age of 65 are alive today. Aging experts Allan Pfifer and Lydia Bronte observe, "When this revolution has run its course, the impacts will have been at least as powerful as those of any of the great economic and social movements of the past."[1] It's time we take an unflinching look at the shape of things to come.

Global aging will transform the world into societies that are much older than any we have ever known or imagined.

For nearly all of human history, until the industrial revolution, people aged 65 and over never amounted to more than 2 or 3 percent of the population. In today's developed world,[2] they amount to 14 percent. By the year 2030, they will be reaching 25 percent and in some countries closing in on 30 percent. In the days of Hammurabi or Julius Caesar or (indeed) Thomas Jefferson, your odds of a random encounter with a person aged 65 or over was about one person in *every forty*. Today, the odds are about one person in *every ten*. A few decades from now, they will be one person in *every four*—or perhaps (in a few extreme cases, like Italy) one in *every three*.

Been to Florida lately? You may not have realized it, but as you gazed upon the vast concentration of seniors there— nearly 19 percent of the Sun State's population—you were

Florida: a demographic benchmark every developed nation will soon pass.

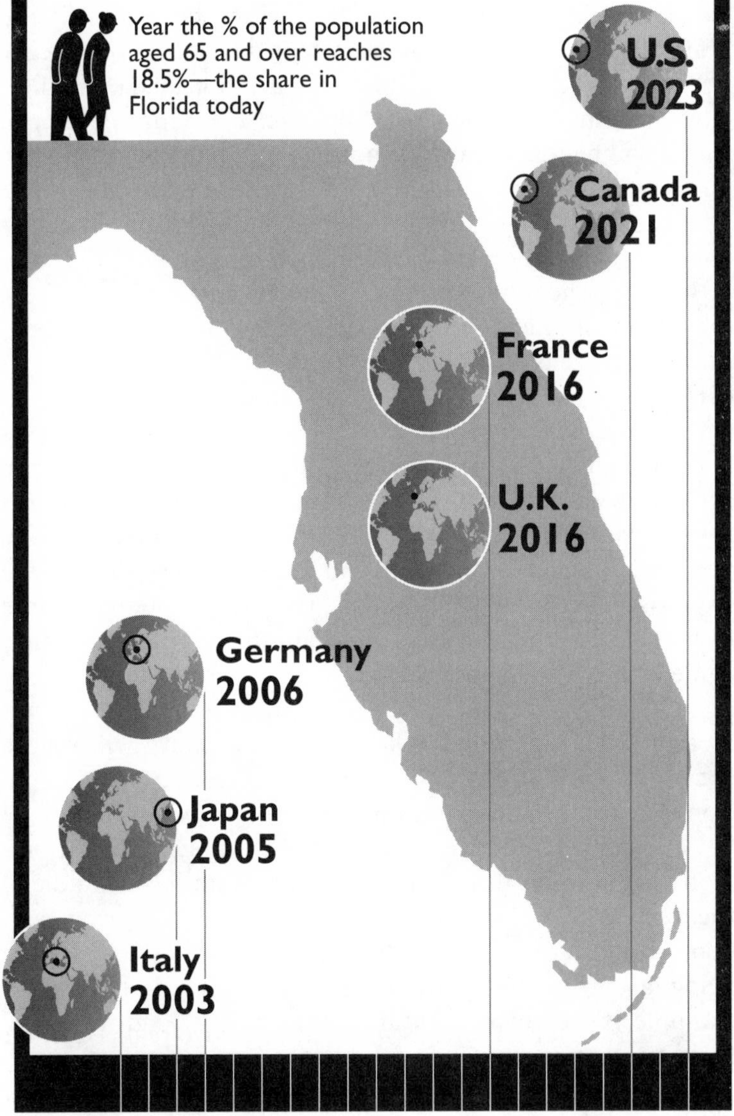

Year the % of the population aged 65 and over reaches 18.5%—the share in Florida today

U.S.
2023

Canada
2021

France
2016

U.K.
2016

Germany
2006

Japan
2005

Italy
2003

SOURCE: OECD (1996)

looking at humanity's future. Today's Florida is a benchmark that every developed nation will soon pass. Italy will be there as early as 2003, followed quickly by Japan (in 2005) and Germany (in 2006). Significantly, these are the countries in which fertility declined earliest during the postwar era. France and Britain will pass present-day Florida a decade later, around 2016. The United States and Canada will hit it later still, in 2021 and 2023. By then the entire developed world will be much older than it has ever been before.

North America will age more slowly because of its large postwar baby boom and substantial immigration. Boomers will keep the elder ratio nearly flat from now until the early 2010s. Yet once these boomer cohorts start hitting age 65, the ratio will jump. Over the coming decade, about two million U.S. citizens will be celebrating their sixty-fifth birthdays each year, a number that will reach 4 million once the Woodstock retirement is in full swing. North America may never become quite as old as Europe. But when its gray dawn arrives, it will do so with shocking suddenness: During the twenty years between 2010 and 2030, the share of the U.S. population aged 65 and over will increase more than it will have risen between 1930 and 2010. Just as boomers once overwhelmed the schools as children, the job market as they came of age, and the housing market as mature adults, so too are they on track to overwhelm America's retirement systems as they enter elderhood. The boomer age wave will rock a society whose fiscal promises to the old rest on the assumption that youthful taxpayers will multiply inexhaustibly.

Developing countries, starting with younger populations, won't begin to hit the Florida benchmark until the middle of the next century. But since they have experienced such a sudden drop in fertility, many developing countries are actually aging faster than the typical developed country. In France, for example, it took over a century for the elderly to grow from 7 to 14 percent of the population. South Korea, Taiwan, Singapore, and China are projected to traverse this distance in only about twenty-five years.

To understand these stunning changes better, consider the underlying shifts in population by age. Over the next thirty years, according to the OECD, the developed world will *gain* 89 million people aged 65 and over and *lose* 40 million under age 65. When you put weight on one side of the seesaw while taking it off the other, everything tips very fast. Oscar Wilde once remarked that "youth is America's oldest tradition"—and, indeed, as recently as 1940 college-age youths (18- to 21-years-old) outnumbered the elderly in the United States by 9.6 to 9.0 million. Yet forty years from now, the Census Bureau projects the number of college-age youths will grow to only 20.2 million while the number of elderly will swell to 75.2 million. When the retirement-home crowd outnumbers the fraternity-home crowd by nearly four to one, America's youth tradition may be little more than a memory. In most other developed countries, these ratios will be even more lopsided by 2040, ranging between five to one and ten to one.

Although the developing populations are considerably younger, their size and rapid aging will produce staggering absolute increases in the size of their elderly populations. Over the next fifty years, the global population over aged 65 will grow by over one billion, nearly one-half of the total expected population growth. In some of the largest countries, even a modest rise in the elder share makes for a huge absolute number. For example, by 2050 the number of Chinese aged 65 and over is projected to reach 330 million. As recently as 1990, that was the elderly population of *the entire world.*

As the number of elderly explodes, global aging will place an unprecedented economic burden on working-age people.

A common indicator of the social cost of supporting the elderly is the ratio of working-age people (aged 15 to 64) to elderly persons.[3] This so-called "aged dependency ratio" offers a crude idea of the number of wage earners or caregivers

By 2030, the developed world will gain nearly 100 million elders—while the number of working-age adults shrinks.

Total change in the population of the developed world

Aged 65 and over: +89 million

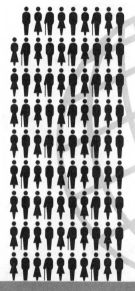

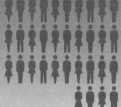

Aged 15–64: –34 million

SOURCE: OECD (1996)

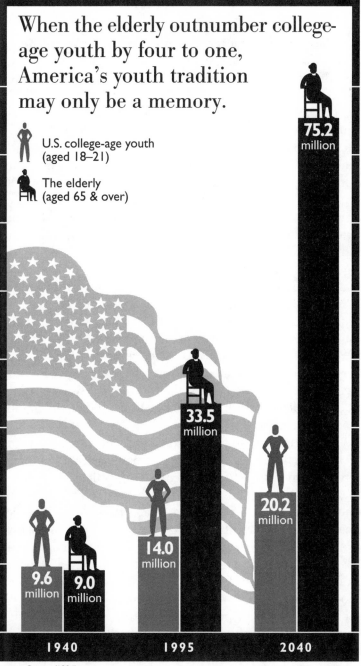

When the elderly outnumber college-age youth by four to one, America's youth tradition may only be a memory.

U.S. college-age youth
(aged 18–21)

The elderly
(aged 65 & over)

75.2 million

33.5 million

20.2 million

14.0 million

9.6 million

9.0 million

1940

1995

2040

SOURCE: Census (1996)

available to support each dependent retiree. As recently as 1960, this ratio was 6.8 to 1 in the developed world. Today, it has fallen to 4.5 to 1. By the year 2030, it is projected to drop to 2.5 to 1.

This may look like a linear decline, but it's not. The percentage decline in the dependency ratio is actually getting much steeper over time. Look at it this way. Over the past quarter-century, the developed world added nearly three working-age adults (120 million) for each additional elderly person (45 million). Soon those numbers will be reversed. Over the next quarter-century, the developed world is projected to add fourteen elderly persons (70 million) for each additional working-age adult (5 million).

Yet even this trend understates the seriousness of the challenge. Since the end of World War II, the retirement age in all developed countries has fallen dramatically, making many more elders (and a rising share of near-elders) dependent on benefits derived from taxes on those who still work. In 1950, for example, the average age at which U.S. workers started collecting their Social Security retirement pensions was 69; today, it's 64.[4] Back then, three in five U.S. men in their late 60s were still in the labor force; today, the number is only one in five.

In continental Europe, the retirement age decline has been especially steep. In France, Germany, and Italy, a mere 5 percent of men aged 65 and over are now officially employed. Meanwhile, disability benefits have grown so fast, especially among government employees, that "disability" is widely regarded as just another route to early retirement. Thirty years ago, employment over age 65 in developed counties was common and pensions for anyone *under* age 65 were rare. Today, in most developed countries, there are far more people under age 65 who are collecting retirement and disability benefits than people *over* age 65 who are working. As the rising cost of public benefits drives payroll tax rates upward, more working-age citizens avoid legal (that is, tax-paying) employment. And as companies move to low-cost

There will be ever fewer working-age adults available to support each elder.

Ratio of working-age adults (aged 15-64) to the elderly (aged 65 & over) in the developed world

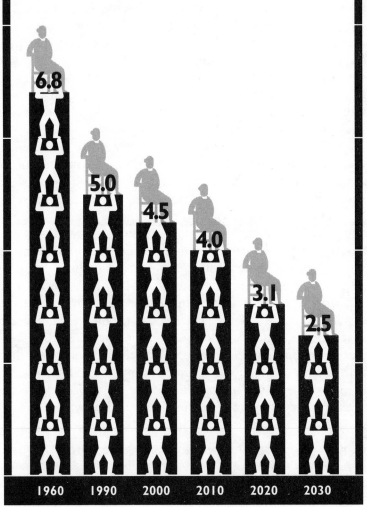

SOURCE: OECD (1996)

economies—often outside the developed world—the fiscal drag on the home economy is exacerbated even further. All this leads to an even heavier burden on those who pay taxes.

As a result, the ratio of taxpaying workers to retired or disabled pensioners is much lower—and has been dropping much faster—than the aged dependency ratio (a strictly demographic measure) would indicate. This ratio of money givers to money takers, nearly 3.0 in the developed world today, is projected to fall to 1.5 by 2030. In some European countries, it will fall beneath 1.0—meaning that there will be more beneficiaries receiving payments than taxpaying workers making them. The extreme case is Italy, where this ratio *has already fallen* to 1.3. Its pension funding crisis, which has helped topple the last few Italian governments, offers an instructive glimpse of the fiscal and political future of the European Union.

To the extent that tomorrow's nonworking elders finance their retirement out of their own savings today, one might argue that they won't really constitute an economic burden. By living off the income from such savings, they are not consuming wealth that would have existed in their absence—which is another way of saying that the pennies they save (and consume in old age) are the pennies they earn. But the point is moot, since few people retire mostly on saved income. Unfunded, pay-as-you-go pensions,[5] not funded personal savings, have become the bedrock institution of retirement security throughout the developed world.[6] Thus, unless major policy changes are enacted, the typical working couple in the year 2030 will indeed feel the burden. On top of all their other taxes, they will, in effect, be required to fund the full cash and health-care needs of at least one anonymous retiree, in addition to whatever voluntary support they can also give their own parents.

Global aging is what happens when people start living much longer.

One major force behind global aging is that singular triumph of the late twentieth century: the unprecedented

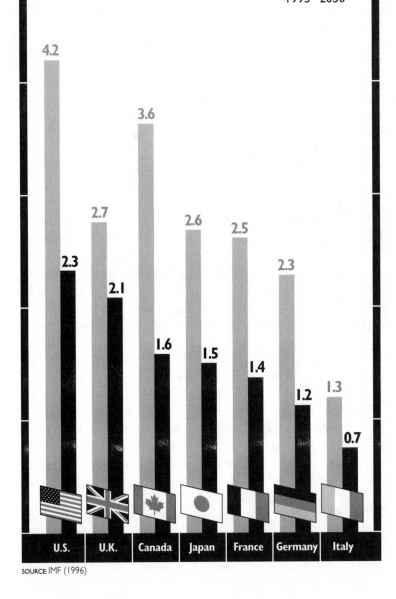

There will be even fewer taxpayers to support each retired pensioner.

Ratio of contributors to retired pensioners in public pension systems

1995   2050

	1995	2050
U.S.	4.2	2.3
U.K.	2.7	2.1
Canada	3.6	1.6
Japan	2.6	1.5
France	2.5	1.4
Germany	2.3	1.2
Italy	1.3	0.7

SOURCE: IMF (1996)

advance in human longevity. Because of stunning progress in public health and medical technology—everything from chlorinated water to miracle vaccines and heart-bypass surgery—global life expectancy has risen from around age 45 to age 65 since World War II. This is a greater gain in fifty years than civilization had achieved over the previous five thousand years. Over the same period, life expectancy in the developed world started higher, around age 65, and has risen to unprecedented heights, all the way to age 75. Japan, the world's longevity leader, last year became the first nation on earth to reach a life expectancy at birth of 80 years. Japanese women who reach age 65 can now expect to live *on average* until age 85. Over the next thirty years, global life expectancy is projected to rise by another seven or eight years. This advance alone will cause the number of elderly to increase by roughly one-third.

These trends have affected women more than men. As modern medicine has reduced the risk of dying in childbirth, women's natural biological edge (combined with their greater aversion to violence and physical risk) has translated into a sizeable and growing lifespan advantage. A century ago, the life expectancies of the two sexes didn't differ much. Today, on average, women outlive men by seven or eight years in the developed countries and by about three or four years in most of the developing world. Inevitably, this gender gap in lifespans has led to the "feminization" of the elderly and a well-known mismatch in the ratio of old widows to old widowers. (Today's senior living community is a bachelor's paradise!) In the typical developed country, women comprise 60 percent of the population aged 65 and over—and nearly 75 percent of the population aged 85 and over. One German study of five-generation families frequently found three generations of widows.[7]

Among both men and women, the longevity revolution is shattering long-standing personal expectations. "Most people my age are dead," declared Casey Stengel in 1964 at age 73—a quip that is still funny but no longer true in today's world of zestful senior living communities. Soon, the longevity

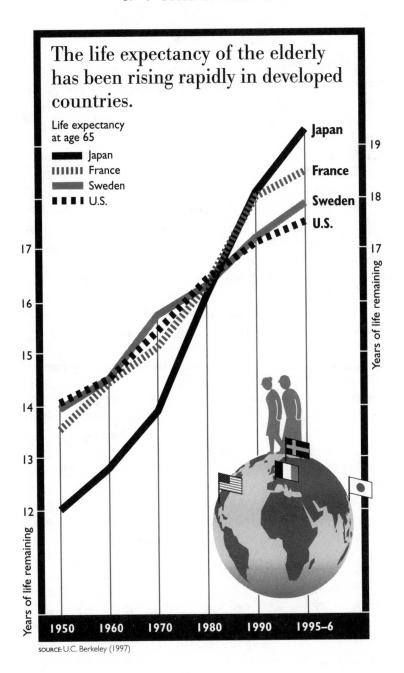

The life expectancy of the elderly has been rising rapidly in developed countries.

Life expectancy
at age 65

▬▬▬ Japan
|||||| France
▬▬▬ Sweden
▰▰▰ U.S.

Japan
France
Sweden
U.S.

Years of life remaining

Years of life remaining

1950   1960   1970   1980   1990   1995–6

SOURCE: U.C. Berkeley (1997)

revolution will also shatter long-standing public policies. Back when the western nations created their public retirement systems—from Bismarck's Germany in the 1880s to FDR's America in the 1930s—the number 65 was often chosen as the "normal" eligibility age because so few people were likely to achieve it. The average lifespan fell well short of age 65—and those workers who reached the age (said the actuaries) weren't likely to live much longer.

When Social Security was founded in 1935, the typical U.S. worker at age 65 could expect to live another 11.9 years. By the year 2040, say today's official projections, the typical worker at age 65 can expect to live at least another 19.2 years.[8] If the normal retirement age had been "indexed" to longevity since 1935, today's workers would be waiting until age 73 to receive full benefits and tomorrow's workers even longer.

In reality, over the past half-century, workers throughout the developed world have been retiring earlier, not later—often in response to legislation that has lowered the effective eligibility age. France, Italy, and Germany, for instance, all now allow full retirement benefits at age 60 for broad categories of workers. Typically, the demand for earlier retirement originates among the aging membership of politically powerful unions who are naturally worried about their own income security. On the assumption that early retirement creates more employment for everyone else, younger workers are persuaded to go along—though most economists wonder how, in the long run, higher payroll taxes are going to cure unemployment. With longevity rising and the retirement age falling, the economic burden of retirement dependency has been growing rapidly. Even a rising share of prison inmates are now receiving retirement benefits, and geriatric wards are being added to correctional facilities.

In most societies, people disagree about whether an increase or decrease in fertility rates is desirable. Yet nearly everyone agrees that that lower mortality rates are a blessing.[9] Indeed, longer and healthier lifespans are probably the greatest personal advantage we moderns enjoy over our ancestors. I rejoice for myself, and for tens of millions like me, who are likely to live to ages that most people could never hope to attain a half-century ago. I also celebrate the enrichment of families and communities that comes from living around more elders. As demographer Nicholas Eberstadt observes, "The aging of human populations is a necessary corollary of the 'health explosion' we have been so fortunate as to enjoy. . . . Would anyone seriously consider trading in the impending problems of aging for a return to nineteenth-century levels of health and mortality?"[10] Certainly not.

Furthermore, as we contemplate how we can afford longevity, it is well to remember that the developed countries are faced with crises in their pension and health-care systems, not because they are poor, but because, by any historical standard, they are exceedingly rich. As Professor Robert W. Fogel of the University of Chicago said about OECD countries in a recent speech, "It is the enormous increase in their per capita incomes over the past century that permitted the average length of retirement to increase by five-fold, the proportion of a cohort that lives to retire to increase by sevenfold and the amount of leisure time available to those still in the labor force to increase by nearly four-fold."[11]

But the question remains: Is the developed world prepared for the full implications of much longer lifespans—not just fiscal and economic, but also social and cultural?

Even among the elderly, the number of "old old"
(aged 85 and over) is growing much faster than the
number of "young old"—a phenomenon demographers
call "the aging of the aged."

Longer lives mean not just more elderly, but disproportionately more in each successive age bracket over 65. This is because there are relatively fewer people in the oldest brackets to begin with. Thus, as longer lifespans cause all the brackets to fill up, the oldest will necessarily fill up at the fastest rate.

By the year 2040 in the United States, for example, the Census Bureau projects that the population aged 65 to 74 will grow by roughly 80 percent—but the 85-and-over age group will grow by 240 percent. Over the long run, the growth multiples for this "old old" population are phenomenal. In 1900, U.S. residents aged 85 and over numbered a mere 374,000. Today, they number nearly 4 million, and by 2040 they will exceed 13 million. That same year, Americans *aged 80 and over* are projected to outnumber all American children *under age 5*. At the very oldest ages, the multiples soar. Centenarians are projected to grow from 63,000 to over 834,000 between now and 2050, a *thirteenfold* increase over the next fifty years.

Similar growth rates are expected in other developed countries. In France, officials worry that the grown children of its burgeoning old old population are *themselves* likely to be retired, with adequate time but insufficient resources to be effective caregivers. Japanese aged 75 and over have increased from 2 percent of the total population in 1970 to 6 percent today and will almost certainly hit 10 percent by the year 2010. By 2050, Japan will have the highest concentration of centenarians of any society on earth: For every three Japanese infants under age one there will be one elder aged 100 or over.

Worldwide, from now until 2050, the United Nations projects that the number of people aged 65 to 84 will grow from 400 million to 1.3 billion (a *threefold* increase); the number aged 85 and over from 26 to 175 million (a *sixfold* increase); and the number aged 100 and over from 135,000 to 2.2 million (a *sixteenfold* increase). By then, thirteen countries will have people aged 80 and over comprising at least 10 percent of their populations. In Italy the share will be 14 percent. By way of comparison, the world leader today is Sweden—with a mere 4.8 percent.

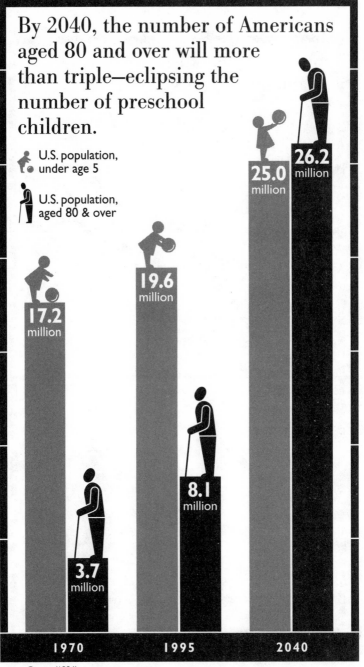

By 2040, the number of Americans aged 80 and over will more than triple—eclipsing the number of preschool children.

U.S. population, under age 5

U.S. population, aged 80 & over

17.2 million

19.6 million

25.0 million

26.2 million

3.7 million

8.1 million

1970

1995

2040

SOURCE: Census (1996)

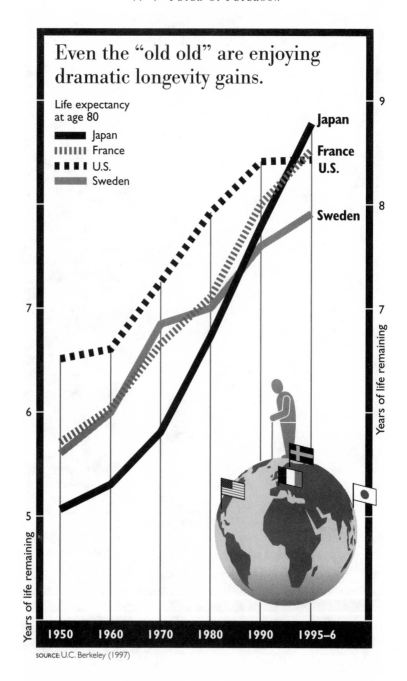

Even the "old old" are enjoying dramatic longevity gains.

Life expectancy at age 80

- Japan
- France
- U.S.
- Sweden

Japan
France
U.S.
Sweden

Years of life remaining

1950 1960 1970 1980 1990 1995–6

SOURCE: U.C. Berkeley (1997)

Extreme age no longer surprises. In Japan a 100-year-old woman was ticketed for riding a motorcycle without a helmet. Her excuse—that her 79-year-old son, the driver, was wearing her helmet—failed to mollify the police. In 1986, upon the death of Japan's Shigechigo Izumi at age 120, the Guinness Book of World Records announced that the title of the world's oldest person shifted to France's Jeanne Louise Clement, who was born in 1875 and remembered meeting Vincent Van Gogh as a teenager. After Mrs. Clement died in 1997 at age 122, so many other supercentenarians have claimed the title that no one under age 110 any longer merits consideration. Thirty years ago, the Queen of England sent her personal congratulations to any British citizen reaching age 100. Today, that gracious ritual has been relegated to a bureaucratic agency.

This "aging of the aged" adds an extra multiplier to the economic burden of global aging, since virtually every measure of disability, dependence, and health-care expense rises with increasing age. With each passing year of age, declining health inevitably results in substantial increases in prescription drugs, hospital admissions, medical tests, operations, transplants, rehabilitation, and physical therapy, as well as the need for assistance with daily living. Total per capita health spending in the United States on the old old (aged 85 and over) is three times as much as that on the "young-old" (aged 65 to 74).[12] For specific types of health care, this multiple varies greatly—from twice as much for hospital spending to over twenty times as much for nursing homes.

In virtually every developed country, the share of the elderly receiving institutional care rises from less than 5 percent among those under age 75 to between 20 and 50 percent for those aged 85 and over. Such long-term care is extremely costly—and now averages about $40,000 annually per person in the United States, an amount exceeding the median household income. According to one study, the number of nursing-home residents in the United States will roughly double by the year 2030 while the total real cost of nursing homes will grow almost fivefold. *By then, the United States will be spending more on nursing homes (in real dollars) than it spends on Social Security today.*[13]

Some experts claim that this cost growth will slacken in future decades as our "health spans" lengthen along with our lifespans and the ills of old age are relegated to a brief (and inexpensive) period of declining vigor in the final years of life. Other experts disagree. According to the "failure of success" hypothesis, the main effect of modern medicine has been to increase the number of "marginal survivors" in the population. Longer lifespans, they say, will therefore be accompanied by a *rising* incidence of chronic illnesses, including arthritis, osteoporosis, deafness, blindness, heart and circulatory disorders, and various forms of senile dementia, including Alzheimer's—which afflicts 5 percent of elders under age 80 but 20 percent of elders over age 80. These chronic illnesses have been relatively resistant to cure, are relatively expensive to treat, and often require labor-intensive personal care for which there are no technological substitutes. Although it is still unclear which medical model is correct, one thing is for certain: The share of old old receiving institutional care continues to grow rapidly in most developed countries, and the cost per resident continues to climb at least as fast as worker pay.

Much of the growing cost of long-term care is absorbed by assorted general-purpose health budgets, often designed around the acute medical needs of indigent families. In the United States, Medicaid pays for roughly half of all nursing home stays even while many middle-class families are bankrupted by the cost they must pay out of their own pocket. But as the aggregate cost grows—and as most households with disabled elder relatives come to expect government assistance—many political leaders talk about breaking nursing care off into its own program. In 1994, Germany set up a separate agency with its own payroll tax revenue to provide long-term care benefits. Japan has plans to do something similar by the year 2000. Most countries (including the United States) are experimenting with home health benefits and other means of allowing the old old to "age in place." It remains to be seen, however, whether current reforms will slow this cost juggernaut—or hasten it by galvanizing voter support for universal long-term care benefits.

Global aging is also what happens when people start having fewer babies.

It's easy to see how longer lifespans can raise a society's average age. But this is only part of the story. As lifespans increase, fewer babies are being born. This "birth dearth" has been even more sudden—and has had even greater quantitative impact on global aging—than the rise in longevity. As recently as the late 1960s, most experts could detect hardly any real movement in the worldwide total fertility rate (that is, the average number of lifetime births per woman).[14] It stood at about 5.0, well within the range that had prevailed since time immemorial. Then came a behavioral revolution, one that shocked demographers. It was driven by rising affluence, urbanization, feminism, rising female participation in the workforce, widespread acceptance of new birth control technologies[15] and legalized abortion,[16] and (in some countries, most notably China) government policy. The result: an unprecedented decline in the global fertility rate. Today the global rate stands at about 2.7—meaning that it has fallen three-quarters of the distance to the "replacement rate" of 2.1. (The replacement rate is what is required merely to maintain a stationary population.[17]) In some countries, the decline has been astonishing. From the late 1960s to the late 1990s, the fertility rate in Mexico has dropped from 6.8 to 2.8; in India, from 5.7 to 3.1; and in China (with its well-known one-child-per-family rule, or "one child norm" as it is officially termed), from 6.1 to 1.8.[18]

Fertility in the developed world has followed the same downward trend, but with one big difference: Birthrates in most "industrial" societies had already entered a gradual decline that dates all the way back to the Victorian era, when urbanization and a broadening middle class began to dull people's enthusiasm for large families. By the early twentieth century, the developed world already had relatively low fertility rates, which makes the recent sharp drop even more startling. In the early 1960s, women in the developed world were averaging 2.7 births over their lifetime; today, the number has fallen to 1.6. Back then, every developed nation was at or above the 2.1 replacement rate; today, every developed nation has fallen beneath it. Leaders in the developed world who had once regarded lower birthrates as an urgent goal now view dropping birthrates in their own countries with growing anxiety.[19]

With a total fertility rate of right around 2.0, the United States stands at the very *high end* of the developed world. Yet 2.0 is a big drop from the U.S. postwar peak of 3.7 during the baby boom.[20] Since the "baby boom" will soon become a "senior boom," the United States (and other English-speaking countries like Canada and Great Britain) will actually age more rapidly in the future than other countries that did not experience a baby boom. At the other extreme are countries that experienced little or no postwar boom and whose fertility has now plunged to the lowest rates ever recorded except during episodes of famine or war. Japan's fertility rate has now fallen to 1.4, and since 1995 there have been fewer births annually in Japan than in any year since 1899. Germany's rate has fallen to 1.3, and Germany now produces fewer babies each year than Nepal, with a population only one-quarter as large. Italy, whose rate has fallen to 1.2, is at the extreme lower limit of global fertility. Fertility rates this low mean that each family generation is little more than half the size of its parents' generation. The traditional population pyramid, as it grows top-heavy with elders, is being turned on its head.

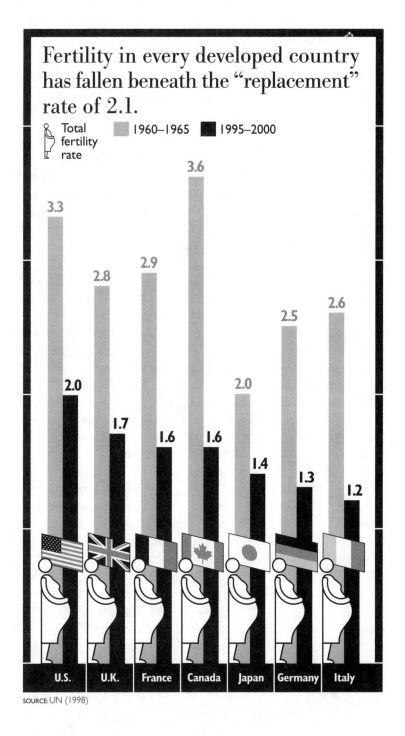

Fertility in every developed country has fallen beneath the "replacement" rate of 2.1.

Total fertility rate   1960–1965   1995–2000

U.S. 3.3 / 2.0
U.K. 2.8 / 1.7
France 2.9 / 1.6
Canada 3.6 / 1.6
Japan 2.0 / 1.4
Germany 2.5 / 1.3
Italy 2.6 / 1.2

SOURCE: UN (1998)

Global aging is pushing the developed world—and perhaps even the entire world—toward eventual population decline.

The logic is inexorable: Absent sizable immigration, every population in which women average less than 2.1 births per lifetime must eventually shrink. In the 1990s, the growth rate of the working-age population throughout the developed world has been decelerating, and in one country, Italy, this rate has already turned negative. During the next decade, the labor force will decline in Germany as it will in Japan, where the number of workers under age 30 is expected to fall by a whopping 25 percent between 2000 and 2010. By the 2010s, the working-age population will be contracting at nearly 1 percent per year in Italy, Germany, and Japan—and will begin turning negative in all of the developed countries combined. By the 2020s, working-age populations will shrink in every developed country, with the possible exception of Ireland. By then, with the workforce in some countries falling as fast as productivity rises, much of the "industrial world" will face a secular stagnation or perhaps even decline in real annual GDP, with unprecedented impacts on housing, business investment, infrastructure, asset prices, and even national defense.

By the late 2020s if not before, the total population of the developed world will likely peak and then begin to fall in absolute numbers. While this decline will be mild or may not happen at all in North America, elsewhere the downward trend may be dramatic. Western Europe and Japan, unless their fertility rates rise again, will shrink to one-half of their current population before the end of the twenty-first century. As Italian demographer Antonio Golini recently declared, "If Italy's fertility remains at the same level for 30 or 40 years, the Italian population will be reduced by one-third."[21] Dr. Shoichiro Toyoda, chairman of Toyota Motor Corporation and one of Japan's most influential business leaders, predicts (only half-jokingly) that—800 years from now—there won't

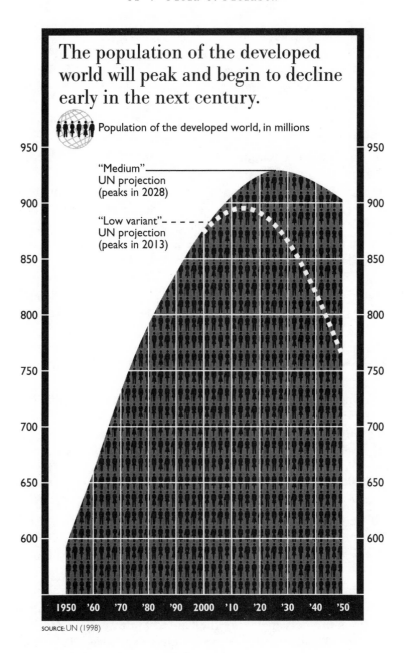

The population of the developed world will peak and begin to decline early in the next century.

Population of the developed world, in millions

"Medium" UN projection (peaks in 2028)

"Low variant" UN projection (peaks in 2013)

SOURCE: UN (1998)

be any Japanese left at all. In a recent report, Japan's Ministry of Health and Welfare tersely points out: "If we dare to make the calculation, Japan's population will be . . . about 500 people in the year 3000 and 1 person in the year 3500."[22]

Will the total world population begin to decline as well? Forty-four percent of the world's population already lives in countries with fertility below the replacement rate. According to a growing number of demographers, this share could rise much higher if fertility trends in the developing world continue to follow the developed-country example. According to one best-guess scenario, designed to reflect the assumptions held by the world's leading demographers, the world population will peak no later than the 2070s.[23] According to the so-called "low-variant" projection published by the United Nations, which assumes somewhat lower fertility than the "official" UN projection, this global population peak would occur (at 7.5 billion) around the year 2040.

An eventual convergence in global fertility, followed by a downturn in global population, is, of course, largely speculation. It won't happen soon, and it may not happen ever. What is certain is that over at least the next half-century an ongoing growth gap will persist between a demographically stagnant developed world and a relatively younger developing world whose fertility may never fall to replacement—and whose aging may never "catch up" to our own. How will these global trends play out? Since 1950, the developed world has shrunk from 24 percent to 15 percent of the world's population. Over the next fifty years, it will shrink to 10 percent—while the Mideast, Central Asia, Africa, and Latin America increases from 48 to 60 percent. In 1950, six of the twelve most populous nations were in the developed world: the United States, Japan, Germany, France, Italy, and the United Kingdom. Russia, technically not a "developed country," was also among the twelve. By 2050, the United Nations projects that only the United States will remain on the list. Replacing the others will be Nigeria, Pakistan, Ethiopia, Congo, Mexico, and the Philippines. In 1950,

A stunning number of countries are projected to lose population over the next fifty years.

	1998	2050	
Austria	8.1	7.1	Population in millions
Belarus	10.3	8.3	
Belgium	10.1	8.9	
Bulgaria	8.3	5.7	
Croatia	4.5	3.7	
Cuba	11.1	11.1	
Czech Rep.	10.3	7.8	
Denmark	5.3	4.8	
Estonia	1.4	0.9	
Finland	5.2	4.9	
Germany	82.1	73.3	
Greece	10.6	8.2	
Hungary	10.1	7.5	
Italy	57.4	41.2	
Japan	126.3	104.9	
Latvia	2.4	1.6	
Lithuania	3.7	3.0	
Netherlands	15.7	14.2	
Poland	38.7	36.3	
Portugal	9.9	8.1	
Romania	22.5	16.4	
Russian Fed.	147.4	121.3	
Slovakia	5.4	4.8	
Slovenia	2.0	1.5	
Spain	39.6	30.2	
Sweden	8.9	8.7	
Switzerland	7.3	6.7	
Ukraine	50.9	39.3	
U.K.	58.6	56.7	
Yugoslavia	10.6	10.5	
TOTAL	784.8	657.7	

Countries projected to lose population between 1998 and 2050

SOURCE: UN (1998)

The developed countries will make up an ever-shrinking share of the total world population.

Developed world population
as a % of the total world population

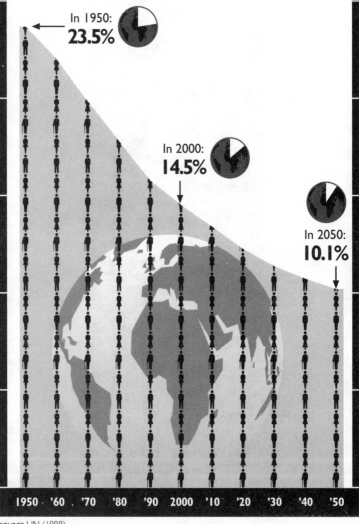

In 1950:
23.5%

In 2000:
14.5%

In 2050:
10.1%

1950 · '60 · '70 · '80 · '90 · 2000 · '10 · '20 · '30 · '40 · '50

SOURCE: UN (1998)

Africa's population was less than half of Europe's (including Russia's). Today it is roughly the same. By 2050, it will be over three times larger.

This disparity in population growth rates could lead to profound consequences for the developed world. Perhaps the most predictable consequence will be massive immigration pressure on older and wealthier societies facing labor shortages. If this pressure results in high and sustained rates of immigration, it will cause the share of ethnic and racial "minorities" in the developed-country populations to rise steadily. This will happen first in the youngest age brackets—adding an extra dynamic to the aging of developed countries. Immigrants are typically young and tend to bring with them the family practices of their native cultures.[24] At least for a while, they maintain a fertility rate higher than the average in their host countries. In the United States, for instance, Mexican-Americans have a fertility rate of 3.2—versus a rate among non-Hispanic whites of only 1.8.

With most developed countries experiencing an immigration surge over the last two decades, this dynamic is already underway. In the United States today, the foreign-born share of people in their 20s is nearly twice the share of people in their 60s. Hispanics and nonwhites now comprise 28 percent of the nonelderly and 15 percent of the elderly. By the year 2050, the U.S. Census Bureau expects that these shares will rise to 51 percent of the nonelderly and 34 percent of the elderly. In many European countries, non-European "foreigners" now make up roughly 10 percent of the population. This includes 10 to 13 million Muslims—nearly all of whom are working-age or younger. At current immigration rates, this foreign share is due to rise throughout Europe. In Germany, according to one recent projection, by 2030 foreigners will comprise 30 percent of the total population and over half the population of major cities like Munich and Frankfurt.

Global aging means that immigration will be a major issue for decades to come. Policy experts will debate the economic costs and benefits. Culture wars will rage over the

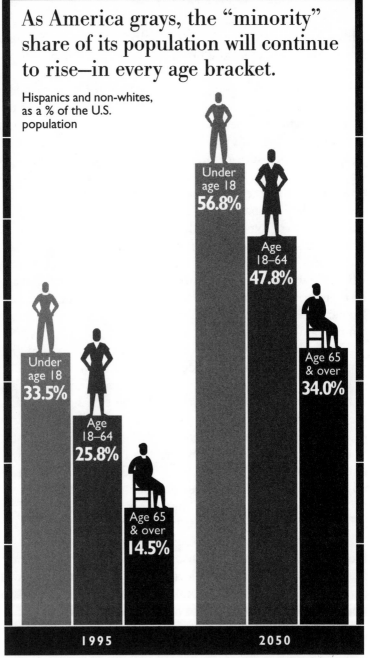

As America grays, the "minority" share of its population will continue to rise—in every age bracket.

Hispanics and non-whites, as a % of the U.S. population

Under age 18
33.5%

Age 18–64
25.8%

Age 65 & over
14.5%

Under age 18
56.8%

Age 18–64
47.8%

Age 65 & over
34.0%

1995

2050

SOURCE: Census (1996)

balkanization of language and religion. Politicians will seek to placate or vilify ethnic groups. Émigré leaders will sway foreign policy. Even the fiscal politics of pay-as-you-go retirement programs will be transformed—if the transfer of income between age groups comes to be viewed as a tribute exacted from struggling young newcomers for the benefit of privileged native-born elders.

Global aging will revolutionize the family, by drastically narrowing and lengthening its shape.

Throughout history, most people who reached old age came to know personally far more of their descendents than their ancestors. In the near future, this will be reversed. It is likely you will never get to know as many of your children (and all their progeny) as of your parents, your parents' parents, and so on. You will consider yourself lucky, indeed, if your entire extended family consists of more than three or four people your age or younger. In many of today's lowest-fertility societies—such as (former) East Germany or urban China—at least one of every two youths is an only child. In another generation, more than one in every four will have neither aunts, uncles, or cousins, nor brothers or sisters. An aging world will be filled with people whose genealogical trees are all stem and no branch.

While the family tree narrows, the surge in life expectancy will make the tree taller. Early in the next century, there will be more grandparents than grandchildren in many developed countries. The number of people who are some living person's child or grandchild will decline—and the number who are some living person's *great-grandchild* will rise. Once a rarity, four-generation families are becoming commonplace. American demographers are already predicting that the baby boom will ultimately give rise to an unprecedented great-grandparent boom.

Already, people are adjusting to an entirely new set of lifecycle expectations and family living patterns. Many elders raised in large families are surprised (and sometimes saddened) by their grown children's decision to have no or few children, while many younger adults find large families undesirable or unaffordable. Many couples have as many aging parents to care for—during as many years—as they had children. A whole new "sandwich" generation of fifty somethings is learning how to cope simultaneously with needy 75-year-olds and 25-year-olds—all of whom may at some point "boomerang" back home.

In the future, such trends will grow stronger. With each passing decade, the number of family "caregivers" available to help each dependent elder will decline steadily, increasing the time and money burden on mature adults and putting extra pressure on governments to pick up the slack. Today, America's boomers are typically able to share the task of taking care of mom and dad among many siblings. But when the boomers themselves grow old, they and their peers in the developed world will be much more likely to have no child or only one child (or to be never-married, widowed, divorced, or estranged from spouse or children) even as they live much longer. As of 1995, 20 percent of U.S. women aged 35 to 39 were childless, nearly twice the percentage registered by their parents at the same age.[25] For boomers unable to purchase at-home or institutional care, a rising share will have no informal alternative to public programs. Moreover, as families get narrower, even the nonelderly may find themselves turning more to government to replace whatever assistance today's "kith and kin" networks provide (in finding a job or recovering from financial or health emergencies). In an era of fiscal austerity, shrinking family size will create new *public needs* on practically every front.

Global aging is ushering in a profound transformation of the world's largest geopolitical institutions. Yet it will also have an unprecedented impact on the world's smallest social unit, the family. No one can be sure how this will play out. In virtually every society we know of, the extended family has served as a vital institution of socialization and mutual assistance. Its atrophy could have major unforeseen social and political consequences, especially combined with further breakdown in nuclear families. Here too we journey into the unknown.

The official projections may err on the side of optimism, since they assume that the underlying causes of global aging will weaken over time.

Unlike many predictions about the future, global aging is about as close as social science ever comes to a certain forecast. Absent a Hollywood catastrophe—a colliding comet or an alien invasion—it will surely happen. In fact, it is already happening. The reason is simple: Future 65-year-olds are already born. And although the number of younger people cannot be projected as precisely, few demographers believe that the current downward birth trend will reverse itself. As three top demographers recently observed in *Nature,* global aging is no mere hypothesis: "A strong increase in the proportion of elderly people is virtually certain, with the low end of the 95 percent confidence interval showing almost a doubling of today's level." Noting that these trends "could bring serious consequences for social security systems," the authors concluded that "the focus of public, political, and scientific concern will continue to shift from global population growth to population aging."[26]

Far from overstating global aging, today's official projections may well *underestimate* its true future magnitude. On longevity, for example, none of the official fiscal projections assume that life expectancy will continue to rise at its historical pace (let alone speed up); instead, they all assume it will grow more slowly in the decades to come. This assumption sometimes leads to almost surreal results. In the United States, for instance, newspaper headlines report unflagging progress against major killer diseases, such as the announcement that in the 1990s the incidence of cancer has been declining for the first time since the 1930s. Yet the

Social Security Administration continues to assume that U.S. longevity at age 65 will grow 60 percent more slowly in the future than it has over the past quarter-century—meaning that Americans by the year 2050 will have a life expectancy no greater than the Japanese *already have today.*

There is no sound basis for this slow-growth longevity prognosis. The U.S. Social Security Administration now projects that the number of Americans aged 85 and over will grow from 4 million in 1998 to 15 million by 2050. But this stunning growth trend is actually slower than the findings of most other academic demographers and government agencies (including the Census Bureau), who project from 20 to 40 million or even more in 2050.[27] To support the higher numbers, these experts point to the historical trend as well as the recent progress on the genetic origins of illness (especially cancer) and on the biochemistry of human aging. In the 1990s, entire new industries, specializing in everything from organ replacement to gene splicing, have emerged. Firms are poised to take advantage of what some entrepreneurs are calling a "golden age" of biomedical discovery. As yet, few go so far as to announce the imminent arrival of "postmortal" societies—with lifespans of 120 years or more.[28] Should that happen, humanity will truly be entering a brave new world. But even if we entirely discount these revolutionary claims, it seems foolish to suppose a future in which medical advances slow down.

Likewise, on fertility, most government and global agencies assume an eventual return to the replacement rate of 2.1 births per woman, no matter how far below that rate the developed countries have already drifted. In the United States, the Social Security Administration assumes that the fertility rate will continue to hover indefinitely at 1.9, just below replacement. Yet this too can be regarded as optimistic, since 1.9 is higher than the current fertility rate in 19 of the other 22 developed countries (excepting only New Zealand, Ireland, and Iceland). Even the SSA's "pessimistic" or "high-cost" scenario assumes an ultimate future rate of

The number of "old old" could far exceed the official projections.

Americans aged 85 & over in 2050, according to alternative projections

Assumption in official U.S. fiscal projections →

Projection by
SSA

14.6 million

Projection by
Census

18.2 million

Projection by
Ronald Lee*

21.4 million

Projection by
James Vaupel*

39.0 million

Projection by
Kenneth Manton*

48.7 million

SOURCE: SSA (1996); Census (1996); NIA (1996) *Research funded by the National Institute on the Aging

1.6—*which is greater than the average rate in Europe today.*
Demographers now know of nothing that is likely to reverse
a long-term fertility decline which—with a few episodic
exceptions, such as the postwar U.S. baby boom—has been
underway for well over a century.

This is not to suggest that the experts have a very good
track record at predicting up or down swings in fertility. They
don't. In the late 1930s, for example, most experts in the
developed world extrapolated from declining fertility trends
and entirely missed the postwar baby boom. In the late 1950s,
they extrapolated from rising fertility trends and entirely
missed the "baby bust" of the late 1960s and 1970s. As
demographer Nicholas Eberstadt elegantly notes, "The paradox of long-term demographic forecasting is that its methods
combine superb technique with an almost complete lack of
viable predictive theory."[29] Yet to admit past mistakes is not to
confess absolute ignorance no matter what the evidence. For
one thing, each of those earlier mistaken forecasts was based
on trends that were only twenty years old. Today, we're looking at trends that are nearly *forty* years old. For another, none
of today's official fertility forecasts assumes that future rates
will continue to decline; indeed, most assume they will rise.

This raises an obvious question: What would the long-
term demographic future of the developed world look like if
we did not assume that fertility rates will gradually drift back
to the replacement rate of 2.1? Well, as it turns out, the
United Nations regularly publishes just such a projection. It's
called the "low-variant" UN scenario. It assumes that fertility
rates in every developed country will eventually stabilize at
somewhere between 1.35 and 1.50, that is, at about what
European fertility is today. And it draws a far more stunning—not to say alarming—picture than the "official" UN or
OECD numbers normally relied on by everyone (myself
included) who writes about the aging challenge. In the "official" developed-world projection, the median age rises from
37 today to 46 in 2050. This is amazing enough—but in the
"low-variant" projection it rises all the way to 51 in 2050.

And this is just the average. In Germany, the median age is projected to reach 53; in Japan, 54; in Italy, 57. And what about the ratio of working-age adults to elders? In the "official" projection, it will fall to 2.5; in the "low-variant" projection, it will fall to 2.0. Meanwhile, the *average* ratio of taxpaying workers to pensioned beneficiaries would fall to 1.0—a figure reached only by a few countries in the "official" projection.

I won't insist on this low fertility scenario. But I must confess that it seems quite plausible. Even conceding our ignorance of the unknown, it is hard to imagine—absent radical policy changes or a major cultural shift[30]—a substantial easing in the "modernizing" social forces that now seem to link rising affluence with smaller families in most societies throughout the world. One such force is the feminization of the global workforce. According to the UN's International Labor Organization, women are the primary source of income in about 30 percent of the world's households. Another force is the extent to which affluent countries have socialized the cost of growing old while keeping the cost of raising children private. One traditional motive for having children—preparing yourself for a secure old age—has thus been weakened, while one of the greatest challenges of parenting—preparing your child for an adequate livelihood—has been made more daunting than ever. As our societies age and as our fiscal burdens mount, this fertility disincentive may help lock in the very scenario that endangers our economy.

As we try to face up to the full magnitude of the global aging challenge, it's important to keep in mind how it arose—not as a strange historical accident, but as the byproduct of a trend toward affluence, individualism, and secular progress that the vast majority of the world's population seems to welcome. Many demographers believe that every society embracing this trend sooner or later moves from high fertility and high mortality (the traditional norm) to low fertility and low mortality (the modern norm). They even have a name for it. They call it "the demographic transition." It is modernization's defining rite of passage, and thus far it appears to be irreversible. "This is the first time humans have altered the age structure of the population," observes the noted demographer Jay Olshansky.[31] It remains to be seen whether humankind can gracefully accommodate the new realities the demographic transition is bringing in its wake.

3

Fiscal Realities

"Boy, I'm sure glad I got up here before
Medicare started running low."

THE POLITICAL ECONOMY OF ANY SOCIETY MUST PROVIDE FOR dependents and prepare for the future. Global aging promises to make both tasks much more difficult by increasing the relative number of dependents and by shifting society's resources and attention away from its future. All regions will be affected, but global aging poses a special fiscal challenge to the twenty-three so-called developed nations. Here is where we find the oldest populations, the largest welfare states, the most generous retirement promises—and the least sustainable budgetary projections. Here is also where we see many variations on a single theme called fiscal duress. Elsewhere, the situation is more diverse. In some poor countries, aging by itself is not a critical issue. In others, it is—though often for reasons that have more to do with the struggle to modernize a traditional society (for example, setting up a retirement safety net for a newly urbanized workforce) than with the rising fiscal cost of past promises.

UNSUSTAINABLE LONG-TERM PROJECTIONS

In the developed world, global aging translates predictably into explosive growth in government outlays for pay-as-you-go elder benefits. According to nearly all official agencies or think tanks that have studied the simple arithmetic of dependency ratios and pay-as-you-go systems, the long-term fiscal projections are staggering.

They are so staggering, in fact, that we might reasonably conclude they could never come to pass. They are, after all, projections not predictions. They tell us what is likely to happen *if* current policy remains unchanged; they don't tell us whether it is likely or even possible for this condition to hold. In all probability, economies would implode and governments would collapse before these projections could materialize. But this is exactly why we must focus on them—for they raise the paramount question: How and when will we change course? Will we do so sooner, when we still have time to control our destiny? Or later, after unsustainable economic damage and political and social trauma lead to a wrenching and involuntary upheaval? Thus, the relevant questions raised by "unsustainable" trends have to do with the nature and timing of the adjustments necessary to reach a more sustainable path. My purpose in discussing these trends is to rouse the public from an indifference fostered by too many politicians telling them not to worry. I do this hoping that we can avoid a tragic outcome.

It is also true that long-term fiscal projections, even assuming current policy remains unchanged, are subject to considerable uncertainty. No serious policy expert would deny this. And if the projections pointed to a problem of only modest size, I might be inclined to agree with those who say, well, no one knows for sure—so why not just wait and see? Unfortunately, the projections point to a problem of alarming dimensions. It's hardly a question of looking at the third decimal point. The numbers for future cost growth are of such magnitude that no plausible changes in the economic and demographic assumptions underlying the projections would make the outcome sustainable.

This is true even if we limit ourselves to cash pensions—despite recent trivial efforts to ratchet down future cash benefit formulas, for example, by gradually raising the "normal" retirement age. Consider the latest OECD projections, which include only the largest national public pension programs in each country.[1] According to these numbers, the fastest-aging countries will experience the fastest cost growth. In Japan, where the age wave has already arrived in force, government pension spending is projected to double as a share of the Japanese economy, from 6.6 percent of GDP in 1995 to 13.4 percent by the year 2030. In continental Europe, the climb will be slower, but since these countries have more generous systems to begin with, the total projected GDP rise will be nearly the same. In Germany, pension costs are projected to rise from 11.1 to 16.5 percent of GDP; in Italy, from 13.3 to 20.3 percent. For most countries, it is possible to recalculate these costs as a share of taxable worker payroll by multiplying the GDP numbers by about 2.5—so that in Japan, for instance, the payroll tax rate on covered workers would have to increase from about 17 to 34 percent in order to pay for future pensions. The long-term projections for Spain, Portugal, the Netherlands, Norway, Finland, and Austria are roughly similar. The projections for France, Denmark, and Sweden are only marginally better.

On the other hand, those countries which are aging later and have less expensive (and better-designed) pension systems face a somewhat less daunting cost challenge. In the United States, for example, the Social Security Administration projects that Social Security will rise from 4.6 to only 6.8 percent of GDP by 2030. I use the word "only" as a relative qualifier. This extra cost is equivalent to a 48 percent hike in the payroll tax rate. If this total swing of 2.2 percentage points of

GDP were payable starting next year, it would amount to roughly $200 billion annually—more than we could generate by raising federal personal income tax rates by 25 percent. Finally, deserving perhaps their own special category, there are a few countries where pension costs as a share of GDP are expected to rise only slightly (Australia) or even *decline* (Britain and Ireland). This fiscal good fortune is not due to any special demographic trend, but to reforms in these countries that allow new benefit awards to shrink as a share of average wages in future decades.

In most countries, global aging thus promises to heap enormous costs on future taxpayers. But wait: Pensions aren't the only public costs that rise as populations age. Health benefits could turn out to be an even bigger burden. Old people consume three to five times more health-care services per capita than younger people—and, as a rule, have most of their medical bills picked up by government. Meanwhile, the "aging of the aged" will push up per-capita costs even faster. Stir these multipliers together, and public health spending on the elderly is likely to rise at least as fast as public pension spending. According to OECD projection data, demographic aging alone will increase total public health spending in the typical G-7 nation[2] from about 6 to 9 percent of GDP by the year 2030.

Even this projection is an underestimate: It assumes that health spending per retiree will grow no faster than taxable wages per worker, whereas historically this spending has greatly outpaced wages almost everywhere. In the United States, to take the most conspicuous example, Medicare outlays per enrollee have grown at least 4 percent per year faster than wages during every decade since the program began. Assuming that, in the future, outlays continue to outpace wages by only a small margin—say, by a mere 1 percent per year—the typical G-7 public health bill will rise from 6 to 12 percent of GDP by 2030.

None of these projections includes the large extra cost burden for health services that public budgets don't cover. The

Graying means paying much more for pensions and healthcare.

Public spending on pensions and health benefits, as a % of GDP

1995   2030 official projection

Country	1995	2030
U.K.	10.5%	15.5%
U.S.	10.5%	17.0%
Japan	11.5%	23.1%
Canada	12.6%	22.5%
Germany	17.3%	28.8%
France	17.6%	25.8%
Italy	19.7%	33.3%

By comparison, total G-7 public spending on defense, education, and R&D was 8.1% of GDP in 1995.

SOURCE: OECD (1996, 1997); Census (1997); author's calculations

biggest *uncovered* item is *long-term care* for elders who don't or won't qualify for public assistance. And this is a big item indeed. In the United States, the growth in total spending on formal long-term care over the next forty years is expected to amount to roughly 4 percent of GDP. Government now expects to pay for only half of this cost increase—and provide no help for the even greater increase in informal care within ordinary families. In an aging world full of two-earner couples and short of potential caregivers, government may be forced to pay a much larger share of the long-term care burden.

Both of these fiscal kickers—health cost inflation and the political demand for more long-term care benefits—will be at work throughout the developed world. But nowhere do they threaten to raise public spending so dramatically as in the United States, whose relatively lower public pension costs may be entirely overwhelmed by a health-cost explosion without parallel elsewhere.

All told, most developed countries will have to spend at least an extra 9 to 16 percent of GDP annually to fulfill their old-age benefit promises. This vast increase is three to five times what the United States currently spends on national defense. It also comes to an extra 25 to 40 percent taken out of every worker's taxable wages—in countries where total payroll tax rates often exceed 40 percent already.

The economic burden imposed on future workers can also be gauged by looking at the total value of future old-age benefits earned to date by today's adults for which nothing has been saved. This is called an "unfunded benefit liability." In every major developed country, the unfunded liability *for public pensions alone* amounts to 100 to 250 percent of GDP—an amount far greater, in each country, than its official public debt. (In the United States, this unfunded liability amounts to roughly $100,000 per household.) Public budgets worldwide are run on a cash-in, cash-out basis. But if governments had to account for accrued pension liabilities according to the same rules private firms typically use in accounting for their own—which means amortizing them as

The developed countries have accumulated massive unfunded pension liabilities—on par with the debt burden of nations at war.

Unfunded public pension liabilities in 1990, as a % of GDP

U.S.	Canada	U.K.	Germany	Japan	France	Italy
113%	121%	156%	157%	162%	216%	242%

SOURCE: OECD (1993)

expenses over 30 or 40 years—most public budgets would show an additional annual charge against revenue amounting to 10 percent or more of GDP. If the U.S. federal government, for example, were to start using private-sector ERISA[3] regulations to account for all of its pension programs, *annual* recorded costs would jump by $750 billion. (Including unfunded Medicare liabilities, they would jump to roughly *$1.5 trillion.*) Political leaders might have a greater incentive to control the rising cost of unfunded retirement promises if these figures were included in current budgets and made public.

Liabilities that even approach these levels are usually piled up by nations only at times of extreme crisis. From 1939 to 1946, for example, the official U.S. public debt rose to 125 percent of GDP while the British public debt rose to about 200 percent of GDP. Observes financial expert David Hale, "The only good analogy to the magnitude of the fiscal challenge posed by the aging of Europe's population is war."[4]

That the developed world is moving more or less in the same direction does not mean that industrial countries are moving in the same way or at the same speed. In each nation, the trend takes on a special spin that reflects the history, culture, and political system of the society in question.

JAPAN: FIRST TO ENCOUNTER THE "AGING SOCIETY PROBLEM"

Japan is an early-warning test case because it is already aging so rapidly. Twenty years ago, Japan was the *youngest* society in the developed world. By 2005, it will be the *oldest.* By 2007, the Japanese population as a whole will begin to shrink. By the year 2010, Japan's ratio of working-age adults to elders will be the very first to sink below 3.0. Marketers around the globe now study Japan to find out what happens at the cutting edge of global aging. Among Japan's losing industries: pediatrics, toys, education, housing starts. Among the winners: nurses, leisure cruises, pets, religious icons.

Why is Japan aging so soon? One reason lies buried in the rubble of Hiroshima and Nagasaki—and the trauma of postwar reconstruction: After 1945, the Japanese no longer saw themselves as an expanding empire in need of an ever-larger rising generation. Not only was abortion legalized in Japan in 1948—much earlier than in other developed countries—but the law permitted abortions when the pregnancy posed any risk to the mother's health or to the family's ability to support itself. Ever since, abortion has ceased to be a religious or political issue. By the 1950s, a national "population control" movement was flourishing,[5] and soon parents were having fewer children. Elsewhere in the developed world, birthrates boomed or at least plateaued in the two decades following World War II. Japan, however, experienced a baby bust, and by the 1960s its birthrate had fallen to half of what it was in the late 1940s. Elsewhere, elementary schools began emptying in the 1970s. In Japan, they began emptying in the 1960s, and ever since 1970 the worker-support ratio has been falling at an accelerating pace. Remarkably, in the fifty- year period between 1945 and 1994, the share of Japanese below the age of 15 fell from 37 percent to only 16 percent, so that today there are more elderly than there are children under the age of 15.

Even apart from its early timing, the aging of Japan is shaped by long-term demographic forces that promise to pose daunting fiscal challenges over the next several decades. Japan's current fertility rate (last year falling to 1.4) is not the world's lowest. But it has languished at or beneath the 2.1 replacement rate for so long—over four decades—that single-child families have become the new social norm. For this reason, few experts expect Japanese fertility to rise again soon.

Since 1950, the unmarried share of all Japanese women aged 25 to 29 has expanded from one-third to two-thirds. Masahiro Yamada, a sociologist at Tokyo Gakugei University, calls these young unmarried women, most of whom still live at home with their parents, "parasitic singles"—or more charitably, *shinguru kizoku*, the "single aristocracy."[6] These young adults typically contribute only a few hundred dollars a month toward rent, food, and other expenses. That permits them a very attractive lifestyle, with the bulk of their income available for pleasant discretionary expenditures such as clothing, eating out, traveling abroad, and entertainment. By contrast, as these women contemplate a marriage in which a couple with their children live on only one income and pay extraordinarily big rents for very small spaces, the marriage option can look like a serious downgrade in lifestyle. Why else do they resist marriage? Many resent the wife's traditional and onerous obligations to the husband's extended family. Others are put off by the male-dominated "Japanese corporate culture," which (observes a recent government report) "requires husbands to put work before family,"[7] and in which men rarely come home until late in the evening, often work on weekends, and when they do come home are often unwilling to help with domestic chores and the children. And today, with more women receiving college educations and pursuing careers, they are less dependent on marriage for economic support. Among those who don't marry, social stigma discourages out-of-wedlock births to a greater extent than in other countries (such as the United States). Even among those who do marry, small, crowded, and extraordinarily expensive housing—particularly in cities—limits family size. Given Japan's traditional aversion to newcomers, it's unlikely that there will ever be enough young taxpaying immigrants to pick up all this slack.

Meanwhile, salutary dietary and lifestyle habits (including a national diet very low in fat, making Japan the most heart disease-free society in the world) have raised the Japanese life expectancy to record heights. Again, extreme longevity doesn't just multiply the number of elderly; it multiplies them fastest at the ages when they are most likely be alone, dependent, ill, or disabled. Having overwhelmed Japan's meager nursing home system, this wave of old-elders has given rise to widespread "social admissions," that is, long-term stays at acute-care hospitals.

In addition to its extraordinary demographic future, Japan faces severe economic problems in the wake of the collapse of its "bubble economy." Still lingering in the recessionary aftermath, Japan in the 1990s has been forced to lower its future projections for real wage growth—which in turn means raising its future projections for benefit costs as a share of payroll. Meanwhile, the financial crisis in Southeast Asia has deferred any hope of early revival for Japanese financial markets. The depressed market value of Japanese real estate and business equity and Japan's moribund banking system not only hinder a sustained economic recovery, but also pose a vast (yet still largely hidden) underfunding crisis for Japan's private pension plans. According to some estimates, the current gap between private pension assets and accrued pension liabilities is equal to 20 percent of equity in many large corporations. Should the government decide to bail out these plans, younger Japanese taxpayers will face yet another bill from their elders.

Despite all of these challenges, Japan possesses genuine social and institutional advantages. Japanese wage earners stash much of their year-end bonuses into bank-run thrift accounts, which boosts Japan's national savings rate to the highest in the developed world. In turn, the Japanese don't expect large public pensions, which keeps the long-term cost projections from rising even higher. Public pensions typically replace between 45 and 50 percent of Japanese preretirement pay, well beneath European standards. Though they live longer, Japanese retirees receive benefits for fewer years, since they retire later. Well over one-third of all Japanese men work past age 65 (often at part-time jobs, and at lower wages, after their formal "retirement").

Most important, an ethic of family piety—similar to Chinese "Confucian values"—encourages children and their parents to take personal responsibility for each other throughout their lives. At last count, some 65 percent of Japanese elders lived with their grown children. That's down from 80 percent in the 1950s, which reflects how affluence, "westernization," and careers for women erode traditions, especially the custom allowing elders to tyrannize over their daughters-in-law. Still, it helps to keep in mind that the U.S. figure is a mere 15 percent. No other country does as well as Japan in enabling families to satisfy many of the elderly's daily needs, including simple human contact, that otherwise would require a costly army of nurses and social service agencies.

The prevalence of multigenerational households has also had a positive influence on policy debates over elder benefits. In other countries, such debates are either politically taboo or become instantly seized by the rhetoric of entitled "rights" to benefits. In Japan, *koreika shakai mondai* ("the aging society problem") is widely and realistically discussed, with plenty of references to "generational equity" and without the inhibiting presence of any sizeable senior lobby. In this atmosphere, Japan's political leaders can proceed more boldly than their counterparts abroad. Since the early 1980s, they have responded to the demographic bad news by making significant cuts in promised pension benefits and by enacting a so-called "Gold Plan" expansion in nursing homes and home-care assistance to hard-pressed families—all to little controversy. Does all this reflect some rare brand of political courage? From the same politicians who don't dare say no to bankers or retailers or rice farmers? Hardly. What it illustrates, instead, is an emerging public consensus—indeed, a cultural predisposition—that may yet help Japan confront a daunting fiscal future.

ITALY: THE WORLD'S WORST-CASE PENSION SCENARIO

In Italy, politics and demography are already conspiring to produce what may be the world's worst-case pension scenario. To begin with, imagine a pension system so generous that it awards new retirees indexed cash benefits equal to 80 percent of pretax wages during their last five years of employment, which means that many people are better off retired (when they no longer have to pay payroll taxes) than at work. Next, imagine a retirement age so low that people can retire with full benefits at age 55—and many are eligible for "reduced" benefits even earlier, in their early fifties for private-sector workers and in their early forties for vast legions of government workers. And finally, for those impatient to wait even this long to retire, imagine medical guidelines so lax that disability pensions can be procured by influential professionals (or distributed widely to entire towns) in return for political favors.

Welcome to retiring, Italian style. Costing over 15 percent of GDP—that's 33 percent of worker payroll—Italy's cash pensions are the world's most expensive. Having expanded by 5 percentage points of GDP over just the last fifteen years, they may also be the world's fastest growing. They have pushed other forms of national social spending—on everything from schools to unemployment—into a shrinking budgetary corner. Already, the number of Italian public pensions actually *exceeds* the number of contributing workers. This situation is economically (if not fiscally) bearable only because two or more pensions often go to the same person, which means that fewer people are actually retired, and because many who do receive pensions continue to work in the "submerged" or nontaxpaying economy. Every Italian leader acknowledges the need for reform, and most agree that recent cost-saving measures enacted under the Dini and Prodi governments are too little and too late. Yet serious reform remains gridlocked. The labor-linked "parties of the left" don't want to spoil a deal that works well for their union members—roughly half of whom, incredibly, are already retired. Right of center, reformers aren't sure how to wean the country from its overwhelming dependence on unfunded public benefits. Much of the Italian public has no familiarity with any sort of private or funded substitute.

Still worse, Italy's long-term fiscal future is in the grip of ruinous demographic trends. Italy recently became the first nation in history with more people over age 60 than under age 20. The problem? Italians aren't having nearly enough babies. Forget the old *mamma mia* stereotype of the overflowing and faithfully Catholic Italian family. Italy today is a highly secular society in which contraception, abortion, and divorce are legal and widespread, where over half of all mothers with small children are employed,[8] and where many young people put marriage and family formation on hold. In fact, Italy is gripped by a "bambini bust"—the lowest fertility rate, 1.2 children per woman's lifetime, of any nation in the world. And even that figure is a national average. Take away the somewhat larger families south of Rome in what Italians like to call their *Mezzogiorno,* and we're left with a fertility rate in the north at slightly less than 1.0. In Bologna, a prosperous northern city with a higher share of college-educated women than any other Italian city, the fertility rate has reportedly fallen to 0.8. On its current course, Italy's industrial heartland will lose over half of its native younger workers with each new generation.

Even the official projections show that the cost of Italy's pensions alone will exceed 50 percent of worker payroll by 2030. In the sober words of Massimo Liv-Bacci, professor of demography at the University of Florence, "We have the best pension system in Europe and the worst system for family support. Rich old people supported by the labor of poor young people. No wonder nobody wants to have a family."[9]

Italy has a few offsetting advantages. It spends no more on health care than the developed-country average. Because disabled Italian elders are generally cared for within the extended family, which is the norm in most Mediterranean countries, it spends little on long-term care. (In general, the popularity of nursing homes declines as you move south from Scandinavia.) Meanwhile, despite the lack of funded private pensions, Italy enjoys a high household savings rate—which allows the government to run sizeable budget deficits without grave economic consequences. Yet, on balance, Italy faces an extraordinary fiscal gauntlet—as does much of the rest of continental Europe. From Oslo to Vienna, legislators are grappling with similar issues that seem to chase each other in a vicious cycle: declining birthrates, generous cash benefits, early retirement, lenient disability, towering payroll tax rates, the slashing of other budget functions, a union and labor-party fixation on "defending" pensions, zero job growth, and youths waiting endlessly for careers to open.

Italy's fertility rate may be the rock bottom, but it has many close runner-ups among its European neighbors: Spain, the Czech Republic, Romania, and Bulgaria (also at 1.2), Germany, Greece, Latvia, Estonia, Slovenia, and Russia (at 1.3), and Portugal, Austria, Hungary, Ukraine, and many others (at 1.4). In fact, according to the United Nations, twenty of the world's twenty-three nations with fertility rates beneath 1.5 are located in Southern, Central, and Eastern Europe. Economists warn that escalating young-to-old income transfers may eventually plunge societies into a downward demographic spiral, in which deteriorating economic performance and declining birthrates begin to reinforce each other. No one knows when that point is reached. But Italy and its environs are worth careful examination: We may already be looking at one or more societies in which that dynamic is underway.

AMERICA: LAND OF THE HEALTH COST EXPLOSION

Finally, let's turn to the United States. People everywhere should be thankful that the developed world's most populous and productive nation possesses several enviable advantages in meeting the aging challenge. The United States is now the youngest of the G-7 nations. By a narrow margin, its fertility rate is the highest. By a wider margin, its net immigration rate from the developing world is the highest. This should ensure that it *remains* the youngest of the G-7 for decades to come and that its aged dependency ratio stays well under the developed-country average.

Even aside from demographics, the United States is not an expensive place to run a public pension system. The typical

U.S. retirement age is well above average, in part due to more flexible labor markets and better enforced age-discrimination laws. The spectacle of seniors still working in American stores and offices often surprises European (though not Japanese) visitors. Along with later retirement, benefit levels are relatively modest. The United States also has a long tradition of private plans—thrift accounts, insurance policies, and employer pensions (covering nearly half of America's workers)—to supplement the retirement income of middle- and upper-income families. This hasn't done much to raise national savings, since U.S. households borrow so much and save so little outside of their pension plans. In fact, the U.S. national savings rate is the lowest in the developed world. But these private plans take some political pressure off the government's pay-as-you-go system. U.S. Social Security, while generous to low-income married workers, provides relatively less than other countries at higher income levels (and to singles). The typical American worker receives a benefit equal to 40 to 45 percent of preretirement wages, a bit below Japan and barely half the level of Italy and France. Compared to Europe, to put it another way, the U.S. federal government currently saves nearly 2 percent of GDP—or some $150 billion annually—through its advantage in benefit levels alone.

Yet for all this good news, the United States labors under two major disadvantages. The first is its very low national savings rate, which will severely restrict the ability of future Congresses to deficit-finance any sizable portion of rising benefit costs. During the 1990s, the U.S. rate of net national savings, at under 5 percent of GDP, was not only lower than that of any other developed economy—it was lower than any earlier decade in postwar U.S. history. (In 1998, the U.S. personal savings rate may come in near absolute zero.) This may seem hard to believe at a time when the Dow Jones Index is at relatively high levels and many Americans feel they're "saving" plenty in their investment accounts. But asset appreciation is not the kind of savings that matters in the long run. A stock-market boom, for all its benefits, does not release new real resources from consumption uses to investment uses, nor does it add to the nation's real capital stock. In practice, the stock market reflects many factors other than the efficiency of business capital—and, historically, it has proven to be a poor indicator of future productivity growth.[10] That is why most economists still subscribe to the official measure of national savings, which is the share of current income dedicated to net new investments. According to this measure, the U.S. performance is dismal.

The second U.S. disadvantage is the cost of its health care. After decades of rapid growth, U.S. health-care spending is now more than twice the developed-country average as a share of GDP. In most other countries, governments set broad health priorities and expect doctors and hospitals to work within *fixed* overall budgets. Only in America have the health-care professions been so free to define what treatments are necessary. Only in America are cost-benefit trade-offs so frequently ignored. Only in America is the insuring and litigating of medical malpractice a major industry. And only in America are medical technologies employed with such limitless abandon to "do everything we can." This open-ended arrangement pleases patients, enriches doctors—and bankrupts taxpayers. On a per capita basis, for example, the United States has eight times as many MRI units as Canada and four and a half times as many open-heart surgery units as Germany.

This national cost explosion translates directly into a rising fiscal burden. True, U.S. government spending on health care is generally limited to the elderly. So vast is the U.S. cost per capita, however, that even these outlays (at nearly 7 percent of GDP) exceed what most other developed-country governments spend on universal plans covering *all* age groups. Precisely because U.S. health-care programs target the old, aging will have a far greater impact on their cost, which is why many experts project much larger growth in public health costs for the United States than elsewhere. A common figure for the major European countries is a rise of about 3 percent of GDP over the next 40 years; whereas the

U.S. Congressional Budget Office concludes that U.S. costs will rise by 7 percent—and even this estimate rests on optimistic assumptions. So while it's true that Social Security's cost growth will be relatively "modest" between now and the year 2030 (from 11 to as much as 21 percent of payroll), adding in the projections for Medicare and Medicaid for seniors could boost the total cost to well over 50 percent of payroll—an unsustainable Italian-sized projection. As health economist Victor Fuchs recently observed: "Although people justifiably worry about Social Security, paying for old folks' health care is the real 800-pound gorilla facing the economy."[11]

So America will be facing big challenges after all. Will the U.S. political system be able to handle these challenges? It's at least possible that America's traditional belief in economic self-sufficiency will deter citizens from overdependence on government and dissuade voters from repeating the fiscal excesses of social democrats abroad. Then again, it might not. Experience teaches, unfortunately, that the preference for personal ownership can easily be expanded (through popular fictions such as "contributions" and "trust funds") to include *un*funded government benefits. As such, a personal "entitlement" may be no easier to trim in Washington, D.C. than a "social contract" is to negotiate in Paris. In Europe, elders influence policy through unusually strong unions and political parties. In America, home of the world's most powerful self-standing senior lobby, the American Association of Retired Persons (AARP), elders exercise power directly by organizing retirees to defend what many believe they have bought and paid for. It's hard to say which situation is more dysfunctional politically.

Timing is also a double-edged sword. Whereas Japan will be the first developed nation to experience rapid aging, the United States will be the last. This delay could be an advantage, since it gives U.S. political leaders more time to plan ahead, to enact gradual policy changes, and perhaps to learn from fiscal disasters abroad. It also gives U.S. households more time to prepare personally for what lies ahead. On the other hand, this delay could breed complacency and encourage endless discussion by face-saving commissions. Americans have grown used to thinking about "the age wave" as something to worry about "way out there" when boomers retire. If the United States responds to its challenge no sooner than other countries respond to theirs, it could find itself worse off—for it will be forced to respond more quickly in a far less forgiving global environment. In the 1980s and 1990s, nations slow to take their fiscal medicine have been able to borrow abroad and run large deficits without irreparable harm. That may not be possible for any economy in the 2010s and 2020s—least of all for a very large economy having a very thin reservoir of national savings.

Much of the social and demographic environment shaping U.S. pension policy is shared by the rest of the English-speaking world—including Britain, Ireland, Canada, and Australia. All of these countries have relatively high rates of fertility and (Ireland excepted) high net immigration. All had a significant post-World War II baby boom, and thus all will age somewhat later and more rapidly than elsewhere. In all of them, the typical retirement age is late, the typical public pension formula is modest, capital markets are deep, the ethic of self-sufficiency is strong, and private retirement vehicles are popular. In all of them, at least half of all workers participate in a funded private pension plan (which is true nowhere else except Switzerland, the Netherlands, and Denmark). Britain and Australia are taking this approach a step further than any other country by gradually shifting all pension benefits (above a national floor of protection) to privately owned funds.

On the health-care front, there's more diversity. Canada spends rather heavily on health care and, like the United States, can expect to face tough choices once its age wave hits. Britain, on the other hand, is famously frugal with doctors. The money it saves on doctors, together with its radical pension reform, distinguishes Britain as better situated than any other nation to weather the global aging storm. According to most official projections, Britain can look forward to little if any growth in future public spending. Thirty years from now, according to the OECD, *the British government will have entirely paid back its national debt*—even while the national debt in France and Germany is projected to rise to staggering levels. While few were looking, the country that invented the "social welfare state" in the 1940s may have figured out how to preserve its fiscal health in the 2040s.

THE DEVELOPING WORLD: A LOOK AT TWO EXTREMES

In the developed world, the most predictable consequence of global aging will be a direct and massive increase in fiscal pressure. In the developing countries, the story line is more complex. Here, the sheer size of the fiscal burden is not the paramount issue. Besides being poorer, these societies also tend to be demographically younger, culturally more traditional, and less connected to the market economy—with stronger families and smaller government sectors. The big issue, instead, is the remarkable *speed* with which many of these countries are aging, urbanizing, and modernizing. As their population of dependent elderly mushrooms, will their living standards and formal retirement systems grow fast enough to accommodate the burden? And can they succeed in the early twenty-first century without the assistance of a fast-aging developed world, which by then may no longer be able to extend the global security or capital exports provided by today's great powers?

Since the developing world encompasses an enormous diversity of circumstances, the urgency of such questions differs among regions.

At one extreme, consider Africa, the Mideast, and Central Asia—population, just over one billion—where global aging poses few direct challenges over the foreseeable future. With the world's highest fertility rate (just over 5.0) and lowest life expectancy (about age 50 south of the Sahara),[12] these countries have only about one elder for every fifteen younger adults. Even by the year 2030, the elder share of these populations is expected to reach only half the elder share in the developed world today. (In that year, for instance, when half the Italian population will be over age 52, half of the Iraqi population is projected to be under age 25.) Fewer than 10 percent of these elders, moreover, are covered by any formal pension system—and these tend to be retired government workers in urban enclaves. The rest remain semi-employed in traditional kinship groups, over 80 percent of whom reside with younger family members who themselves live at near-subsistence levels in the poorest economies on earth. Most governments in this region, challenged by widespread disease, illiteracy, hunger, and violence, have yet to formulate any effective "retirement" policy at all. Even in the more modern and affluent Islamic societies, public authorities typically promote large and loyal families as the best old-age insurance policy.

At the other extreme, consider the former Soviet empire and the Warsaw Pact nations of Eastern Europe—population, 400 million. They aren't waiting to meet the aging challenge. They've already met it head on, and failed. During the early postwar decades, the leaders of these nations enlisted all citizens into universal public retirement systems and touted them as cornerstones of a cradle-to-grave workers' paradise. By the Brezhnev era, these systems had acquired all the fiscal burdens of their western European neighbors—pay-as-you-go financing, generous benefits, early retirement, lax disability standards, and plunging fertility rates—without the economic growth necessary to keep them solvent.

Then, with the end of the Cold War, there arrived the economic shock that turned these systems into fiscal wrecks. It was a double whammy, as I learned on a recent trip to Kazakhstan and Russia: The state-owned business pensions were as unfunded as the universal government pension. A floodtide of unemployed workers began "retiring" onto pensions just as businesses downsized and economic output contracted. As the support ratio of taxpayers to pensioners plunged beneath 2.0, governments let high inflation erode the real value of benefits until today most pensioners receive a "minimum" (when benefits are paid at all) that is often not enough to keep frail veterans or widows out of abject poverty. Even so, pension outlays as a share of GDP now match the highest levels in Western Europe, payroll-tax evasion is widespread, and very low fertility rates make long-term projections futile. In the laconic language of the World Bank: "All reform countries in Central and Eastern Europe require rapid and drastic restructuring of their public pension schemes."

From Warsaw to Prague, Budapest to Riga, political leaders are debating radical new pension ideas. The proposals typically include further sacrifices from past contributors and the introduction of a whole new "funded" tier of benefits for future retirees. These efforts are proceeding even in the midst of economic depression. The prevailing social hardship is underscored by stunning declines in average longevity due to collapsing public health services, widespread alcoholism, personal stress, and an epidemic of "heart and circulatory diseases." Between 1990 and 1994, the life expectancy of Russian males declined from 64 years to 58 years, which was the life expectancy of U.S. males in 1920.[13] Whatever the outcome, Eastern Europe's pension crisis provides an awesome vision of how something similar may someday happen to the developed countries. The gory details are all there— beginning with budgetary emergencies and a sinking economy and culminating in a shrinking population, the betrayal of an entire generation of retirees, and a devastating collapse of civic trust.

LATIN AMERICA AND ASIA: COUNTRIES AT THE CROSSROADS OF REFORM

The rest of the developing world consists mainly of South and East Asia and Latin America—and includes some 3.5 billion persons, about 60 percent of the world's population.

Unlike the "African" case, most of these countries have experienced swiftly growing lifespans and swiftly declining fertility rates over the past three decades. In East Asia and Latin America, the average fertility rate is now 1.8 and 2.7, respectively—versus 5.1 for the continent of Africa. These trends translate nearly everywhere into a rapid rise in the dependency ratio of elders to working-age adults. In East Asia, the rise will be somewhat delayed over the next two decades due to a very large post-World War II generation (much like the U.S. baby boom, though it was caused by a rapid decline in child mortality rather than by a rise in fertility). As this "boom" generation reaches elderhood in the 2020s, however, the dependency ratio in East Asia will shoot upwards as well. China and America have this much in common: They both expect age waves that will hit late but hard.

In these developing countries, rising dependency ratios will greatly increase the economic burden of aging—especially when combined with the social changes that accompany modernization. As their market economies expand, more workers will pay into formal pension systems. As their living standards rise, so too will expectations of longer and more comfortable retirements. Meanwhile, the massive population shift from country to city will continue to separate grown children from their parents and strip elders of their social status and economic role. Today, 37 percent of the population in developing countries are urban dwellers; by the year 2025, according to the United Nations, that figure will climb to 57 percent. In effect, virtually all the developing world's population growth is expected to occur in (or migrate to) cities. The traditional system of informal family support, while still strong, is showing signs of stress. Already, governments are trying to fill the gaps with retirement tax breaks, widows' benefits, nursing homes, and senior health clinics.

Unlike the "Eastern Europe" case, few of these Latin American and Asian countries have overcommitted themselves to universal unfunded benefits. Typically, less than half the workforce is covered by public systems, and these offer modest benefits. Hence total pension spending throughout this core category averages only 2 percent of GDP, only a small fraction of the developed-world norm. Although many systems are poorly designed, with widespread payroll-tax evasion and periodic episodes of insolvency (especially in Latin America), they seldom threaten to overwhelm the economy by their sheer size. As a result, most of these countries still have plenty of time to experiment, reform, plan, and prepare.

Many of these developing countries are unwilling to follow the Eastern European (or developed world) example by accumulating vast unfunded liabilities. Instead, they are deliberating over radical new approaches that promise to prevent future retirement security from becoming a burden on future wage earners. One approach is to reinforce filial piety within the extended family (the Asian or "Singaporean" model). Another is to fund the system by financing benefits with personally owned and accumulated assets (the Latin America or "Chilean" model).

China, its vast size aside, faces an especially challenging future. China's public pension system currently offers comparatively generous benefits to retirees from (mainly urban) state-owned enterprises on a strictly pay-as-you-go basis. It requires, depending on the enterprise, a stiff 20 to 25 percent payroll tax rate on participating workers. For now, the system's total cost, at approximately 2 percent of GDP, is affordable because it covers only one-fifth of China's workforce. But without reform, disaster looms. By the early 2030s, the payroll cost rate of the current system is projected to climb to somewhere between 40 and 50 percent.

And even this figure doesn't reflect the troubled economic outlook for China's notoriously inefficient state-owned enterprises (which still employ nearly two-thirds of urban workers but now account for only one-third of industrial output). In order to become more efficient and profitable, these companies—which have been kept afloat by loans from state banks—will have to downsize. But ironically, in doing so, they will reduce the employee base for funding retired worker benefits. As an estimated 30 million state-sector workers are laid off over the next decade—one hopes to be rehired by private businesses—the payroll burden on those remaining will rise sharply. An obvious solution would be to extend the current pay-as-you-go system to the private sector. But this would merely delay the day of reckoning. And if the extension should include a large share of today's enormous rural labor force (as peasants move to cities and become wage earners), the ultimate total cost as a share of GDP would become unmanageable.

Because of China's large postwar generation, the country is still demographically young. The aging burden doesn't become severe until around 2015. Thereafter the aged dependency ratio rises very suddenly—as the "Red Guard" generation retires and today's unusually small and largely single-child cohorts, born during the era of China's draconian birth-control policies, replace them.

When China's age wave hits, it will do so with startling speed. Improved nutrition, sanitation, modernized health care, and relative affluence are greatly lengthening average life expectancy. Meanwhile—in a society in which the vast majority of women have an IUD inserted after their first birth and are sterilized after their second[14]—China's birth control policies are having remarkable success. Even in the country-side, where rigorous enforcement is difficult, village populations are only barely replacing themselves. In the major cities, where only the wealthy can "buy" the right to a second child (by paying a hefty fee, which in Shanghai amounts to three years of both parents' wages), fertility rates have fallen to Italian levels. In Beijing, they may have dropped below 1.0—and may now even rival the super-low rate in bambino-bust Bologna. As Nicholas Eberstadt has observed, "China's age structure is about to shift radically: from the 'Christmas tree' shape so familiar among contemporary populations to something more like the inverted Christmas trees we set out for collection after the holidays."[15] There are now 140 Chinese children under age 5 for every 100 Chinese aged 65 or older;

by 2025, the official projections show 250 elders for every 100 young children. Meanwhile, the median age is projected to climb from today's still-youthful 27 to 40 or older. This will not make China the oldest country in the world: Japan's median age, for example, is already 40 and rising. But Japan's real GDP per capita is eight times higher than China's. No matter how much economic growth China experiences between now and 2025, it is likely to be the poorest country ever compelled to cope with developed-world rates of old-age dependency. As a Chinese writer, Lin Ying observes, "Whereas the now-developed countries first got rich and then got old, China will first get old."[16]

China's aging burden will be even more serious because of the striking deficiency of females among its young "buster" birth cohorts, the result of the easy availability of abortion—and its selective use against girl babies. Each year, it is estimated, the Chinese give birth to one million fewer baby girls than the natural ratio of newborn boys to girls would otherwise yield. In most societies, there are ordinarily around 105 to 107 boys born for every 100 girls. In China, the sex ratio as of 1995 was perhaps the most anomalous the modern world has ever seen in a major population group: 118 boys under the age of 5 for every 100 girls. Some of this may reflect the concealing of baby-girl births by parents who still hope to have a boy. But much of it is a result of the tragic practice of targeted abortion and infanticide against girls. This practice is especially common in rural areas where sons are favored, not only because of their economic value in working the land but also because of the expectation, rooted in China's traditional Confucian ethic, that elders will be supported in their later years by their sons' families. Where rural families are constrained by government limits on family size, the parental incentive to get rid of a baby of the "wrong sex" can be very strong.[17] One likely outcome will be a future lack of women of marriageable age. Another outcome will be a future lack of females of all ages—those who are the traditional caregivers for frail or disabled elders.[18]

Nicholas Eberstadt has analyzed this growing gender gap in China in provocative detail:

> In China's tradition, virtually all men and women who are able to get married ultimately do so. For a society with a presumption of near-universal marriage, however, the arithmetic implications of unnatural imbalances between the supply of prospective husbands and wives are straightforward, and unforgiving. If there are 116 young Chinese men for every 100 young Chinese women, and if (say) 2 percent of those young women never marry, then one out of every six of these young men must find a bride from outside of this cohort—or fail to continue his family line.
>
> In theory, this problem could be finessed simply by marrying outside one's cohort—for example, by finding a younger bride . . . In the coming decades, given today's regimen of low and sub-replacement fertility, China's rising youth groups will typically be smaller than the cohorts born just before them.
>
> Thus, to the degree that China's young men in the coming century manage to solve their mating problem by marrying younger women from within their country, they will concomitantly intensify the eventual "marriage crisis" facing Chinese a few years their junior. Searching abroad for Chinese wives, for its part, will be a strategy of distinctly limited promise. By 2020, for example, the surplus of China's males in their 20s will likely exceed the entire female population of the island of Taiwan!
>
> In many settings throughout history—including most of early modern western Europe—bachelorhood was an acceptable social role. China, however, was never one of those settings, and is not one of them today. Unless it is swept by a truly radical change in cultural attitudes toward social values about marriage in the next two decades, China is poised to experience an increasingly intense, and perhaps desperate, competition among young men for the nation's limited supply of brides.

What forms will this competition take, and how will the Chinese society be affected by it? Contemplating the country's future gender imbalance, a 1997 essay in the journal *Beijing Luntan* predicted direly that "such sexual crimes as forced marriages, girls stolen for wives, bigamy, visiting prostitutes, rape, adultery, . . . homosexuality . . . and weird sexual habits appear to be unavoidable."

Not a few of China's young men, moreover, might also be struck by the bitter irony of their paradoxical national circumstances: At a time when (in all likelihood) their country's wealth and power would be greater than ever before, their own personal chances of possessing the wherewithal necessary to establish their own family not only look poor, but appear to be steadily worsening.

It is easy to imagine how such a paradox could invite widespread dissatisfaction—or even discontent . . . As *Beijing Lutan* intoned, the involuntary bachelors from China's rising cohorts will "handle [a] punishment they have received as a result of the social and natural imbalance created by the mistakes of the previous generation." How they handle that "punishment" remains to be seen—and it will bear directly on the character and behavior of the China that awaits us.[19]

To prepare for the future, Chinese leaders are working to minimize dependency costs by reinforcing the traditional Confucian ethic of family solidarity in a country where the vast majority of elders still live with grown children. Parental control over children's marriages and careers receives official sanction, and the government continues to limit the out-migration of farmers from rural areas. Leaders dread the specter of countless millions of uprooted farmers swarming into major cities where they will not only threaten the social order, but swamp public-benefit programs that already have trouble making ends meet.

With so many bloated state-owned enterprises slated for privatization and downsizing, and untold millions of their workers soon to be unemployed, China's leaders are considering a plan to replace the current pension system with a new three-pillar system. It would consist of a scaled-back pay-as-you-go system, a compulsory funded system of individual savings accounts, and a voluntary option for supplemental contributions. At the moment, this plan makes no explicit provision for investing personal contributions in stocks, even though stock markets in China have already attracted 25 million household investors since they were established earlier in this decade. Rather, all contributions would be directed into bank savings accounts, which in times past have sometimes been recycled into imprudent loans—subsidies really—to notoriously inefficient state-owned enterprises and into speculative real-estate bubbles.

It's still an open question whether China's new system will eventually allow workers to invest their contributions in stocks and other approved financial assets. If it does, China would be better able to channel its abundant savings—China's gross national savings rate is now roughly 40 percent—toward productive investment by business and industry. One encouraging sign is the determination of China's leadership to broaden and deepen the nation's capital markets. However, while allowing households to pick their own investments offers big advantages for the economy, such personal control would constitute a challenge to the entrenched political elites who still manipulate (and sometimes profit personally from) the allocation of much of China's savings. China's effort to reform its retirement system could pose a critical test of its willingness to democratize political and economic power.

Like so many similar efforts elsewhere, China's struggle to prepare for global aging is running into strong cultural crosswinds. Reinforcing filial piety means resisting the perceived tide of "western" (or simply, American) values that emphasize personal autonomy and rights. Moving toward funded contributory systems means affirming personal foresight and responsibility—and forging stronger ties to "westernized" global capital markets. Many far-sighted leaders in the developing world want to avoid repeating western mistakes. But as they design new aging strategies, they often find themselves struggling to harness some western ideas even as they reject others.

No two people grow old the same way. Likewise, in the coming era of global aging, no two societies will grow old the same way. One can point to certain broad similarities within groups of nations—rich or poor, fast aging or slow aging, modern or traditional. Yet each society faces its own unique problems and opportunities, and must in the end chart its own course.

4

No Easy Choices

"Just what exactly is _your_ generation going to
do about _my_ generation's social security?"

THE OFFICIAL PROJECTIONS ARE STARK. MOST DEVELOPED
countries will have to undertake fundamental reform of senior
benefits or else experience a fiscal meltdown early in the next
century. Given this choice, it's not surprising that many
politicians prefer denial. While just about everybody acknowledges that global aging itself is inevitable, there are plenty on
both the left and the right who insist the cost can be avoided.

THE HOAX OF FASTER ECONOMIC GROWTH

A typical claim is that economies are bound to grow faster
than projected, making current benefit promises more affordable. As evidence, optimists point to the long-term real GDP

growth forecasts by national and international agencies, and note that they are well beneath what the developed world has achieved historically. This is true, but it doesn't mean what the optimists suppose. Remember: GDP equals the number of workers times product per worker. Thus, when the number of workers grows more slowly, so must real GDP (assuming no change in productivity growth). When, for example, the U.S. Social Security Administration projects that U.S. real GDP growth will eventually fall from 2.5 percent annually (since 1980) to 1.4 percent (during the 2020s), it is not assuming a decline in productivity growth but a modest productivity *improvement*. The entire decline in GDP growth is due to the slowing rate of employment growth, from the 1.5 percent annually since 1980 to a mere 0.1 percent annually during the 2020s. With the labor force due to plateau (in the United States) or contract sharply (in Japan, Italy, and Germany), GDP growth will necessarily slow down or even turn negative—unless productivity growth greatly accelerates. This is not pessimism, but arithmetic.

The more relevant question is whether the official assumptions about productivity (or output per worker) are reasonable. Generally, the projections for developed countries assume a long-term productivity growth rate of about 1.5 percent per year, which (surprise!) is roughly equal to their track record over the past twenty-five years. To be sure, productivity may pick up dramatically over the next decade or two—but is there any reason to think it likely? According to "new economy" optimists, ongoing advances in computer and information network technologies promise to trigger quantum leaps in economic efficiency. But as yet, this promise remains unproven. As the Nobel laureate economist Robert Solow has famously observed, "you can see the computer age everywhere but in the productivity statistics." And even if productivity growth does pick up, the improvement would have to be enormous in order to offset much of the rising burden of senior benefits. Closing just the long-term U.S.

Social Security deficit, according to Federal Reserve Chairman Alan Greenspan, would require *tripling* current rates of productivity growth. Closing the long-term U.S. Medicare deficit as well would require a larger multiple.

There are equally plausible arguments that productivity growth will *slow* in the future. The economist William Baumol holds that services resistant to productivity improvement (especially personal services such as teaching, medicine, counseling, law, and entertainment) naturally tend to grow as a share of the economy as living standards rise. Over time, therefore, the very growth of such services inhibits improvement in overall productivity growth. Many experts think that this dynamic, sometimes called "Baumol's disease," helps explain disappointing productivity throughout the developed world over the last quarter-century. Another reason to expect slower productivity growth is more closely linked to the fiscal pressure of aging itself. Just think of the economic consequences of leaving senior benefits on autopilot—widening budget deficits, soaring interest rates, evaporating national savings, and declining investment, both public and private. The official projections usually ignore these negative economic feedbacks, which is sufficient grounds for regarding them as a best-case scenario.

Aside from raising productivity, another way to increase GDP growth is to raise employment—that is, to add more working bodies to the economy. Increased immigration is often billed as an easy fix for the developed world's aging burden. Immigration, some claim, could dramatically expand the tax base and lower the aged dependency ratio. Why? Because families who leave one country to come to another include a disproportionate share of young adults and children. Immigration thus works much like a higher fertility rate.[1] But it also works much faster, since most immigrants become taxpayers right away—and it may even be cheaper, to the extent that some other society bears the cost of raising and educating them.

Higher immigration is surely part of the solution in some countries, but few nations are likely to tolerate—politically or socially—the extra immigration needed to make a real difference. If the United States wanted to achieve the long-term equivalent of raising its fertility rate by 25 percent, that is, from 2.0 to 2.5, American voters would have to accept an *extra million* immigrants annually, more than *doubling* the current net rate of legal and illegal immigration combined. Or consider a more ambitious goal—entirely closing Social Security's operating deficit through the year 2030. In this case, American voters would have to accept an *extra four million* immigrants annually, more than *quintupling* the current net rate of legal and illegal immigration combined. To meet this target, America would need to accept enough immigrants to repopulate the state of Tennessee every year. Such a massive increase—to a rate of immigration more than twice its historic high tide during Teddy Roosevelt's presidency—seems highly unlikely. At least one-third of today's inflow is illegal; thus, the total inflow is already much greater than what the law allows. Ironically, the U.S. Social Security projections assume an indefinite continuation of this "other-than-legal" immigrant stream (to use the actuaries' delicate phrase) even as other federal agencies are urgently trying to shut it down!

In America, as throughout the developed world, a growing share of voters wants to restrict immigration *beneath* current levels. At least for now, most governments are raising, not lowering, the drawbridge. In the future, political leaders may be forced to look more favorably on immigration as fiscal pressures mount and shrinking labor forces (especially in Europe and Japan) generate increasing demand for young workers. Electorates may also become more willing to accept large cumulative shifts in the ethnic mix of their societies. But even if immigration is allowed to rise well above today's levels, it will not significantly slow the aging of the developed world as a whole. Even in America—a country whose projected public pension deficit is relatively modest—more immigration by itself won't come close to solving the fiscal problem. In other countries, the fiscal impact would be even less noticeable.

Another obvious way to add to the labor force is to encourage workers to retire later, a reform I support. But, as we shall see in the next chapter, it is wrong to underestimate the cultural and political obstacles in the way of such a change. Despite steady gains in health and longevity since World War II, the average retirement age in the developed countries has been falling. Working longer is not a way to avoid the hard choices. It *is* the hard choice.

UNFUNDED PRIVATIZATION— JUST ANOTHER FREE-LUNCH FANTASY

"Privatization" is a much-touted solution. Just break the chain letter of young-to-old transfers, allow workers to invest their current contributions in the stock market, and presto, say enthusiasts, the fiscal costs of global aging will painlessly disappear. With all their hype about personal investing, the privatizers *seem* to be advertising a funded system. And indeed, a genuinely funded retirement system would offer great advantages—not just higher national savings, and hence higher wages during the working years, but higher returns on contributions, and hence higher incomes during the retirement years.

The problem is, what the privatizers offer is rarely genuine. Their typical plan assumes that pay-as-you-go taxes can be redirected effortlessly into savings. But this is a free-lunch fallacy. In developed countries, workers will have to keep paying for retirees in the old system even while they put aside *extra* money into the new system to prefund their own retirement. It's nonsense to imagine that the same money can be spent twice. In developing countries, setting up a universal funded retirement system often means that most workers will be putting money aside regularly for the first time. Either way, pain precedes gain: Saving more necessarily entails consuming less—at least until the benefits of higher savings and higher productivity kick in.

Pension reformers call this required extra savings a "transition cost," and in developed countries it's a big political obstacle. How big? Well, if we want to replace the old system entirely while honoring all of its promises, the transition cost will equal the present value of all future public pension benefits that have already been credited to today's workers and retirees. In the United States, this comes to about $10 trillion,[2] which is several times greater than the inflation-adjusted cost of U.S. participation in World War II. For all developed countries, it comes to about $35 trillion. This is what governments would have to set aside and invest right now, *today*, in order to fund the pay-as-you-go benefits that workers have already "earned" under current public-pension programs. The $35 trillion represents roughly 150 percent of the developed world's GDP and is triple the size of its existing public debt. The figure would be about twice as large if we tried to prefund health benefits to the elderly as well as pensions. U.S. Federal Reserve Chairman Alan Greenspan has urged Congress to make these implicit unfunded liabilities explicit and not to hide them "off the books." The U.S. Congress seldom mentions the federal government's $10 trillion of unfunded pension liabilities, even though it often expresses alarm over unfunded *private pension* liabilities that are less than one-hundredth as large.[3]

The privatizers are hazy about how countries like the United States are supposed to handle this mountain of debt. Some suggest ignoring these future benefit costs until they come due. As the old pay-as-you-go system winds down, they hint that money will "somewhere" be found to pay off the remaining benefits—but they don't say where. Others claim to be shocked by such irresponsibility. They suggest that Treasury borrow all or most of the money now, and that Congress find budget savings to make room for the permanent debt-service charge—but they don't specify where these budget savings will come from. Still others, while agreeing that existing benefit liabilities be recognized up front, propose a different solution. Instead of issuing debt to the public, they say, the old system's benefit liabilities should be translated into "recognition bonds" that would be paid (along with interest payments on those bonds) directly into the workers' new accounts. But this would require government to raise huge amounts of cash to pay off the bonds-plus-interest once they come due upon each worker's retirement. A $10 trillion liability requires an amortization charge of $750 billion per year—several times more than the current cost of servicing the U.S. national debt. So how are we better off with a formal debt instrument than with an unfunded liability?

In one way or another, too many privatization plans end up nullifying their purported objective. Sooner or later, whatever workers save by making smaller contributions to a pay-as-you-go plan they'll have to sacrifice in higher taxes to pay off existing pay-as-you-go liabilities. Either that, or government will have to repudiate these liabilities by canceling promised benefits. The only remaining option is to run future deficits and roll over the liabilities into other forms of public debt. But to the extent privatizers lean on debt, their reform won't be funded and thus won't fulfill its objective. "Recognition bonds," by locking in future liabilities, would even make the fiscal outlook worse than it was to begin with. Unfunded privatization may allow politicians to delay the hard choices. But national savings will not rise, and today's pay-as-you-go chain letter will continue.

A few privatizers openly concede that their plans may not raise national savings—but then argue this doesn't matter. Yes, they know that government will have to borrow to pay off benefit liabilities under the old system. But apparently they believe that workers' private accounts would forever earn greater returns on the new equity assets than would be lost on the new debt liabilities. Assume, for instance, that government can borrow funds at a 2 percent real rate of return and that workers can invest their personal assets in a broad portfolio of stocks at a 6 percent real rate of return.

The 4 percent difference looks a lot like manna from heaven—since the workers, in effect, can fully cover the government's debt service charge with only a third of the annual gains on their personal accounts.

Cashing in on this so-called "equity premium," however, poses a real dilemma for free-market privatizers. On the one hand, they can surmise that the 4 percent spread is a rational estimate of the true extra risk of owning equities. But if so, how does their reform make the economy better off over the long term? If the premium reflects the true risk, that means somebody sooner or later incurs real losses by holding equities. Or else the privatizers have to conclude that markets are fundamentally irrational. Why else would markets not permanently bid down the price of bonds or bid up the price of stocks? Yes, some financial analysts claim that this is precisely what has happened during the great bull market of the 1990s. But if they are correct, and the equity premium has disappeared, then the future return on stocks carries no further advantage over the future return on bonds. And the privatizers are right back at square one.

Despite such logical quandaries, the historical spread between stocks and bonds is so tempting that most privatizers can't resist taking advantage of it. Indeed, even many defenders of pay-as-you-go systems (particularly in the United States) now advocate taking part of the payroll tax receipts or any annual surpluses in those systems and investing them in private equities rather than in public debt. Apparently, the political and economic dangers of having the central government own a large share of the nation's corporate equity doesn't bother them.[4] If there's a free lunch to be had, they reason, why give it all to privatizers? Why shouldn't government get some too?

But such financial alchemy can't possibly work. For one thing, it ignores the likely impact on financial yields. If millions more workers start buying up stocks on a large scale and government starts selling new debt (either public debt or "recognition bonds") on a large scale, the yield on bonds will rise and the yield on stocks will fall. This would narrow the favorable spread on which the plan depends (and add enormously to interest costs in public budgets). More importantly, to the extent the spread remains, it will probably reflect the true extra risk of owning stocks. Until recently, with a great bull market roaring, much of the public and indeed many experts no longer seemed to take this risk seriously. Today, with new talk of bear markets, they are relearning an age-old lesson. Let's not forget an earlier 15-year period, between 1967 and 1982, in which the Dow Jones industrial average fell about 40 percent in real dollars—or the catastrophic performance of Japan's Nikkei average over the last decade. Stocks are great long-term investments, but they can also be risky, especially in the short term.

All of these issues aside, there's a more fundamental problem. Suppose it is true that the risk-adjusted return on private equities remains forever higher than the return on public debt. This would simply mean, under a privatized system, that whatever the smart stockowners gain (within the new accounts) will be lost by the dumb bond-owners (outside the new accounts).[5] *Unfunded* privatization is a revolving door that cannot leave society as a whole any better off.

Let's face it: If this sort of large-scale financial arbitrage could work, it would make sense entirely apart from any plan to prefund retirement programs. It would be every nation's standard fiscal policy.[6] Governments would issue trillions of dollars in debt, invest the proceeds in the stock market, and refund the effortless profit to taxpayers. But it doesn't make sense, which is why no nation has ever tried it.

SPENDING LESS ON DOCTORS: NOT AS EASY AS IT LOOKS

Against all experience, many optimists still claim that with a few grand changes in our national health-care systems we can greatly ease the cost of global aging. Simply get rid of all the waste, fraud, and abuse, they say, and cost control will be within reach. Most experts, however, disagree. Health spending in developed countries is not growing so fast due to the proliferation of useless medical services. It is growing because of the continuous introduction of expensive new technologies and treatments that are beneficial but expensive. As health economist Victor Fuchs has written, "There is substantial consensus among health-care experts that the driving force behind increasing health expenditures is new technology—new methods of diagnosis, new drugs, new surgical procedures, and the like. In a survey of 50 leading health economists in 1995, more than four out of five agreed with the statement, 'The primary reason for the increase in the health sector's share of GDP over the past 30 years is technological change in medicine.'"[7] Not incidentally, this technological change is contributing to extended longevity worldwide.

The world is in the midst of a medical revolution that shows no signs of abating. One of my earliest childhood Nebraska memories is of good old Doctor Edwards carrying a black bag filled with all the tools of his trade. If he couldn't help us with a stethoscope and hypodermic needle, my family made a rare visit to a community hospital, which may have boasted an X-ray machine. There wasn't much that medicine could do, and most of that wasn't very expensive. Doctor Edwards would never have comprehended what has happened since: the growth of a U.S. medical-industrial complex that now spends more research and construction dollars each year than the total cost of the U.S. space program from Sputnik to Apollo 11.

Medical miracles unimagined only a decade or two ago are now commonplace. Some of these technologies screen for low-probability risks (from space-age imaging devices to genetic testing). Others improve the odds for low-probability cures (from organ transplants to powerful new AIDS therapies). Others help alleviate debilitating chronic conditions (from insulin-pump implants to microchip hearing and seeing devices). Still others simply enhance our quality of life (from sports medicine to the Viagra vogue). And the pace of innovation may be accelerating. Pointing to an enormous bow wave of biomedical research now on the horizon, health technology expert William Schwartz insists that few governments have any idea what's about to hit them. "Everything that's happened up until now in medicine is a prelude," he reports. "What's really ahead is stunning. It's going to be . . . very expensive."[8]

"Good health," moreover, is not a fixed target, but a subjective standard that rises over time as society becomes more affluent, less tolerant of risk and discomfort, and more secular—that is, more apt to see happiness in the here-and-now as life's ultimate goal. As this rising standard interacts with medical advances, it is transforming the practice of medicine. While once health care meant an occasional visit to the doctor, it is today becoming a lifelong process of diagnostics and fine-tuning in which any extra dollar spent is likely to confer *some* benefit.

All of these cost drivers, along with demographic aging itself, make cost-savings very difficult. In the United States, the situation is compounded by open-ended insurance systems that often shield patients and providers from meaningful trade-offs between health and other priorities.

Every country experiences occasional pauses in the upward trend in health-care spending. Yet when these pauses are the result of limits on access, the public reaction often speaks volumes about its expansive sense of entitlement to the highest quality, most convenient, and least intrusive treatments available. In the mid-1990s, for example, the U.S. "managed care" revolution was temporarily successful in limiting private-sector health spending, but this led to abundant and heated complaints about loss of "choice" and declining "quality of care." Had today's typical HMO suddenly appeared thirty years ago, it would have been celebrated as the dispenser of miracle cures. Now, it is routinely attacked for violating the basic rights of its patients. In any case, with HMO premiums surging again in the late 1990s, the underlying cost drivers are again gaining the upper hand. The age wave and its special cost multipliers still loom over the horizon. Yet over the last two decades, a benign demographic period in America in which boomers have only progressed from youth to middle age, U.S. national health spending has already risen by a staggering 5 percent of GDP. Now imagine what will happen as they transition from middle age to elderhood if Americans remain unwilling to tolerate any restraint on health-care spending.

Even if we give the optimists everything they hope for and suppose that dramatic and painless savings are possible, this still might not deflate the official projections. What the optimists fail to realize is that these projections *already build in* the expectation of slower cost growth. This assumed slowdown is especially dramatic in the United States, where the Health Care Financing Administration (HCFA) projects that the growth in real per capita Medicare spending will decelerate from its historical rate of 5 percent per year to just 1 percent per year by the 2020s.[9] HCFA does not point to any specific change in technologies or policies that might explain this cost slowdown. It simply assumes that *someday, somehow,* costs must be controlled if Medicare is not to consume the entire economy. As the economist and sometimes-humorist Herb Stein is fond of saying, things that are unsustainable tend to stop. Indeed, they do. But merely to assert that something must happen begs the real question: How will we make it happen—and after how many years of fiscal and economic damage?

THE "TOTAL DEPENDENCY" FALLACY

Well, say the optimists, maybe the growing number of dependent elderly does pose a daunting cost challenge. But let's cheer up: In an era of low fertility, a steep drop in the relative number of dependent children will largely neutralize this challenge. Of all the arguments for complacency, this is

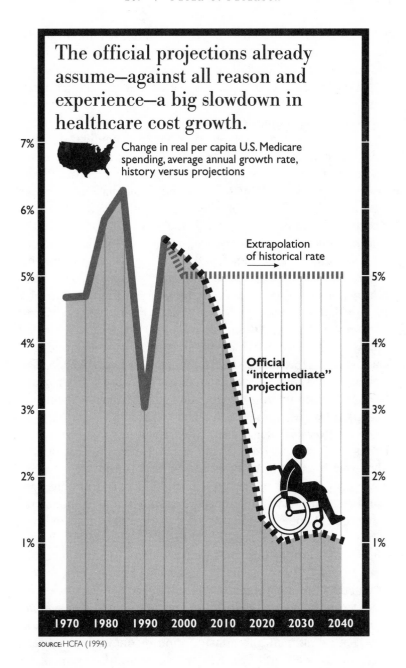

The official projections already assume—against all reason and experience—a big slowdown in healthcare cost growth.

Change in real per capita U.S. Medicare spending, average annual growth rate, history versus projections

Extrapolation of historical rate →

Official "intermediate" projection

SOURCE: HCFA (1994)

perhaps the most wrongheaded. As economist John Shoven recently put it, "Simply adding the number of children and elderly together is kind of ridiculous."[10]

As a factual matter, the ratio of *all* dependents (children and elderly) to working-age adults will still rise steeply in every developed country over the next thirty years. Back in the 1950s, to be sure, the relative number of dependent children was a lot higher than it is today or will be in the future—especially in the United States and a few other postwar "baby boom" countries such as Canada and Australia. But that was an era in which the developed world did not socialize much of the cost of dependency. Today it does—and it does so for the old to a much greater extent than for the young. Even including cash and in-kind benefits from all levels of government, per capita public spending on the elderly (aged 65 and over) relative to spending on the non-elderly ranges from a low of 5 to 1 in Canada to a high of 11 to 1 in the United States. Within the U.S. *federal* budget alone, each elder consumes on average nearly ten times as much in benefits and services as each *child* ($15,600 versus $1,700 in fiscal year 1995). The bottom line is that elder dependency is far more costly to public budgets than youth dependency. This fact is entirely obscured by the "total dependency" concept.

Sometimes the dependency theorists argue that what matters is total spending on dependents, private as well as public. Yet even by this broader measure, the typical old person consumes more than the typical child. Apart from the raw numbers, moreover, this measure assumes that it makes no difference to the economy whether income is transferred privately within families or publicly through government. It also implies that any income that workers spend on anyone other than themselves represents an equivalent burden—regardless of whether the spending is a voluntary sacrifice for *one's own* children or a tax-and-transfer payment to some *anonymous retiree*. Most fundamentally, it ignores the distinction between investment and consumption. Money spent on senior benefits is essentially pure consumption. Money spent on

Public benefits everywhere strongly favor the elderly.

Social welfare spending* in 1990:
per capita benefits to the elderly
as a % of benefits
to the nonelderly

*All levels of government; includes
pensions, health, unemployment,
and family benefits

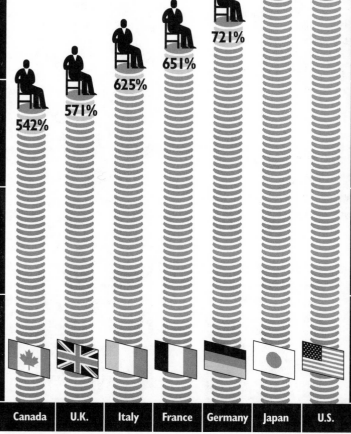

1079%

853%

721%

651%

625%

571%

542%

| Canada | U.K. | Italy | France | Germany | Japan | U.S. |

SOURCE: OECD (1988 & 1994); NTUF (1998)

The U.S. federal budget dispenses nearly ten times as much in benefits to each senior citizen as it does to each child.

Per capita
U.S. federal spending
on children
and the elderly
in fiscal year 1995

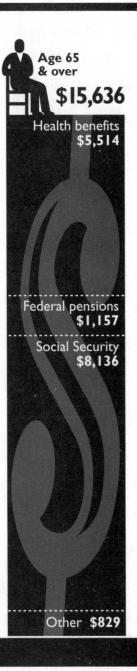

Age 65
& over
$15,636

Health benefits
$5,514

Federal pensions
$1,157

Social Security
$8,136

Other $829

Under
age 18
$1,693

SOURCE: CBO (1997); OMB (1996); NTUF (1998)

children is an investment. In the *Washington Post,* Richard Leone of the Twentieth Century Fund expresses puzzlement that Americans await the coming age wave with anxiety but didn't consider the 1960s an era of "deprivation,"[11] even though the U.S. total dependency ratio was higher in 1960 than it will be in 2030.[12] The difference, of course, is that thirty-five years ago adults were sacrificing through families to build the future, while thirty-five years from now they will be sacrificing through government to reward the past. What happened then was investment; what is scheduled for our future is consumption.

LETTING DEFICITS GROW: THE ROAD TO GLOBAL FINANCIAL MELTDOWN

In the end, one suspects that the counselors of complacency are merely searching for a pretext to postpone reform. But as the projections indicate, doing nothing is not a realistic choice. Just imagine total benefit spending going up 9 to 16 percent of GDP with no commensurate increase in revenues—and then keep in mind that most developed country governments are already running red ink. What would happen by the mid-2020s? Virtually everywhere, the result would be deficits of unprecedented size and public debts exploding to Weimar levels. For any one country, this course would be economically ruinous. For the entire developed world, it would be impossible. There aren't enough creditors to allow it to happen. Soaring interest rates or government defaults would intervene to cut the experiment short.

I recently looked at the public pension systems of the G-7 countries and asked what would happen if we ran them all out on autopilot, leaving benefits and taxes unchanged except for reforms already scheduled in law. What I found was that the growth in the operating deficits of these systems, together with accumulated interest charges, would add 60 percent of GDP to the publicly held debt of G-7 governments by 2030. Meanwhile, the collective budget deficit of these governments would rise by 7.4 percent of GDP. (This figure naturally averages a broad range of deficit swings, from just 2.8 percent in Britain to 14.7 percent in Japan.)

For those who find GDP shares too abstract, let me put the bottom line in more concrete terms. By 2030, the extra G-7 red ink would, in today's dollars, come to $2.4 trillion *annually*—a sum several times greater than today's combined G-7 public-sector deficit.

Borrowing at anywhere near these rates is unsustainable. From 1985 to 1994, the rate of net national savings in the G-7 countries has averaged 8.6 percent of GDP. Assuming this baseline, current pension policy will consume 86 percent of net G-7 savings by 2030—and 141 percent by 2040. To finance their widening pension deficits while maintaining even a minimum level of domestic investment, the G-7 countries will thus have to borrow heavily from the developing world—an ironic reversal of the policy recommendations of the 1970s. To maintain investment at just half of today's level would by 2030 require capital imports totaling roughly $1 trillion annually in today's dollars—many times more than what the world's largest debtor, the United States, has ever raised in foreign capital markets. And this time, with Japan and Germany among the borrowers, who will be the creditor? We cannot sustain the unsustainable, nor can we finance the unfinanceable.

Not only will current fiscal policy be unsustainable through the year 2030; it will wreak economic havoc on nations going down this path. As populations age, widening budget deficits will erode national savings. As the savings rate declines, either domestic investment will fall or capital inflows will grow. Both are likely to happen together. Interest rates will rise as domestic loanable funds get scarcer and as foreigners exact a larger risk premium from domestic borrowers. Over time, productivity growth will decline, and so will living standards. The price to be paid for larger capital inflows will be rising debt-service payments to foreigners—and, perhaps, an erosion of national autonomy.

Widening public pension deficits are on track to consume the economic savings of the developed world.

Change from 1995 in the combined G-7 budget balance attributable to projected public pension deficits,* as a % of G-7 GDP

2000 0.1%	'05	'10	'15	'20	'25	'30	'35	'40

-0.2%

-0.9%

-1.9%

-3.3%

-5.1%

A deficit swing of 8.6% of GDP would consume entire G-7 net national savings**

-7.4%

-9.9%

-12.1%

* Assumes no change in taxes and other spending; includes interest on prior-year pension deficits
** Assumes all other savings continues at 1985–94 annual rate

SOURCE: OECD (1996); author's calculations

This isn't just theory. According to numerous empirical studies, there is a positive correlation between the ratio of public debt to GDP and the real interest rate. This correlation is strong for any individual country and, not surprisingly, even stronger for the developed world as a whole. According to one study,[13] each one percentage point increase in the developed economies' debt-to-GDP ratio raises real interest rates by as much as one-quarter of a percent. If this estimate is even close, the no-policy-change scenario—in which the G-7 debt-to-GDP ratio rises 60 percentage points by the year 2030—implies runaway interest rates, perhaps 15 percentage points higher than today's, even assuming inflation remains unchanged. "The deterioration in government fiscal positions," concludes a recent research survey by the OECD, "is seen as probably the major reason for the rise in world real interest rates during the 1980s and may be the greatest potential source of pressure in the future."[14] Predicting interest rates decades hence is an inexact science. But many financial experts are intrigued by the widening yield differential between 10- and 30-year U.S. Treasury bonds issued since the mid-1990s—which may reflect, they say, deepening worries about the consequences of current fiscal policies beyond the year 2010.

Some will object that my analysis overstates the deficit threat posed by global aging because it ignores the substantial financial assets accumulated by government pension systems. But these assets deserve to be ignored. Although every major public system in the world possesses some sort of "trust fund," such accounts never pretend to fund more than a small fraction of future benefit liabilities. Even these "assets" typically consist of IOUs from one government agency to another, outside the normal budget process. The term "trust fund"—truly a fiscal oxymoron—implies that annual savings are invested in economic assets which are held in trust and constitute a claim on an existing stock of capital that can later be distributed to beneficiaries. In reality, the annual savings are immediately borrowed and spent on other government programs. All that's left in the trust funds are unbacked claims on future tax revenue—that is, on economic resources that have yet to be created. That's why economists generally agree that these public systems operate on a pay-as-you-go basis[15] and that their trust funds are little more than symbols of government's political commitment to the elderly.

The notorious double-counting of the U.S. Social Security surplus,[16] once when it is spent and the second time when it is credited to the system's trust funds, is by no means the only (or even the most flagrant) example of such budgetary shenanigans. No matter what these public trust funds claim to be saving, future taxpayers bear the ultimate burden. When the time comes to spend down the trust funds, government can raise the cash only by hiking taxes, cutting other spending, or issuing bonds to the public. The U.S. Social Security trust fund is expected to remain technically solvent until 2032, a fact which has encouraged public complacency about the program's long-term prospects. But by 2013 the program's annual outlays will begin to exceed its annual tax revenues, creating a cash shortfall which will have to be met by liquidating trust-fund "assets," namely, U.S. Treasury bonds. By the time these IOUs are exhausted and the trust fund actually goes bankrupt, Social Security will have added a cumulative $6.9 trillion to the publicly held U.S. national debt. The fiscal and economic impact will be the same as if the trust fund never existed. As Social Security Administration's former research director, John Hambor, has written, "The Trust Fund more accurately represents a stack of IOUs to be presented to future generations for payment, rather than a build-up of resources to fund future benefits."[17] U.S. Senator Daniel Patrick Moynihan, a sponsor of the 1983 legislation that gave rise to today's large trust-fund surpluses, now concludes that trust-fund accounting is "thievery." In sum, trust-fund solvency is irrelevant. What really matters is government's total annual borrowing from the public and its impact on national savings.

U.S. Social Security will run widening operating deficits well before its official "bankruptcy" in 2032.

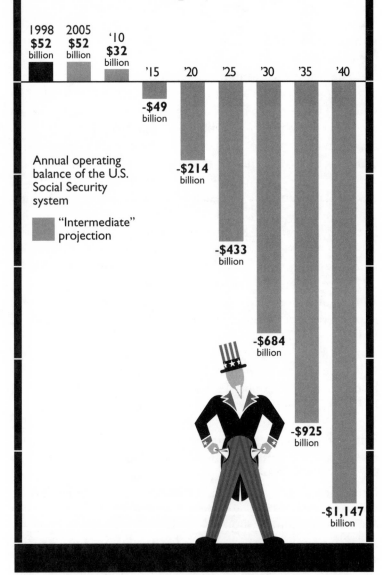

1998	2005	'10	'15	'20	'25	'30	'35	'40
$52 billion	**$52** billion	**$32** billion						

-$49 billion

-$214 billion

Annual operating balance of the U.S. Social Security system

"Intermediate" projection

-$433 billion

-$684 billion

-$925 billion

-$1,147 billion

SOURCE: SSA (1998)

Once we strip away the comforting trust-fund illusions and look at the unforgiving numbers they conceal, the enormous fiscal impact of global aging assumes a new urgency. In fact, my deficit calculations understate the cost of doing nothing. My calculations refer only to pensions. Health care roughly doubles the projected deficits for most countries. My calculations also assume that savings rates elsewhere in the private and public sectors in the developed world will remain the same. More likely, global aging will itself pull down private savings rates as more people enter their harvest years. The OECD projects that private savings in the developed world could fall by 2030 to less than half of today's rate. In the United States, projections show that most large U.S. pension plans will become net dissavers—that is, pay out more to current retirees than they take from current workers—once the boomer generation begins to retire. Not long ago, some American economists hoped for a compensating advantage. They predicted that the eventual U.S. savings decline would be mitigated by a huge household savings boom that was supposed to accompany the middle-aging of the boomers in the 1990s. Yet this household savings boom never materialized: Since the early 1980s, the U.S. personal savings rate has been continuously falling.

RAISING TAXES:
HOW MUCH HIGHER CAN WE GO?

Well, if doing nothing won't work, what about the next path of least resistance—trimming other areas of total public spending? This might help, but to make a real difference governments would have to slash, not trim—and it's not at all obvious where to place the knife. Leaving aside all social insurance programs (such as pensions, health care, and unemployment), interest on the debt (which is uncuttable), and infrastructure (including schools, subways, and satellites—much of which is vital for the future), what remains is an average of only about 10 percent of GDP in developed countries, or roughly one-fourth of total government spending. (In Europe, we'd be left with just one-fifth.) So great is the projected growth in senior benefits that many countries could cut *all* of what remains and still find themselves running widening deficits in the 2020s.

But it can't all be cut. Much of this spending consists of core state services (from police to postal services) that have remained fairly constant as a share of GDP for decades. It also includes national defense. Not long ago, defense would have made a nice target. But since the end of the Cold War, average military spending in the developed world has contracted to a level (under 2 percent of GDP) that history teaches is more likely to rise than to fall in response to future events. Since the late 1980s, this contraction is a principal reason political leaders have been able to allow senior benefit spending to grow without asking for tax hikes. In the United States, where a dramatic fall in defense spending has coincided with a long economic expansion and a temporary leveling off of the aged dependency ratio, fiscal choices have been relatively painless. Over the last decade, the rise in federal benefit spending (2 percent of GDP) has been more than matched by the fall in defense spending. The real question is not whether this trade-off can continue, but how—when new threats to the peace emerge—it can be reversed.

At this point, some will say we'll have to bite the bullet—and raise taxes. Tax increases may help, but taxes are already high. Most developed countries are now clearly at or beyond their threshold of efficient taxation. The United States and Japan, where the total tax take is roughly 32 percent of GDP, are possible exceptions. But in the European Community, total tax revenues average 46 percent of GDP and total payroll tax rates typically run between 30 and 60 percent of wages.[18] How can these nations conceivably raise the extra 9 to 16 percent of GDP—or, equivalently, the extra 25 to 40 percent of payroll[19]—needed to cover the long-term cost of the coming age wave? Already today, few European politicians and even fewer policy experts advocate raising taxes

Raising taxes to cover current retirement promises would impose a crushing burden on future workers.

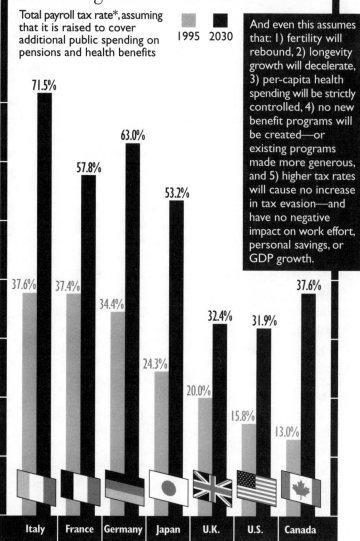

Total payroll tax rate*, assuming that it is raised to cover additional public spending on pensions and health benefits

1995 2030

And even this assumes that: 1) fertility will rebound, 2) longevity growth will decelerate, 3) per-capita health spending will be strictly controlled, 4) no new benefit programs will be created—or existing programs made more generous, and 5) higher tax rates will cause no increase in tax evasion—and have no negative impact on work effort, personal savings, or GDP growth.

71.5%
63.0%
57.8%
53.2%
37.6% 37.4%
34.4%
37.6%
32.4% 31.9%
24.3%
20.0%
15.8%
13.0%

Italy France Germany Japan U.K. U.S. Canada

SOURCE: OECD (1996); SSA (1997); author's calculations
*Tax rate is measured (gross) as a % of total wages, including employer contribution. Includes contributions to all social welfare programs, from pensions and health to disability and unemployment compensation.

any further. Many warn that higher tax rates will slow the economy more than they will raise new revenue. This is particularly true for payroll taxes, since Europe's high structural unemployment can be attributed in part to the high cost of labor. Even in the United States, where the payroll tax burden is relatively light and unemployment is not a big issue, President Clinton has flatly ruled out any increase in the payroll tax rate for Social Security.[20]

High tax rates, indeed, may explain why the cost of Europe's major social insurance programs has recently been rising even faster than the growing number of elderly would suggest. Not only are unemployment and disability benefits to the nonelderly rising, but many working-age people (especially under 30 and over 55) are dropping out of the formal labor market altogether in favor of the untaxed gray market—or more leisure. Meanwhile, many businesses are motivated to move their operations to lower-tax countries. Quite simply, most European countries may already be maximizing their potential payroll tax revenues. So may the United States, given its long tradition of limited government. If developed countries try to raise much more, they are bound to learn the Latin-American lesson: hiking the rate and collecting the money are two different things. They could also trigger a political backlash from younger workers, who are already getting a much worse return on their payroll contributions than their parents. Understandably, they will resent a tax-hike "reform" that pretends to safeguard their future but worsens their return even further—by requiring them to pay more now for the same benefits tomorrow.

This points to another problem with the tax option, entirely aside from whether it is sustainable. Apologists for the status quo often dismiss concerns about huge projected cost hikes with reassurances that the next century's more affluent workforce will be able to afford higher tax rates. The principle implied here—a novel one for western democracies—is that the long-term benefits of economic growth can be confiscated for our own use so long as we leave our children and grandchildren no worse off than ourselves. Apart from the principle, the arithmetic is mistaken. Under the U.S. Social Security Administration's official scenario, if the United States raised taxes enough to pay for the growing cost of old-age entitlements, all projected growth in real after-tax worker earnings over the next half century would be erased. Under an alternative "high-cost" scenario that allows for larger gains in longevity and slower growth in productivity, real after-tax earnings would suffer a catastrophic decline. The prospects in most other developed countries are surely no brighter. According to "generational accounts" research underway in over a dozen nations, future workers in many developed countries are facing even steeper future tax hikes—absent any change in policy—than workers in the United States.[21]

If borrowing won't work and cutting other spending won't work and raising taxes won't work, some might say there's another option: printing money to pay the bills. Inflation, after all, has been the last recourse of princes and empires from the beginning of time—and even today, many regimes (for example, in Eastern Europe) are making ends meet by inflating their spending power ahead of their fixed obligations, including their pension obligations. The problem with inflation, of course, is that it usually ends up destroying social trust and ruining the economy. Even as a short-term palliative, moreover, it won't work in the developed world, where public pension benefits are directly indexed (and health benefits indirectly indexed) to the price level. Deliberate inflation would act like a perverse chemotherapy regimen that ravages the body while leaving the tumor untouched.

FACING UP TO FISCAL AND ECONOMIC REALITY

The time will come when fiscal and economic reality compels developed countries to confront the truth: that their universal pay-as-you-go entitlements cannot survive the coming age wave, and that the generosity of these entitlements must be greatly reduced. Everything will have to be on the table: from retirement age hikes and COLA cuts to new benefit formulas and universal means-testing. Health technology will have to be rationed, health budgets capitated, or health insurance voucherized. Various combinations are possible, but most likely, many of these options will have to be implemented at the same time in order to generate the needed fiscal savings. In recent years, I myself have proposed an entitlement reform plan for the United States that includes the following cost-cutting elements: gradually increasing the full-benefit retirement age to 70, and indexing it thereafter to average longevity; reducing the annual COLA by as much as one percentage point (a "diet COLA"); "affluence testing" all public benefits received by upper-income households; and instituting a global budget and fixed-dollar vouchers for government health benefits, together perhaps with higher premiums, copayments, and deductibles. These measures would greatly reduce projected federal deficits. To further raise national savings, I have also proposed a mandatory and fully funded system of personal retirement accounts.

The developed world may already have begun confronting the truth: In recent years, many legislatures have debated trimming benefit levels and five of the G-7 nations have already scheduled modest future hikes in the normal retirement age. But the cost projections remain unsustainable. The developed world will have to act far more decisively. If this happens sooner, the needed changes can be made with deliberation and foresight, and in a way that strengthens our economy, gives families time to prepare, and secures the safety net for those who really need it. If it happens later, the changes may be sudden and painful—for low-income families most of all—and arrive in the midst of financial crisis and political upheaval.

Most workers, after all, are highly dependent on public retirement benefits. The United States has one of the world's most extensive private pension system, yet barely half of U.S. workers are currently covered by an employer plan—not even by a meager 401(k) that can be cashed out long before retirement. Social Security accounts for over half of the total income of beneficiary households with total incomes under $20,000. Of all U.S. households, half have accumulated less than $1,000 in net financial assets (which exclude housing); even among households in their late fifties, when most workers are preparing to retire, median financial net worth still falls shy of $10,000. One study shows one-third of boomers have saved nothing at all, and another third have saved too little to make a difference in retirement. According to another study, which assumes that Social Security benefits will not be cut, though they most certainly will be, boomers would have to triple their current household savings rate in order to enjoy an undiminished standard of living in their old age. Very few, moreover, are preparing for the extra cost of infirmity in old age (for instance, by purchasing long-term care insurance), though one in three boomers will someday enter a nursing home. Yet this is the generation, according to the surveys, that expects to retire earlier than ever and with no reduction in living standards.

When you think about boomers, those who will be retiring when the age wave hits, don't be fooled by the yuppie stereotype. Yes, some boomers have invested their own money well. But only a minority of this generation rode the Dow up in the 1990s, and only a minority will be able to cash out big. And yes, some are receiving handsome inheritances from their parents, but such bequests are very unequally distributed. In the United States, the median bequest per boomer is estimated at around $30,000—typically enough to cover the costs of settling Dad's estate and paying off a few last medical bills, but not much more.

Once again, the problem facing U.S. boomers is raw demographics. When they reach retirement age and the time comes to sell off their mutual funds, where will they all find enough willing buyers? At home, among the smaller and economically troubled Generation X following behind them? Overseas, in societies where younger households will be even scarcer? Many financial analysts are predicting that a "great depreciation" in financial assets is likely to accompany the boomer entry into elderhood. One needn't subscribe to such views to be genuinely concerned about how most boomers will fare—especially if old-age entitlements have to be slashed across the board. Many ex-yuppies could become what retirement expert Craig Karpel calls "Dumpies"—Destitute Unprepared Mature People—carrying signs reading, "Will Work for Medicine."[22]

The outlook in many other developed countries is worse. Outside of the English-speaking world, only a few small countries (notably, Denmark, the Netherlands, and Switzerland) have funded private pensions systems that cover half or more of the workforce. In the major nations of continental Europe, employers do little or no savings on behalf of workers. Household savings rates in those countries are higher than in the United States, but are very skewed by income. Most working-class households have nothing to count on except the promise of a government check—a fact which has made senior benefits a passionate (and potentially explosive) class issue from Paris and Rome to Oslo and Vienna.

Benefit cuts are thus only the first step in facing up to global aging. A total reform strategy must go beyond fiscal sacrifice—hardly an appealing political platform in any case—and offer a *positive vision* of a society that believes in its future. I am convinced this positive vision must include a durable safety net and a new and secure source of retirement income based on funded and personally owned retirement accounts. But in any case, the new vision must eschew the ritual repetition of political promises, and begin to offer genuine and credible retirement security. It must prepare society to meet the special needs of elders without overburdening the economy or overtaxing the young. While restraining pay-as-you-go promises, it must require people to furnish alternative means of support. We must, in other words, adopt entirely new strategies of providing for the elderly, strategies that are affordable and sustainable in a rapidly aging world.

UNUSUAL RETIREMENT PLANS

1000 · F.A.I.

I'll take a thousand bucks, stick it in a bank, "forget about it," and in thirty years I'll be *pleasantly surprised.*

M.K. Plan

"My Kids" will take care of me. I'm virtually certain of that.

Jackpot Account

I'm not going to need one, because I'm going to be RICH, yessirree Bob.

The ? Plan

Who can plan, like, *next week*? Because an asteroid could smash into the Earth tomorrow, so what's the point?

5

New Strategies

ONLY A HALF-CENTURY HAS PASSED SINCE PAY-AS-YOU-GO entitlements became the dominant means of supporting the elderly in the developed world. This paradigm has culminated in some remarkable successes. It has raised the incomes of the elderly, shielded them from poverty, allowed them to withdraw from onerous labor, enabled them to live on their own, and given them access to the best that modern medicine has to offer. Such dramatic gains would have been unimaginable to earlier generations. The paradigm has also been accompanied by some evident failures: an uncertain dependence on anonymous bureaucracies, a breakdown of the extended family, and for many elderly, social isolation. One particular failure—long-term economic unsustainability—remains mostly abstract, a matter of numbers and projections. But this is the failure that will eventually require the paradigm to be scrapped.

As the pay-as-you-go era ends, a new paradigm will emerge. What will it be? Benefit cuts will signal the decline of the old system. Yet how will the world build a new one? A look at history and at cultures around the world suggests that any workable paradigm will likely be assembled from some combination of six basic strategies.

ENCOURAGE LONGER WORK LIVES

Let's start with the most direct approach: *Reduce dependency among the elderly by encouraging longer work lives.*

Retirement as a socially accepted, even celebrated phase of life is a very recent and western innovation. Until World War II, even in industrial societies, most elderly men remained at work. Old people were expected to be productive as long as they were able, and the very word "retirement" had the negative connotations of what one did with a used-up machine. I recall from my own small-town childhood during the Great Depression that it was utterly unremarkable for men to stay on the job well into their seventies—whether or not they could afford to quit. Pension benefits, then in their infancy, were widely regarded as a regrettable necessity. Indeed, they were sometimes openly defended as a means of clearing out deadwood and—as Senator Robert Wagner declared on behalf of the original U.S. Social Security Act in the 1930s—"to make new places for the strong and eager."

In the mid-1950s, these attitudes began to change. As pension and health coverage expanded and benefit formulas rose, the public perception of retirement grew steadily more favorable. The poorhouse gave way to advertisements for golf and beaches and spas. Voters endorsed reductions in the threshold age at which people could enjoy "resort retirement." Today most workers in the developed world look forward to enjoying leisured years of subsidized dependence which now take up roughly a third of their adult lives. In 1950, the median retirement age was slightly *higher* than life expectancy at birth; today, it's 12 to 18 years *lower*.

Retirement ages have dropped most in continental Europe, where earlier retirement has been actively pushed by unions and political parties for decades. Responding to popular demand for an "early retirement" option, most European countries began to lower their minimum retirement ages (typically, from age 65 to age 60) in the early 1970s. As they did so, incredibly, they made little or no actuarial reduction in the annual benefits to people who choose this option. Thus, any worker who delays his retirement for a year—and gives up a year of benefits—often gets no compensating increase in the annual benefit he will receive later on. Since

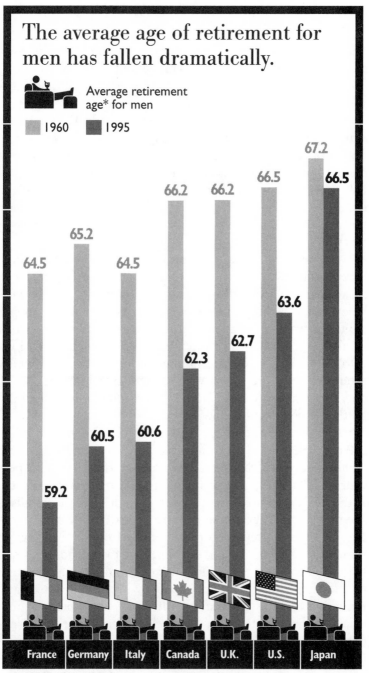

The average age of retirement for men has fallen dramatically.

Average retirement age* for men

■ 1960 ■ 1995

	France	Germany	Italy	Canada	U.K.	U.S.	Japan
1960	64.5	65.2	64.5	66.2	66.2	66.5	67.2
1995	59.2	60.5	60.6	62.3	62.7	63.6	66.5

SOURCE: OECD (1998)   * Defined as age of total withdrawal from the labor force

benefits are so generous, this amounts to a huge lifetime loss. It has been estimated that in France and Italy, for example, the benefits workers forego by staying on the job one extra year past the minimum retirement age amount to 80 percent of that year's after-tax pay. In the Netherlands, they forego a stunning 141 percent of after-tax pay.[1] (In this case, it's greater than 100 percent because the average wage net of payroll deductions is actually smaller than the average pension benefit!) Even these figures, moreover, only take into account the shorter retirement of later-retiring workers; they don't reflect the additional lifetime payroll taxes "contributed" by such workers.[2]

This implicit tax rate on continued employment is a huge incentive for workers to retire early. Where early retirement on regular pensions is not possible, continental Europe provides fiftysomething workers with many alternative stepping stones toward permanent retirement—including generous disability benefits (which often have more lenient provisions for older workers), long-term unemployment benefits (which often don't require older workers to search for a new job), and "special early retirement" (from industries earmarked by the government for downsizing).

And retire earlier they do.[3] One fascinating bellwether is the employed share of all men aged 60 to 64. Over the last twenty-five years, this share has dropped from 70 to 32 percent in Germany, and from 67 to 22 percent in France. Although the shares are somewhat higher in the English-speaking world, surveys show most U.S. workers in their forties, financially prepared or not, expect to retire even earlier than today's "early" retirees. Nine out of ten boomers say they want to retire at or before age 65. Some 60 percent hope to end their careers before age 60—with few expecting any reduction in their living standard! To be sure, there is some evidence that the trend may be leveling off: European governments are beginning to cut back on unaffordably generous disability and unemployment provisions for older workers, and in many countries (including the United States) the

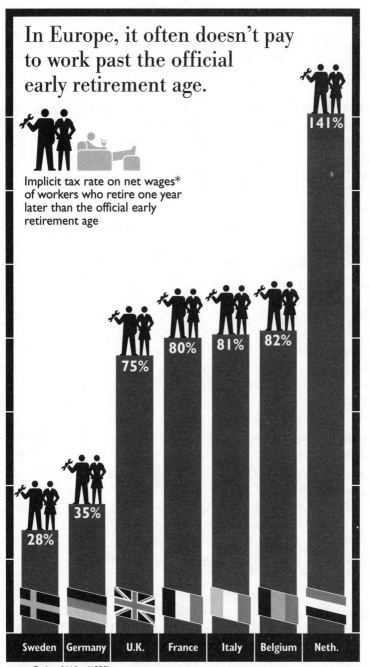

In Europe, it often doesn't pay to work past the official early retirement age.

Implicit tax rate on net wages*
of workers who retire one year
later than the official early
retirement age

141%

82%

81%

80%

75%

35%

28%

| Sweden | Germany | U.K. | France | Italy | Belgium | Neth. |

SOURCE: Gruber & Wise (1998)
* Lifetime pension benefits foregone as a share of yearly wages net of payroll taxes

employed share of older workers has been relatively stable for over a decade. But at this late date, the transformation has already been wrought. Only in Asia—led by Japan—is it still considered normal for a large majority of the "late middle-aged" to work. Although Japanese workers "retire" from their career positions no later than workers in other countries, they typically get new jobs (at least part time) with their old firm or one of its subsidiaries.

It's hard to exaggerate the enormous impact of lower retirement ages and longer lifespans on benefit costs. Although the impact has been largest in early-retiring Europe, even the U.S. numbers are dramatic. In the year Social Security benefits were first issued in the United States, the average age of retirement awards was sixty-nine, when U.S. life expectancy at that age was *ten years*. Today, the average retirement age is sixty-four, when U.S. life expectancy at that age is *eighteen years*. You don't have to be a math whiz to understand the vast cost implications of this shift. On the other hand, getting people to retire later rather than earlier would greatly ease the fiscal burden of aging. (Note that there is a double effect here: Each year retirement is delayed means both one *less* year of benefits and one *more* year of payroll contributions.) For example, the U.S. Social Security Administration reports that raising the minimum age at which people are considered "elderly" (now age 65) by one year per decade over the next forty years would erase two-thirds of the rise in the aged dependency ratio—that is, in the ratio of the elderly to working-aged adults. The OECD makes an equally dramatic calculation: Gradually raising the retirement age to seventy would eventually cut *total* pension outlays by 20 to 40 percent beneath current projections in virtually every country.

The argument for later retirement is not just fiscal. The new thinking among medical experts is that continued work would improve the health and well being of the elderly themselves. As leading U.S. gerontologist Robert Butler puts it, we must develop a vision of "productive aging" in which "work expectancy" rises along with "life expectancy." If people desire satisfying sex at age 70, why not satisfying work as well? In academic circles, the old-fashioned three-box lifecycle—education, work, and a rocking-chair retirement—is giving way to the no-box lifecycle, in which people can revisit education and work at any age. A rising number of European labor experts are calling for an end to "guillotine" retirement. Perhaps it's no coincidence that the Japanese, who enjoy the longest life expectancy and maintain the highest rate of elder participation in the labor force, are also most likely to believe that some form of continued work helps elders to maintain good health. Once retired, even many Americans rethink their vaunted rendezvous with uninterrupted leisure. Most U.S. retirees admit that they miss purposeful work activity, and three-quarters say they would like "some sort of paying job."

Business and government leaders in the developed world are therefore beginning to discuss pro-work policies for the elderly. On the table are bigger delayed-retirement bonuses, an end to "earnings tests" that withhold benefits to working seniors, and partial- and phased-retirement options that allow older workers to remain employed—an approach that Sweden has used very effectively. Also on the table are stricter policies and laws against age discrimination, which sometimes blocks the recruitment of workers over age 50. "Active aging" is now the buzzword at multilateral conferences on the economic future of the developed world. As the 1997 G-8 Denver communique went out of its way to stress, "old stereotypes of the elderly as dependent should be abandoned."

While all these are steps in the right direction—that is, they all help to reverse today's bias toward earlier retirement and expand opportunities for seniors to be productive—policy leaders had better work faster and harder if they want to make a real difference before the age wave hits in earnest. In particular, they need to recognize that the problem of "ageism"—the pervasive view that elders can't or don't want to be productive citizens—is too deep-seated to be solved by equal-opportunity laws alone. Overcoming ageism will require ongoing education and commitment, much as overcoming racism in American workplaces has over the past few decades. An entire stereotype will have to be reversed, along with all the institutional rules and habits of thought that help perpetuate it.

The public needs to be better informed about the good health and productivity of the typical elder worker. Most job studies find that elders compare well against younger workers by most measures of knowledge, output, reliability, and work habits. Where they do sometimes fall behind (for instance, in physical stamina), they make up for in judgment and experience. As the McDonald's chain demonstrated in its highly effective intergenerational ad campaign, the part-time senior service worker can be a huge customer draw.

Businesses need to think more strategically about a long-term future in which young workers will be scarce. They can start by identifying tasks which older workers may actually perform better than younger workers (for instance, customer service) and by finding ways to retain elder careerists by allowing them to work fewer hours, with lighter duties, and for reduced salary. In most developed countries—with the notable exception of Japan—employers face many obstacles to such arrangements, including discrimination laws, union rules, long-established seniority pay systems, and the very design of the defined-benefit pension plans traditionally favored by large corporations (which encourages career workers to retire early). Pension expert Sylvester Schieber enumerates some of the problems facing the developed countries generally and the United States in particular:

> In the U.S. we have a major problem in our pay structure being related to age. Defined-benefit pension accounting rules and funding patterns discourage early funding and make these plans more expensive as workers age. Even 401(k) plans have match rates which raise the cost for older workers, who typically contribute at higher rates than

younger ones. Employer-financed health costs are higher for older workers. Leave programs award workers with longer tenures for time not worked. Older workers have longer tenures than younger ones. Disability and workers' comp costs rise with age. All of these facets of the pay system reduce older workers' relative profitability. Yet discrimination laws preclude employers from reducing pay on an age-related basis. Thus employers structure retirement plans to get older workers to retire in their mid-50s to early 60s because they are no longer economically profitable.[4]

Unions need to move beyond their traditional focus on getting better pensions for older workers and do more to improve their employment opportunities. They must also repudiate the pernicious official doctrine, widely held in Europe, that ever-earlier retirement improves the long-term employment prospects for younger workers. This backward notion seems to assume that the size of the economy is fixed—and that young people should welcome the chance to pay generous pensions to older workers in order to take over their jobs.

Meanwhile, political leaders—and the benefit lobbies that so often tell them that later retirement is a hardship—need to guard against perhaps the worst form of "ageism" of all: the assumption that most elderly, due to their manifold infirmities, cannot possibly move in the direction of greater economic independence. Governments need to reduce the heavy implicit tax on public pensions received by elders who retire later, and should consider providing tax credits to encourage employers to hire and train older workers, increasing direct government funding for training older workers, and allowing part-time employees to receive a proportionate share of fringe benefits. One especially controversial reform would be to require that private employer pensions be made age-neutral—in other words, that no financial penalty apply to those who work beyond a pension plan's "normal" retirement age.

Public benefits, moreover, need to be better integrated with employer benefits. In the United States, for example,

Medicare is a "secondary payor"—and thus will not pay workers aged 65 and over for any medical expenses covered by their employers. This means that keeping such workers compels employers with health plans to pay for what taxpayers would otherwise pay for (namely, the cost of Medicare insurance) if the workers simply retired. Making Medicare the "primary payor" for everyone age 65 and over, working or not, would make elder workers more cost competitive with younger workers in the eyes of their employers.[5]

Although later retirement is an important strategy, no country will ever control the fiscal burden of aging solely through this means. The obstacles in its path are simply too profound. For one thing, developed market economies cannot reverse the clock and integrate elders seamlessly into mainstream productive life in the manner, say, of a rural village in a developing country. The informal economy of the old *Walton's* homestead, in which grandma and grandpa just naturally fit in, is gone for good. For another, the idea of compelling workers to retire later remains very unpopular with the public, whose attitude seems to be: Let me have the *choice* of working later—but also the *right* of retiring earlier.

In part, the public's attitude is influenced by the predicament of workers whose strenuous occupations or declining health make later retirement a genuine hardship. Richard Trumka, President of the United Mine Workers of America, served with me on the President's 1994 Commission on Entitlement and Tax Reform (better known as the Kerrey-Danforth Commission). He used to admonish lawmakers about the need for early retirement benefits by telling the story of his father, who retired as early as he was able (at age 62) after contracting black lung disease. Trumka advised anyone in favor of later retirement to take what he called "the Trumka test"—which was to run up three flights of stairs holding your mouth and one nostril shut.

Though he presents his case eloquently, Trumka overstates it as a general proposition. Every developed country maintains one or more separate programs that provide benefits to disabled workers of any age. And most workers never become disabled. When retirees are asked whether they retired because of poor health, the overwhelming majority say no.[6] It makes no more sense for a government to design its overall retirement policy around the needs of the broken-down miner who legitimately chooses to retire at age 62 than around the needs of the policeman who retires with a gunshot wound at age 42 or the knee-injured football star who retires at age 32. Nonetheless, the developed countries are averse to a redefinition of retirement that might hurt some of their hard-working citizens who, for whatever reason, find it difficult to qualify for disability benefits.

These issues may explain why very few countries have yet to raise the minimum retirement age for most workers. It is true that many countries (including Italy, Germany, and the United States) have scheduled modest rises in their so-called normal retirement age. But that is something different: The normal retirement age is simply the age at which the *full-benefit* formula applies. In the United States, for example, the normal retirement age is scheduled to rise from 65 to 67 between the years 2000 and 2022—but the minimum benefit age will remain at age 62. Raising the normal age (but not the minimum age) is in effect equivalent to a proportional cut in the initial benefit awarded to workers retiring at all ages. Yes, such raises do reduce future budget outlays, but they don't require anyone to work longer before receiving benefits—and indeed the official U.S. cost projection assumes that relatively few workers will do so. This in turn suggests that the economy won't benefit from longer work lives and that elders won't have any substitute for the benefits they lose.

The scheduled hike in the U.S. Social Security normal retirement age is a step in the right direction—but it doesn't go far enough. So long as we are raising the normal retirement age so gradually (as we should, to give people time to prepare), why not raise it all the way to age 70—and index it to

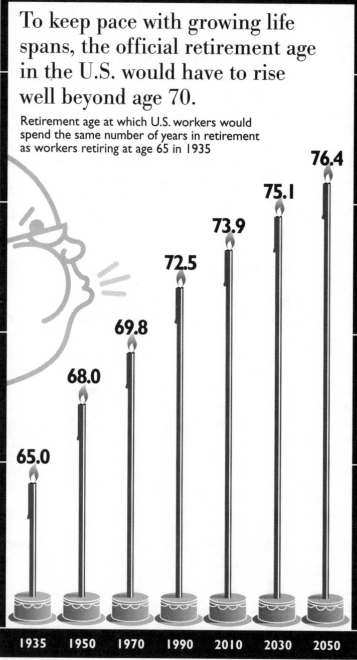

To keep pace with growing life spans, the official retirement age in the U.S. would have to rise well beyond age 70.

Retirement age at which U.S. workers would spend the same number of years in retirement as workers retiring at age 65 in 1935

1935	1950	1970	1990	2010	2030	2050
65.0	68.0	69.8	72.5	73.9	75.1	76.4

SOURCE: SSA (1992); author's calculations

longevity increases thereafter?[7] At the very least, this hike would achieve much needed benefit savings. It could do a lot more. Because the benefit reductions for early retirees would be steep, they may help to reduce elder dependency by extending work lives.

I have no illusion, however, that getting people to retire later is simply a matter of cutting their benefits. Advocates of "productive aging" have a big job ahead of them: Neither governments, nor business, nor labor unions, nor for that matter the elderly themselves, have taken anything but token steps towards making longer work lives an economically sensible, socially accepted, and personally comfortable norm. A vast behavioral inertia still surrounds the expectation of early retirement throughout the developed world.

INCREASE THE SIZE OF THE WORKING-AGE LABOR FORCE

A second and related strategy is to *encourage more work from the nonelderly—either by getting working-age citizens to work more or by increasing the inflow of working-age immigrants.*

Policies that expand the labor force are sure to receive growing support (or at least spark growing debate) as the shortage of young workers becomes more painfully apparent in the years ahead. Pro-work and pro-immigrant policies are similar to policies encouraging later retirement in one important respect: They all have the advantage of offering an instant payoff. Unlike pronatalism or investing more in children (strategies I will turn to shortly), they don't require a long lead-time. To the extent societies can find and assimilate working-age adults who are prepared to take a job tomorrow, they need not wait a generation to grow or educate new taxpaying workers from scratch.

Consider the first part of this strategy: encouraging working-age citizens to increase their employment—by getting jobs if they're not currently employed or by working longer hours if they are. Ordinarily, policymakers in liberal democratic societies aren't in the habit of telling people how much they should work. If citizens face rising taxes, the assumption is that they can decide for themselves whether they want to work more to offset some or all of the extra burden. A large exception must be made, however, in cases where public and private institutions now tilt the playing field against employment.

Developed countries, for example, often discourage work through disability, unemployment, and welfare programs that offer generous benefits but few incentives to find new jobs. This is especially true in continental Europe, where only a few governments have started to reform these programs—and most have yet to learn from such remarkable success stories as the U.S. overhaul of its welfare system in the 1990s. Governments also discourage employment by enforcing a regulatory thicket of wage laws, mandated fringe benefits, and professional licensure rules. Some governments have gone so far as to adopt a national policy of reducing the average work week. (In France, for example, the recent campaign to cap the work week at 35 hours has led to gendarmes raiding businesses to make sure workers aren't logging too much overtime.) For countries in which retirees are projected to multiply ten times or more faster than workers, such policies are fiscal insanity. In fact, many governments and political parties would be well advised to start ratcheting up their definition of the full-time work week—even if this runs against the current of recent labor legislation and social trends. There appears to be ample room for change in many countries, given the large international disparity in work habits: The average manufacturing work week in Japan, for instance, is 40 percent longer than in Sweden; in the United States, it's 20 percent longer than in France.

Two segments of the labor force deserve special attention. With regard to working women, we must confront reality. To the extent that generational promises to elders have been redefined in terms of cash benefits and paid health providers—rather than personal care within the family—the developed world can no longer be indifferent to whether women are enlarging the tax base. At least two major nations facing very large fiscal challenges (Japan and Italy) also happen to have very low rates of female employment. These countries may soon have to challenge their traditions and actively encourage more women to work. Another critical issue is the declining labor-force participation of young adults. In part, this trend reflects more years of training and higher education, and so is not a problem. Also in part, it is a reaction to very high payroll taxes—and bringing these down must await overall reform of retirement benefit programs. Nonetheless, there are many measures which can be taken right away, such as better training and apprenticeship programs, an end to two-tier pay scales, and macroeconomic policies based more squarely on the premise (too often ignored) that youth opportunity depends upon new firms launching new products in a growing economy. Leaders who ascribe to these policies must somehow find the resources to invest in future productivity and wage growth and refuse to let their economies be held hostage by unsustainable economic projections.

The second part of the larger-labor force strategy is immigration. On this issue more than most, governments will no doubt have to balance the conflicting views of different constituencies. Voicing their collective self-interest, big business may come out in favor of more immigration and big labor will likely be opposed. The general public will hold mixed views: Many people are tolerant of new immigrants, but then again many are skeptical or negative. Nearly every developed country with significant immigrant minorities has experienced episodic popular backlashes—for example, in Germany (against Turks), France (Algerians), Italy (Albanians), Britain (Indians), the United States (Mexicans), and Australia (Southeast Asians).

Meanwhile, economists will try to settle the argument one way or the other with cost-benefit analysis. To date, their research has produced few clear conclusions. Most studies tend to show that immigration results in a short-term fiscal loss but a long-term economic gain (especially when the tax contributions of the immigrants' *children* are taken into account). And of course, from the standpoint of the developing nations, those who emigrate are often better skilled, better educated, and more enterprising than those who don't. Their departure thus represents a permanent economic loss to the societies they leave. What economists cannot address are the perceived social and cultural changes that often worry the public in countries receiving (and sometimes even countries supplying) large numbers of immigrants.

No one can foresee how the developed world will reconcile these conflicting views, though it is likely that different countries will gravitate toward different positions according to their cultural traditions. Consider the contrast between the United States, a high-immigrant society whose history and very identity are bound up with the image of a lamp lifted "beside the golden door," and Japan, a low-immigrant society that has always emphasized racial and social cohesion. Nicholas Eberstadt has noted that, during the 1990s, fewer immigrants have been naturalized in Japan than in tiny, reclusive Switzerland. (Japan's experience with second-generation Koreans whose parents were imported during World War II, or even its recent welcome to ethnic Japanese returning from Brazil, has been fraught with difficulty.)

Where nations seek closer cooperation, as in continental Europe, national traditions that hinder immigration pose a serious problem—since economic integration depends vitally upon the free movement of labor across borders. Workers have to be free to find employment where it may be, as millions of U.S. workers do between the states. European parochialism (how many Parisians would gladly move to Munich—or vice versa?) is a major concern to the European

Union leadership. If new populist pressures force governments to shut down immigration from North Africa, Turkey, and Eastern Europe, immobility could easily worsen. Most studies show, ironically, that these immigrants tend to move around within Europe far more readily than native Europeans do—so that a sizeable immigrant workforce may itself contribute to the success of the European Union.

The preferences of immigrants themselves may also make a big difference. The most prosperous economies will likely attract the greatest number of young, skilled newcomers, making them still more prosperous. Along with the economic advantages, high-immigration countries will have to accept the political challenges of managing a "clash of civilizations" within their own borders. One major challenge will be the reluctance of fast-growing non-native groups of immigrants, most of whom send income abroad to their own elder parents and families, to comply with "generational contracts" designed to transfer yet more of their income to affluent elder natives. Meanwhile, the most troubled economies may tip in the opposite direction. They may close their borders and embrace a more homogeneous self-image.

Yet the biggest problem with higher immigration as an aging strategy lies in the numbers. As I've already noted, immigration would have to double, triple, and even quadruple over today's levels—and remain at these higher levels permanently—to sizably reduce the fiscal burden of aging. This would be wrenching for any society, but will be especially traumatic for host populations that are no longer reproducing themselves, since even a small influx will cause the foreign-born to grow rapidly as a share of the labor force. Even for nations facing economic hardship—some might say especially for such nations—the social adjustment may be too painful. Public education and planning may help, but attempting to overcome the developed world's demographic constraints through immigration will surely strain the cultural fabric.

For these reasons, the possibility of substantially more immigration into the United States and other developed countries seems unlikely *today*. But this could change. For one thing, future immigrants will not necessarily come from where they have in the past. In the European Union, more opportunity-seekers may come from Poland and Hungary than from Morocco and Turkey.[8]

As the developed world approaches its aging crisis, moreover, higher levels of immigration may be perceived as an economic necessity. This may lead to short-term labor importation (or "guestworker") programs, which will no doubt be sold to native citizens as "temporary," but which, history teaches, tend to remain in place indefinitely. It's not hard to imagine the United States sanctioning business requests to hire large numbers of Chinese and other Asian immigrants from populations perceived as hardworking, skilled, orderly, and unlikely to create a social welfare burden. (Raising the special "H-1B" quota for skilled immigrants is now a hot issue before the U.S. Congress.) Even in Japan, historically resistant to immigration, the government may have no choice but to alleviate labor and taxpayer shortages by importing more mainland Asian laborers and Filipino domestics. I am told that there are already tens of thousands of illegal Chinese immigrants working in Japanese agriculture. The view among Japanese leaders is that change will come slowly and incrementally (as is true of all change in Japan). However, as I talk with younger and increasingly westernized Japanese—who will soon bear the heavy cost of an aging population—I sense a more pragmatic view about the benefits of immigration. I suspect that in time the view of today's younger Japanese will prevail.

But even here there's an important catch: To the extent that these new young workers come from countries facing their own future retirement challenge (such as Poland, Hungary, or even China), the immigration solution ends up shifting the aging burden and the shortage of young taxpayers from one country to another. So in the end, while immigration has a place in building a new paradigm of aging, it can be only one part of a much larger project.

RAISE MORE—AND MORE
PRODUCTIVE—CHILDREN

A third strategy for handling the burden of elder dependency is to *raise more numerous and productive children,* so that the cost burden is spread over a larger and more affluent rising generation.

Having plenty of babies, of course, is mankind's most ancient form of old-age insurance. In the poorest countries—where tradition is strong, government is weak, and children often die young—this strategy persists. When people the world over are asked whether they regard their children as a future source of financial support, the share of affirmative answers rises directly with the poverty and birthrate of the country in question. Independently of a country's wealth or poverty, moreover, the generosity of its public pension system also influences birth choice—by freeing parents from financial dependence on their children. Nearly all countries in Eastern Europe and the former Soviet Union have extensive pension systems and low fertility, while the more affluent tier of Islamic nations (Morocco, Tunisia, Turkey, and Iran, for instance), with roughly the same GDP per capita, have meager pension systems and high fertility.

In the developed world, financial support has long ranked vanishingly low on the list of personal reasons that people have babies. Perhaps to remedy this decline in personal interest, many affluent nations have from time to time experimented with policies that favor having babies. "Pronatalism" endures in every tax break or family subsidy that rewards parents with children.

In France, parents at all income levels are eligible for a vast array of monthly cash payments, from a "basic family allowance" to such exotic add-ons as a "housing allowance" or a "beginning of school year allowance." Swedish employers must offer all new parents a combined 450 days of paid leave—including 390 days with payment at 75 percent of earnings. While these policies have many economic and humanitarian objectives—from making it easier for parents to keep their jobs to assuring that children are well-fed and housed—an explicit purpose is to encourage births. In Norway, for example, the per-child cash allowance *increases* with each additional child. In France, many of the cash subsidies begin only after the birth of one's *second* or *third* child. Perhaps as a result, French and Scandinavian fertility rates remain 10 to 20 percent higher than those in the rest of Europe. If this higher level of fertility persists,[9] it will reduce the ultimate cost of old-age benefits by roughly the same percentage range.

Fertility rates, of course, are determined by a lot more than subsidies. Social and economic conditions, to say nothing of the prevailing culture, can overwhelm the direction of government policy. Italy offers new parents a relatively generous menu of cash and workplace benefits, but its already-low fertility rate continues to fall. The English-speaking countries, on the other hand, offer few universal child benefits other than tax preferences for family households (such as the U.S. child deduction and Earned Income Tax Credit) and are notoriously stingy about maternity and family-leave benefits. Nevertheless their fertility rates are among the highest in the developed world. The stunning results of China's one child per family regulation suggests that any birth policy, pursued aggressively enough, can be made to work. In more affluent and democratic societies, however, such extreme policies are not possible. Encouraging people to have more babies can be a helpful strategy, but is of only limited effectiveness and reliability. According to demographers, the verdict on pronatalism ranges from weak to modest.

Over the next few decades, despite these limitations, much of the developed world may try harder to encourage births. Pronatalism may be a sensitive topic so long as overpopulation (and its associated environmental costs) is perceived to threaten the world. Yet many national leaders, particularly in Europe, are beginning to warn that low fertility is also a threat—to their economies, to the affordability of their welfare states, and even to their biological survival. No one should be surprised if Germany, France, and Italy expand their childbearing incentives, even as many developing countries continue to push birth control. Subsidized childcare and parental leave, now discussed mainly in terms of personal empowerment, will be recast in terms of the national interest. Feminist opinion may divide as a result. Some women will fear that pronatal policies will cost them their hard-won gains in the workplace by bribing them to stay home. Others will like the new benefits and the enhanced role of motherhood in public life. Then again, perhaps policies will be devised that avoid undesirable trade-offs between jobs and babies. Sweden, for example, has the world's most generous family benefits—as well as the highest rate of women working outside the home. Along the way, of course, questions about privacy, civil liberties, and the sanctity of child-bearing and child-rearing will be raised by any governmental policy that explicitly seeks to encourage women to have babies in order to serve national goals.

When a society worries about its next generation of children, what's usually at issue is not just their number but how well they are being raised and prepared for the future. Given the developed world's aging challenge, this broad focus is more important than ever—since the future size of the economy (and hence the tax base) depends on the *quality* as well as the *quantity* of tomorrow's workers.

So how well is the next generation being raised? Not well at all, it seems. Different ends of the ideological spectrum emphasize different problems. The right tends to dwell on the deterioration of "family values," the left on the weakening public commitment to schools, job training, anti-poverty programs, and social services. Where both sides agree is that recent decades have witnessed a widespread decline in the adult time and effort, and in the public and private resources, invested in children. U.S. Senator Moynihan wonders if we will become "the first species that forgets how to raise its young," a question that strikes home in societies that have been hit hardest by changes in family structure and that have the weakest traditions of public involvement in child welfare. Leading the list are the English-speaking countries in general and the United States in particular—that affluent superpower whose youth indicators on infant mortality, poverty, nutrition, functional illiteracy, math and science test scores, drugs, and crime often define the outer edge of pathology for the developed world.

Whatever the broader social implications of this trend, the economic implications are clear: The next generation's human capital is in danger, so much so that many experts wonder if an acceleration in the wage-growth prospects of tomorrow's workforce is a realistic goal. Many question whether the next generation of workers will even boost productivity as much as the last—a key assumption underlying today's long-term fiscal projections.

Developed world policy makers are now looking for better ways to invest in the skills and work habits of the young. Thus far, however, their efforts are generating only mixed results. Government programs work best when they provide new resources and opportunities to well-adjusted youths who are eager to learn and work. The results are less inspiring when the youths in question suffer from serious family troubles—a predicament which, unfortunately, describes a growing share of the rising generation. Money alone is often not the issue. Many studies raise troubling questions about whether government programs for disadvantaged children can make a difference no matter how much budgetary funding is available. In the United States, to take one example, the Comprehensive Child Development Program (CCDP) launched the so-called Beethoven Project in 1988. This project provided abundant social services—in particular, extensive counseling—to young poor mothers in Chicago at a cost of nearly $16,000 per family. In the study, half of the families received this service; half, the control group, did not. When the project was over, the research evaluators concluded, "CCDP did not produce any important effects on participating families."

As policy makers learn more, they are likely to adopt more comprehensive approaches. Spending on children (especially disadvantaged children) is not like spending on mature adults—in other words, on beneficiaries who receive money directly and are presumed to know how to spend it in their own best interest. Rather, a program's success depends on its ability to reshape the child's entire social environment—and forge effective alliances with the parents and teachers who act on the child's behalf. Governments will need to experiment with more realistic and cost-effective approaches to assisting, repairing, or (when necessary) replacing dysfunctional families. They will need to raise educational standards and reinforce values that push the lives of children in a positive direction. Most importantly, successful investment in children requires mobilized communities and bully-pulpit leadership at the national level.

Today, throughout the developed world, policies on behalf of children are on the rise—for reasons that may have something to do with the fiscal shadow hanging over our future. Historically, public enthusiasm for such policies has waxed and waned along with public worries about birth rates and about society's long-run need for more children. In the 1930s and 1940s, fears of "population decline" led most developed countries to sweeten family benefits, while in the 1960s and 1970s fears of the "population bomb" had the opposite effect. In the 1990s, the celebration of babies is making something of a global comeback in both the popular culture and legislative policy. From health and education to family responsibility, governments are moving toward stronger protections for children—prompting *Newsweek* to talk of a new wave of "kinderpolitics" sweeping the developed world. Consider an American example. As a share of median family income, the U.S. child tax deduction peaked in the Truman era, fell steadily to a nadir in the early Reagan era, and has since been partially restored by the same recent Congresses that have enacted "Kidcare" and "Kidsave" legislation.

Even while senior lobbies remain powerful—and in some countries are still gaining clout—today's renewed interest in the welfare of children is beginning to express itself politically. Very gradually, this interest is bringing together a wide variety of child advocates with overlapping agendas. In time, the two halves of the pro-child strategy—expanding the quantity *and* quality of tomorrow's workforce—may merge into a single cause.

By the year 2030 and beyond, the success or failure of pro-child strategies will have significant fiscal and economic consequences for the developed world. In the near- and medium-term, the official budget projections are sensitive to a large number of complex variables, from unemployment to inflation. But in the very long term, two simple variables— fertility and labor productivity—dominate all the others (even longevity). Higher fertility and more productivity mean a bigger economy. And nothing would do more to overcome the fiscal challenges of an aging society than a strategy that makes the economy grow faster decade after decade.

But pro-child strategies cannot work alone or substitute for other reforms to reduce the cost of elder dependency. To begin with, the pro-child strategy takes a long time to work. Even a highly successful pronatal policy enacted this year would have negligible fiscal impact until the late 2020s. The same is true for child investment. Most developed countries will hit the fiscal wall well before then.

Pro-child strategies, moreover, come with a large price tag—and it is hard to imagine substantial government funding so long as the cost burden of elder dependency continues to mount. In recent decades, the growth in retirement benefits and interest payments has accounted for more than all the growth in developed-country government spending as a share of GDP. In future decades, these benefits are on track to crowd out what governments *already* spend on new parents and children. Then there's the central question of effectiveness. Even if we find the money and spend it, we can hardly bet the economic future of the developed world on programs which may or may not deliver. That could lead to a nightmare scenario: Pronatalist policies encourage the bearing of more children, but then societies fail to invest effectively in their welfare, education, and training—so that the next generation contributes, not to supporting the elderly, but to an exploding underclass.

Finally, child-policy advocates must confront a fundamental contradiction between helping society raise children and leaving today's retirement programs on autopilot. Throughout history, most societies have prepared for the future by harnessing the dedication with which families prepare their own children. If this dedication is no longer as focused and fruitful as it once was, part of the explanation may be the growth of pay-as-you-go retirement. In most of today's developed countries, *elders do not reap the return on what they've invested in their own children—but on what others have invested in theirs.*[10] Thus, even vigorous government action on behalf of children may be no match for the implicit bias against children in what government already does for elders. At some point, we must ask whether it's possible to redirect society toward future generations while leaving all other public priorities untouched.

STRESS FILIAL OBLIGATION

A fourth strategy is to *stress filial obligation*—that is, to increase the willingness of tomorrow's grown children, however numerous or productive, to support their own elder parents through informal and familial channels.

All cultures traditionally obligate the active young to care for the dependent old. In the Judeo-Christian tradition, this is implicit in the fifth commandment—"honor thy father and thy mother"—mentioned even before the injunction not to kill or steal. Pay-as-you-go entitlements, designed as a public substitute for this sometimes onerous burden, have weakened the sense of personal obligation. In the developing world, where entitlements are meager, most elders live with their extended families and are supported by their children. Very few live alone. In the developed world, where entitlements flourish, roughly twice as many elderly have no spouse and live entirely alone (two in five) as live with their grown children (one in five). Very few receive major financial support from their children. Indeed, the public income transfer from young to old is so large that the direction of private assistance within extended families is often reversed. According to the U.S. Bureau of the Census, American adults aged 25 to 34 now report receiving twenty times more support *from* their parents than they give *to* them; even for adults aged 35 to 44, the ratio is five to one.

The difference isn't just between rich and poor countries, but also between the more individualistic culture of the West and the more corporatist culture of the East. Elders have the weakest ties to extended families in northern Europe and North America, where (according to opinion surveys) both the old and young speak approvingly of their mutual independence. Elders have the strongest ties in Japan, China, and East Asia generally, where most continue to live with their children no matter how affluent the household or the economy.

East Asian children are initiated into this "Confucian" family ethic at an early age, often by growing up with grandparents in the same home. Even in prosperous Japan, 33 percent of elders live in three-generation households—versus only 1 percent in the United States. As in most other Asian countries, Japanese law obligates grown children to look after and, if necessary, provide for their elderly parents (112 Japanese were prosecuted under these laws in 1995). In the United States, government officials encounter withering public criticism for trying to bill affluent children for any portion of the nursing home costs of their destitute parents.

Japan is the only developed country where most elders live with their children.

% of the elderly living with their children

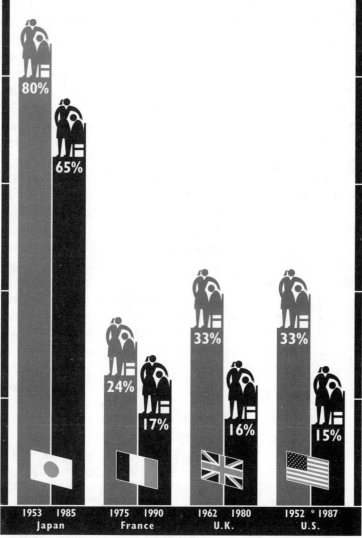

80%	65%	24%	17%	33%	16%	33%	15%

1953	1985	1975	1990	1962	1980	1952	1987
Japan		France		U.K.		U.S.	

SOURCE: OECD (1996)

The East has much to teach the West about filial obligation, although it is not clear that the West is in the mood to listen. In any event, as the age wave hits in earnest, and as the demand for personal care surges along with the number of old-old, Eastern societies will be better situated to provide that care without resorting to anonymous tax and transfer mechanisms. In the West, along with celebrating their greater independence, many young complain of being overtaxed, many old of being neglected. (Even the poshest nursing home can only provide what Bruce Vladeck, former chief of the U.S. Health Care Financing Administration, calls "unloving care.") In the East, where customs and values have traditionally wed the interests of successive generations, the young are more inclined to feel proud, not burdened, and the old to feel honored, not disrespected.

But how to strengthen the extended family? Today, even Asians are worried that global cultural trends are eroding their timeless ethic of filial piety. The Japanese are talking about a new "Me Generation" of young adults who are inclined to put their own lifestyles and careers before their family duties. The Chinese are wondering how filial obligation will change when the large "Red Guard" generation enters elderhood and today's "Peach Generation" of only children become adult caregivers. Will the dearth of siblings strengthen filial attachment to the older generation? Or will the extended family shatter under the great personal burdens placed on the younger generation? The unprecedented shrinkage of the Asian family and the movement of populations from rural to urban areas could reshape the Confucian ethic.

In the West, expectations for a heightened sense of filial obligation must be modest. Perhaps the most promising approach is to focus on the personal needs of elder dependents, where family involvement is most likely to be regarded as a proper and effective substitute for public programs. This could mean creating or expanding tax incentives and social services (like respite care and assisted home care) that help hard-pressed working families tend to the needs of their frail parents. Unconditional long-term care for the chronically disabled will bankrupt any aging society that does not find some way to enlist family support. Making families liable for more of the cost of publicly funded alternatives may be another way to "incentivize" such support—and to be fair to those families who assume the entire burden themselves. Some reformers would go much further. U.S. economist Shirley Burggraf boldly suggests that all payroll-financed benefits be linked in some way to the payroll contributions of each elder's *own children*. Under her proposal, workers would perceive a direct connection between their payments and the support received by their elder parents. Her proposal would also give them a "stakeholder's interest" in their own children's later contributions, which would tangibly reinforce any strategy to increase the number and productivity of the next generation.[11] Filial obligation and parental responsibility, after all, are a two-way street: Parents who sacrifice for their kids are the most likely to have kids who won't mind sacrificing for them.

No one supposes that western societies can or should import the Confucian ethic. But societies that treat the economic interaction between young and old as something other than a group negotiation between strangers (or worse, adversaries) will be better prepared for the challenge ahead.

TARGET BENEFITS ON THE BASIS OF NEED

Beyond trying to increase the carrying capacity of the younger generation, there is a fifth strategy of critical importance—namely, *to save on benefits by targeting them on the basis of financial need.*

During the half-century between Otto von Bismarck's social legislation in Germany and Franklin D. Roosevelt's Social Security Act in the United States, it was taken for granted that "old age" benefits were intended primarily to protect retired persons from poverty. FDR himself coined the phrase "floor of protection," and in fact the acclaimed cornerstone of his 1935 Act was *not* payroll-financed Old Age Insurance (what we today call Social Security), but Old Age Assistance (today part of Supplemental Security Income or SSI), which provided means-tested benefits to destitute elders. Until the early 1950s, this precursor to SSI paid out much more in annual benefits than Social Security. Then came the idea that government should attempt to underwrite a comfortable retirement for *everyone*. Today, Social Security outspends SSI by fourteen to one. A retirement system originally set up to protect against what FDR called "poverty-ridden old age" has since become a universal program disbursing benefits to all retirees regardless of income or wealth.

Today's retirement systems the world over, no matter how much they spend, redistribute little household income from rich to poor—and often offer limited benefits to large numbers of elders who are in dire need. In developing countries, the rural poor often don't qualify for benefits at all, and the rules are rigged to favor powerful urban elites. Even in the developed world, the data lend little support to the often-heard claim that universal social insurance is intrinsically progressive. In the United States, for instance, the most affluent beneficiary households receive more than twice the average government payment as do the poorest households.[12] Some $200 billion in yearly benefits go to the most affluent quarter of all households—while one-tenth of all elders still languish below the official U.S. poverty line. True, the affluent contribute a lot more per capita in payroll taxes. But when the numbers are fully adjusted for factors such as years of work and years in retirement, many academic studies question whether developed countries really offer a better deal to the low-income worker. At most, the progressive tilt is a modest slope. When everything is taken into account, there is, according to the World Bank, "little if any redistribution from the lifetime rich to the lifetime poor."[13]

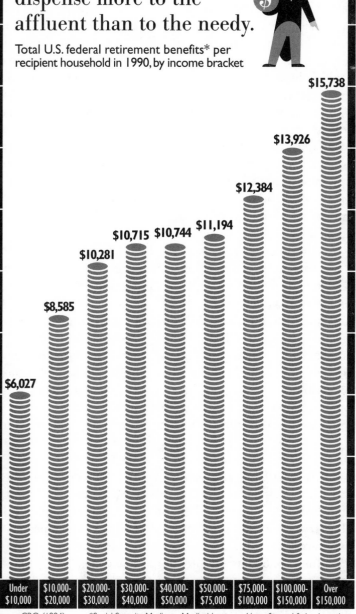

Public retirement systems dispense more to the affluent than to the needy.

Total U.S. federal retirement benefits* per recipient household in 1990, by income bracket

Under $10,000	$6,027
$10,000–$20,000	$8,585
$20,000–$30,000	$10,281
$30,000–$40,000	$10,715
$40,000–$50,000	$10,744
$50,000–$75,000	$11,194
$75,000–$100,000	$12,384
$100,000–$150,000	$13,926
Over $150,000	$15,738

SOURCE: CBO (1994)   *Social Security, Medicare, Medicaid, veterans' benefits, and federal pensions

The targeting strategy would return elder entitlements to their original function—and direct more of their benefits to the poor while reducing their overall cost. This could be done by expanding special types of "first tier" systems that are more progressive than the mainstream contributory systems in which benefits are linked solely to prior wages. This first tier ranges from a flat or fixed-amount benefit to all households (as in Britain and Denmark), to a flat benefit on which a means test is imposed for upper-income households (as in Canada), to a fully means-tested benefit (as in Australia). Also, the caps on payroll taxes could be lifted, cost-of-living-adjustments could be eliminated above some minimum benefit, or benefits could be made fully taxable. Finally, a comprehensive means test could be imposed on all retirement benefits.

A comprehensive means test (what I call an "affluence test") is a central piece of the reform package that I have proposed for the United States. In the interest of fairness, I would impose it on *all* federal benefits no matter what the age of the recipient—including Social Security, military and civil service pensions, Medicare, housing subsidies, and unemployment compensation. Those beneath the U.S. median household income would retain full benefits. Above the median, households would lose 10 percent of their benefit for each additional $10,000 in income. The maximum reduction would be 85 percent, thus ensuring that even the most affluent would retain some minimal return on their prior personal contributions. This reform would save roughly $75 billion annually by the year 2000 and much more in future decades as the total cost of elder entitlements rises. Some of these savings could be used to increase benefits to the elderly poor under SSI. Narrower versions of this approach have been proposed in Congress for a number of individual benefit programs. In 1997, the U.S. Senate adopted an affluence test for Medicare that was nearly incorporated into that year's budget.

Policy experts hotly debate the pros and cons of affluence testing—or, for that matter, any strategy that tilts old-age benefits toward the needy. According to the U.S. Congressional Budget Office, affluence testing "has several pluses: straightforward interpretation, simplicity of design, apparent ease of administration, and some political appeal."[14] The last point is worth emphasizing. Polls show that majorities of every age group—even the elderly—favor affluence testing. For example, in a recent national survey by Princeton Survey Research Associates, the *only* Medicare reform proposal supported by a majority of Americans (65 percent) was having higher-income elderly pay more for health care.

My own experience bears this out. A few years ago, in an event sponsored and filmed by *60 Minutes,* I visited an affluent retirement community and asked residents whether they would be willing to accept somewhat reduced benefit checks if there were a social safety net for them were they to need it and if the budget savings helped to improve the economic prospects of the next generation. To the visible surprise of the TV producers, nearly all the residents raised their hands.

Some critics say that an affluence test would constitute a tax on saving and hence discourage thrift. (In Australia, reportedly, some new retirees spend down their assets in order to qualify for the means-tested pension.) Other critics say that "programs for the poor are poor programs" and that any effort to target an entitlement to lower-income households will erode its political support among middle-class voters. According to this view, the public has to be bribed to support a system whose original focus on the poor no longer has much appeal.

Both of these drawbacks, I believe, are overblown. If an affluence test constitutes a "tax" on savings, the direction of its effect on savings is unclear and, in any case, the magnitude of its effect is small. To argue that an affluence test deters saving presupposes that younger people will choose to accumulate less personal wealth during their working years, thereby ruining their retirement, for the express purpose of picking up a bit more in government benefits many years later. This hardly seems plausible. If one could rule out affluence testing on these grounds, one could also argue—with equally misguided conviction—that welfare benefits ought to go to every family so that well-off families won't impoverish themselves in order to become eligible.

Outside the English-speaking world, few policy makers seriously believe that public programs are unpopular to the extent that they target the poor. And even in bastions of self-reliance like the United States, the history of Social Security indicates that the floor-of-protection concept can indeed capture the public imagination. When it's a question of young single mothers, everyone assumes that means-tested benefits are workable. When it's a question of elder retirees, we can no longer afford to assume otherwise. Let me put it another way: If everybody is invited onto the bandwagon (including the rich), who will be left to pull it? Targeting the needy in all phases of life can and must be a critical strategy for an aging society.

REQUIRE PEOPLE TO SAVE FOR THEIR OWN OLD AGE

And what about societies that want to replace, not merely modify, a retirement system predicated on transferring income from young to old, whether within public budgets or private families? Well, for them there's the sixth and final strategy, which is *to require people to provide in advance for their own old-age dependency—by saving and investing more of their income during their work lives.*

In theory, this saving can be accomplished either collectively (by governments) or individually (by businesses and households). In practice, government saving rarely works. As we've seen, the term "trust fund"—as used in the realm of public retirement policy—is seriously misleading. The assets of government trust funds constitute nothing more than IOUs against future taxpayers. They neither increase national savings nor relieve future workers of the burden of financing rising benefit costs. Because contributions do not belong to the individual workers who make them, governments can and do borrow against them—without any formal notice to workers that their own (or their children's) higher taxes will someday have to make up the difference.

The United States offers a stunning example of government's failure to achieve economic savings by means of budgetary trust funds. Originally, Congress explicitly intended that Social Security would fund much of its future benefits through a large trust-fund build up. But thereafter, Congress repeatedly postponed scheduled payroll-tax increases and enacted generous benefit hikes (including 100 percent cost-of-living allowances), preventing the trust fund from accumulating significant assets. Some experts have called this a "ratchet effect," in which the program is made more generous when there's extra cash flowing in—but, when the cash runs dry, reducing this generosity (by tax hikes or benefit cuts) is "impossible" or "unthinkable." By the 1960s and 1970s, a much enlarged Social Security system had thus become a pure pay-as-you-go operation. Then, in 1983, far-sighted U.S. policy makers decided to change course. Looking ahead at the lopsided demographic trajectory of the baby boom generation, Congress chose to hike Social Security payroll taxes long before the extra cash was needed to pay benefits. Thus the boomers were supposed to prefund a portion of their own future retirement benefits. Yet once again, things didn't work out as planned. Congress soon found ways to borrow the trust-fund surpluses and allocate the money to other programs, including other senior benefit programs like Medicare, while pretending that the trust fund was building up a massive savings reserve. By means of this double-counting, Congress has been able to circumvent the intent of the 1983 Social Security Act and mask the full magnitude of annual federal deficits during the 1980s and 1990s.

The alternative to government saving is private saving. And indeed, giving individuals a real ownership claim on future benefits is the only effective way to create a retirement system that adds to national savings and holds future taxpayers harmless. In a number of emerging-market economies, notably in Southeast Asia, led by Malaysia and Singapore, this is accomplished through "provident funds," personally owned but government-managed savings accounts.[15] In the developed countries, it is accomplished through employer pension and personal thrift plans, institutions that have their longest history and fullest development in the United States and Britain. There, and in Japan, private-plan assets amount to 50 to 75 percent of GDP. In the major nations of continental Europe, by contrast, plan assets nowhere exceed 10 percent of GDP. The private-plan assets of the United States alone exceeds the combined value of private-plan assets in all other countries in the world. Countries such as the United States and Great Britain with well-developed private plans tend to have the broadest public ownership of corporate equity, the deepest and most active stock markets—and the least developed (and often least generous) public pension systems.

During the last decade, developed countries have shown a rising interest in the funded retirement strategy based on private ownership. Where funded private pensions are rare, as in Germany and France, legislatures are enacting some measures to expand them—not just for the benefit of retirees, but to deepen and democratize the public's participation in capital markets. Where funded private pensions are relatively common, as in the United States, the popularity of personal plans like the 401(k), IRA, and Keogh has surged. In 1980, only one U.S. household in twenty owned a mutual fund; today, more than one in three does. In 1997, the majority of an official advisory council recommended transforming part of Social Security into personal accounts. The U.S. Congress is even debating new methods of prefunding health-care benefits—such as long-term care insurance and Medisave accounts.

A few developed countries are implementing reforms that *supplement* their pay-as-you-go systems with funded private

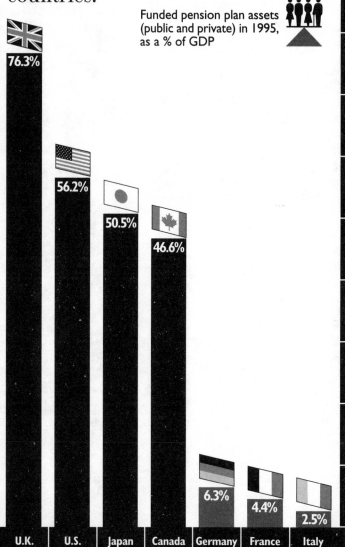

The English-speaking countries and Japan rely much more heavily on funded pension plans than other countries.

Funded pension plan assets (public and private) in 1995, as a % of GDP

U.K.	76.3%
U.S.	56.2%
Japan	50.5%
Canada	46.6%
Germany	6.3%
France	4.4%
Italy	2.5%

SOURCE: Goldman Sachs (1997)

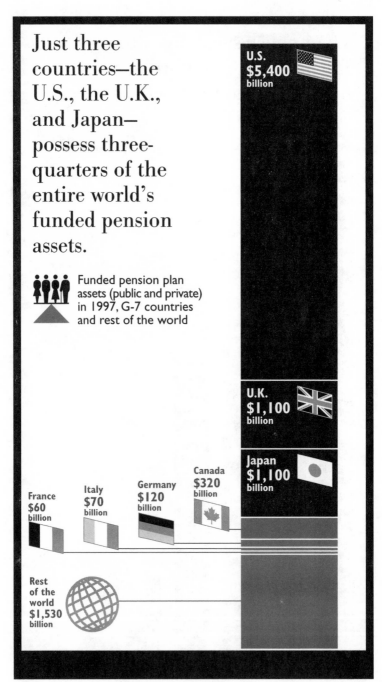

Just three countries—the U.S., the U.K., and Japan—possess three-quarters of the entire world's funded pension assets.

Funded pension plan assets (public and private) in 1997, G-7 countries and rest of the world

U.S. $5,400 billion

U.K. $1,100 billion

Japan $1,100 billion

Canada $320 billion

Germany $120 billion

Italy $70 billion

France $60 billion

Rest of the world $1,530 billion

SOURCE: InterSec (1998)

systems. In Denmark, the Netherlands, and Switzerland, employer pensions have been made mandatory for large segments of the workforce. In Sweden, all workers will soon be required to contribute 2.5 percent of payroll to a new system of personally owned retirement accounts. Part of a broader restructuring of Sweden's overall pension policy,[16] this reform will be at least partially effective for all workers born in 1938 or later and fully effective for all workers born in 1954 or later. Two countries, Britain and Australia, are going even further by implementing reforms that will largely *replace* their pay-as-you-go systems with funded private systems. In both countries, all pension benefits above a flat national floor are being gradually shifted to privately owned funds. Britain is encouraging workers to shift to employer plans while gradually allowing its public pension benefit to wither. Australia is requiring all workers to be covered by a new system of funded pension accounts while tightening up on its means-tested public benefit.

What's happening in Britain and Australia is precedent shattering—and may represent the wave of the future. In Britain, the 1986 Social Security Act enabled workers to opt out of the government's wage-related pay-as-you-go system (the "state earnings-related pension scheme," or SERPS). Workers who opt out must then either contribute into a fully funded employer plan, which has to offer a "guaranteed minimum pension" (at least as good as SERPS), or establish and pay into a personal retirement account. These private options are fully integrated with SERPS, since those who opt out receive a payroll-tax rebate and personal-account owners can earn benefits from both public and private systems. Since 1986 most workers have in fact opted out, and today only 17 percent of the workforce remains in SERPS. A growing share, especially among the young, are migrating to the personal accounts option, which the government has steadily expanded in recent years. At last count, fully one-quarter of all British workers (and a majority of workers under age 30) had personal accounts. Britain is the only major developed country that has ever given its citizens a choice between pay-as-you-go benefits and funded savings—and funded savings has won hands down.

As the years go by, Britain's reform is projected to boost national savings and hugely reduce long-term fiscal costs. Because very few new workers are joining SERPS, Britain is in effect liquidating a large share of its unfunded pension liability. (And to accelerate this process, the government has reduced the ultimate SERPS benefit by 25 percent.) Meanwhile, all retirees remain eligible for a Basic State Pension, Britain's traditional flat benefit with means-tested supplements. But since this benefit is fixed in real terms—that is, is linked to prices rather than wages—it too will gradually shrink as a share of the economy in future decades. Ironically, while Ronald Reagan's American-style conservatism was attracting the most world renown for its colorful invective against "big government" in the mid-1980s, Maggie Thatcher's British-style conservatism engineered a far more enduring policy revolution.[17] Major tax cuts come and go, but major changes in the state's economic and social role are rare and, when they happen, typically last a long time.

Australia has moved along a similar path. In 1986—the same year the initial British reform was enacted—the Australian government began requiring employers to contribute to funded private pension plans for certain groups of workers. In 1992, it expanded this requirement into a "superannuation guarantee" applying to all workers so that now all employers are required to contribute. (For the self-employed, participation is optional.) When the new system, nicknamed "Super," is fully phased-in by 2002, mandatory employer contributions will be 9 percent of payroll, supplemented by voluntary employee contributions plus an additional 3 percent government match for low-earning workers. Unlike Britain, Australia never had a public wage-related pension program. No opting out is necessary, nor is there any unfunded liability to pay off. Like Britain, Australia does have a floor-of-protection benefit, in this case a means-tested "age pension." But its future cost is projected to decline as retiree incomes rise (with Super) and fewer people meet the means test. Thus, Australia too expects to reap huge fiscal dividends.

This kind of reform can have dramatic results, as the British experience makes clear. Over the last fifteen years, Britain's elderly have grown far less dependent on public benefits: For the typical retiree, investment returns and private pension benefits have risen from roughly 25 to 40 percent of income. At the same time, Britain's elderly have prospered. Their per-capita income has risen far faster than that of any younger age group, and their poverty rate has plunged. Back in 1979, the bottom fifth of the British income distribution contained 47 percent of all pensioners; by 1993 it contained only 25 percent. With the typical private pension fund earning double-digit annual returns, today's younger workers can look forward to an even more comfortable retirement. British actuaries are telling 30-year-olds to expect a private pension benefit that is twice the level of SERPS.

Clearly, radical pension reform is an agenda that can be pushed by either side of the political spectrum: The new British policy was launched by a Tory government under Margaret Thatcher, while the Australian policy was launched by a Labor government under Bob Hawke. Yet what's more remarkable is that, over time, pension reform can gain strong bipartisan support. In Britain, a new generation of Labor leaders has embraced the privatization package, and indeed Tony Blair proposes expanding it, especially in the direction of personal accounts for young workers. Australia, which is now permitting workers to put pension contributions into special bank accounts, is moving in a similar direction. It is interesting to note that both countries originally planned to shift from public pensions to employer pensions—yet today are turning their attention to personal accounts, which offer greater flexibility and individual control.

In the developed world, the experience of Britain and Australia remains exceptional, but in the developing world, many countries are overhauling their old (and often bankrupt) pay-as-you-go systems and greatly expanding the role of fully funded private pensions. Chile led the way in the early 1980s,[18] and today roughly two-thirds of all Chilean workers contribute 10 percent or more of their wages into personally owned pension accounts. The typical Chilean worker now retires with a pension benefit equal to 78 percent of pre-retirement pay—more generous than the benefits offered by many pay-as-you-go systems with much higher tax rates. Meanwhile, Chile's gross national savings rate has grown to over 25 percent of GDP, the highest in the Western Hemisphere, while its economy has expanded at a real rate of 7 percent annually since the mid-1980s. The Chilean example is being debated by emerging economies around the world. In Europe and Asia, it has helped pave the way for funded private pension supplements in Hungary, Poland, and Kazakhstan. In Latin America, it has been followed in one form or another by Argentina, Peru, Columbia, Mexico, Bolivia, and Uruguay. Over the past four years alone, total Latin American pension fund assets have risen from $50 billion to about $130 billion. In its recent publication *Averting the Old Age Crisis,* the World Bank extolled the Chilean reform and went so far as to warn developing countries away from the pay-as-you-go road taken by the developed world. Since many of these countries do not now have universal public retirement programs, they can largely avoid the so-called "double burden" problem that confronts most developed countries, that is, paying existing benefits while, at the same time, funding private retirement accounts.

The case for a funded retirement system is simple and compelling. To be sure, switching over to a genuinely funded system requires up-front sacrifice from today's adults, in the form of more personal savings and less public benefits. Unlike "privatization" shell games, however, funded systems will pay for the growing dependency costs of an aging society without placing an extra *fiscal* burden on taxpayers. And in the long run, they will raise living standards, both before and after retirement, for every future generation.

They will do so by raising national savings and by increasing the payback on worker contributions. In the 1950s, when the developed world was expanding today's pay-as-you-go systems (and the developing world was setting them up), neither of these issues seemed to matter much. The reigning dogma of Keynesian economics stressed the importance of aggregate demand and warned of the dangers of "excess savings." Such views now seem quaint. As for the payback issue, economists today nearly all take for granted that the return on contributions in a funded plan (which is equal to *the average rate of return on capital*) is much higher than the return in a pay-as-you-go plan (which, when it matures, is equal to *the average growth rate of the economy*). But this fact was not always considered self-evident. In the early 1960s, high rates of fertility and real wage growth seemed to suggest that the developed economies might henceforth grow faster than the rate of return on capital. Pointing to these trends, Nobel Laureate Paul Samuelson famously declared in 1967 that pay-as-you-go entitlements were "a Ponzi scheme that worked."[19] Later events—especially, the "baby bust" and the global productivity slowdown of the 1970s—exploded this pay-as-you-go optimism.

A funded system that takes the form of personally owned accounts confers yet another advantage—greater security. When today's social insurance systems were established and expanded, young workers generally assumed that government would always make good on its guarantees. Today, increasingly cynical young workers trust the ownership of an asset far more than the promise of a politician. The appeal of personal ownership strikes a special chord in many poor and unstable regimes in the developing world, where ordinary workers have never had much reason to trust their governments.

Along with these advantages, however, comes a caveat: During the transition to a genuinely funded system, the economy as a whole has to save more and consume less. As I have indicated, today's workers will have to fund their own retirement at the same time that they continue to pay for their parents' and close the fiscal gap in the existing system.

Reformers have suggested several ways of accomplishing this. On the one hand, the government could issue "recognition bonds" equal to some *affordable* share of accrued benefits under the old system—and place them as well as all future payroll taxes into the workers' new personal accounts. The government would then hike general taxes to pay off the recognition bonds. By keeping the tax hikes modest and by paying off the bonds slowly, the government could spread the transition cost over several generations. The great peril here is that politicians might defer the tax hikes, leaving future generations with the huge cost of servicing the recognition bonds indefinitely. That would undermine the whole purpose of reform. On the other hand, the government could start a new funded plan on top of the old system by requiring additional payroll contributions—and then cut the old system back while the new funded plan is maturing. (The faster the old plan is cut back, the smaller the add-on contribution would have to be.) This add-on approach does not allow politicians to push any liabilities onto future generations: It requires society to pay for the transition as it occurs. There would be no debt overhang. From day one, the add-on plan would pay out all of its benefits from the return on new economic investments that would not otherwise have been made.

To be successful, any new paradigm must draw on various and diverse strategies—from later retirement, to investing in children, to stronger families, to means testing. But I believe that transitioning to a funded and mandatory system of personal retirement accounts is probably the most essential strategy of all.

Why *funded?* A funded system is the only strategy which, while providing greater retirement security, also strengthens the national economy by raising national savings. There are only two ways to raise national savings: increasing the public savings of government (which, in practice, usually means reducing budget deficits) and increasing the private savings of households and businesses. A genuinely reformed and funded retirement system would do both—by reducing the cost of the government's current pay-as-you-go system and by enlarging the pool of private savings as workers (and perhaps employers) contribute to the new system. In the long run, a funded system can overcome the greatest threat facing the developed economies as global aging sets in—the threat of insufficient national savings.

To be sure, it is often hard to persuade much of the public that they have a stake in capital formation, since they don't own much capital. This points to another advantage of personally owned accounts. Because they turn workers into capitalists—or the reverse, to invoke Peter Drucker's prophecy of "pension fund socialism"—they can merge the interests of workers with those of business, capital markets, and the overall economy. Consider again the British example. The same Labor Party that once assailed the very concept of personally owned pensions now sings their praises. According to one recent Labor pamphlet, funded pensions "are capable over time of producing the best returns each individual can achieve from their hard-earned savings. They have the potential to give people a real sense of ownership . . . ."[20] In addition, a funded system gives society the flexibility to adapt to an uncertain future. Personal accounts are portable, which makes them ideal for a world in which most workers will have to change jobs or even careers many times during their lives. They are also well-suited for a world in which many personal choices (such as retirement age) may have to be altered in response to demographic trends (such as very large gains in life expectancy) that no one can anticipate.

Why *mandatory?* I have come to this conclusion reluctantly. I once assumed that funded retirement security could be achieved by strengthening tax favors and other incentives to encourage workers and their employers to save more voluntarily. After weighing the evidence, I'm far less confident.

Several years ago, I chaired a subcommittee on capital formation for the Competitiveness Policy Council where I asked many prominent economists to evaluate the most popular pro-savings policies. They concluded almost unanimously that voluntary incentives are unlikely to increase national savings much, once the fiscal cost of offering them is taken into account. Moreover, many of these incentives have little impact on the savings of households beneath the national median income. Where U.S. employers now offer defined-contribution (401(k)-type) pension plans, only 36 percent of low-income workers elect to participate—and when these workers change jobs, only 16 percent roll their assets over into another pension plan. These are the very workers most likely to face hardship in retirement even if all of today's public benefit promises could be kept—and, of course, they can't. A voluntary plan would be neither fair nor effective. The funded strategy must include everyone.

Some critics claim there are problems with personal ownership. One danger, they say, is that workers will make bad investment decisions or be misled by less-than-ethical asset managers. In Britain, for example, privatization has led to numerous "pension mis-selling" scandals. "Inappropriate products were sold by inappropriate producers to inappropriate customers," is how David Blake, director of the Pension Institute, has described it.[21] (And with inappropriate sales commissions, he might have added.) But this is largely avoidable through proper government regulation—such as ceilings on fees and rules that require investing in a diversified portfolio or in a limited number of qualified mutual funds.[22]

Another danger, say critics, is that workers will be vulnerable to the roller coaster of the stock market. Do we really want people worrying every day about the impact of the sliding ruble or climbing yuan on their retirement years? For young workers in mature market economies, however, this is not a genuine problem. Ever since 1802, stocks have *invariably* outperformed "safe" fixed-income assets such as money market accounts and Treasury bonds over any 30-year period in the United States. According to Jeremy Siegel, professor of finance at the Wharton School, "Even the *worst* 30-year post-1926 returns for stocks, which occurred from 1960 to 1990, is almost three times the *best* 30-year returns for bonds and bills. You can mix and match any 30-year period in stocks to any in bonds and bills and find it impossible not to find stocks coming out on top."[23] For older workers, the risk posed by market volatility can be minimized by requiring them to shift from equities into fixed-income assets as they grow older. Simulations show that such portfolio rules could protect workers nearing retirement from just about any market decline—even a crash on par with 1929. An economic collapse large enough to short-circuit these safeguards would probably destroy an unfunded public system as well.

Still other critics raise the question of practical feasibility. How, exactly, are citizens to be compelled to save against their wishes? My short answer is simple: The same way all countries compel citizens to pay taxes against their wishes—and the same way it is done in countries that have already adopted mandatory savings plans. My longer answer is that most citizens—especially today's young adults—see a big difference between tax payments and contributions (mandatory or not) which remain personal property.[24] Even those who don't see the difference will find mandatory contributions persuasive once they understand that the alternative is even steeper tax hikes (and lower rates of return) in the future.

Finally, some critics assume that personal accounts would rule out any taxpayer subsidy designed to ensure a minimally adequate pension to low-earning workers. They are wrong. Some reform plans would provide a government savings match for low-earners. Other plans would (and Chile's plan does) "top up" the accounts of workers with insufficient assets to buy a minimum retirement annuity. The effect of these provisions would be to create a funded system that at least duplicates and probably improves the progressive tilt of current pay-as-you-go systems, thereby securing the social safety net—*which is a moral imperative.*

The concept of funded and personally owned accounts is too often equated with total "privatization"—that is, with society abandoning any responsibility for how people are provided for in their old age. The choice, supposedly, is between government either doing everything or doing nothing at all. This dichotomy is unfortunate—for it conceals the fundamental issue at stake. If the challenge is to replace (at least in part) the mandatory unfunded systems we have today, let's make the new system funded but keep it mandatory. The problem with the pay-as-you-go concept is not that it compels people to save, but that the "savings" it compels are a fraud—and that, without reform, its chain-letter benefits are unsustainable and generationally inequitable.

EMBARKING ON REFORM—
WHAT, WHERE, AND WHEN

Understanding these strategies is critical to building a new paradigm of aging. But reform is not just a giant button waiting to be pushed. Nor does it come in a one-size-fits-all package. Designing and implementing a reform agenda means deciding countless practical questions of what, where, and when. Which strategies will prove most popular? In which countries? And on which timetable?

Let's begin with the obvious: Some policy reforms are ideologically better suited to some countries than to others. In continental Europe, where unfunded pensions have long been considered the litmus test of social democracy, reform will have to pay special attention to income equity and class solidarity. In the English-speaking countries, on the other hand, personal autonomy, asset ownership, and high-octane returns will have more appeal. French voters will never split up their state pension system into 30 million 401(k) plans, while Americans will never switch to a universal flat pension—or consent to having a health minister tell them when they can see a doctor.

Or consider differences in attitudes toward family. Scandinavian elders have a long tradition of living apart from their families (a tradition that remains strong even in Minnesota, which has the most nursing-home residents per capita of any U.S. state). They will never be as amenable to living with their grown children as are Japanese elders—or even Italian elders. On the other hand, crowded Japan will never push pronatal policies to the extent Scandinavia already has.

As they are implemented, all of the strategies are likely to reveal new gaps in coverage—and this too will call forth differing policy responses. Universal, pay-as-you-go systems guarantee cash and care to just about every elder who has no alternative to public benefits. (They guarantee this to everyone else too, which is why they're so costly.) But as countries move toward alternative paradigms that allow more choice and require more foresight, this guarantee will be thrown into question. Some people won't be able to postpone retirement; some won't have large or dutiful families; and some may end up without savings. Societies will resist reforms that put their elders at significant risk of unsupported hardship. As it moves toward a new paradigm, therefore, the developed world must improve its social safety net. Most likely the English-speaking countries will prefer to expand their explicitly means-tested programs, while continental Europe will opt for a higher minimum benefit—and, perhaps, Asia will strengthen laws that require families to care personally for destitute elder parents.

In short, there are many roads to reform. As new paradigms of aging emerge, they will reflect the values of the different regions and civilizations of the world.

Then there's the all-important issue of timing. Many aging strategies—including some that would have huge fiscal and economic payoffs in the long term—won't do much at all in the near term. As we have seen, even if a society doubled its birthrate from one year to the next, it would have to incur somewhat *higher* social spending (on education, among other things) for a generation before it begins to see a big reduction in its elder dependency burden. Similarly, the transition to a funded pension system will take a couple of decades to pay off in significantly higher living standards for workers and retirees. Some behavioral strategies, such as raising the retirement age, could in theory produce quicker results. But the social and political reality is that people cannot change their expectations or life plans overnight.

The danger of relying on strategies with long lead times, however, is that they may allow the demographic and economic situation to deteriorate for many years to come. This deterioration could in turn trigger a vicious cycle dynamic which causes everything to get worse even faster than the official projections now indicate—overwhelming the strategy's long-term payoff. There's the adverse debt dynamic, in which countries respond to fiscal pressure by running larger public-sector deficits, leading to higher interest rates, less domestic investment, greater foreign borrowing, and slower growth. There's the adverse tax dynamic, in which countries respond by hiking taxes, leading to less work effort and less formal labor force participation. In both cases, the result is a smaller economy and a narrower tax base, which sets in motion another turn of the cycle. Finally, there's the possibility of an adverse birth dynamic, in which high unemployment or disappointing after-tax wage growth discourages young adults from having as many babies, leading—eventually—to a higher aged dependency burden and even more economic bad news down the road.

We need to learn much more about such vicious cycles. As things stand, most national and international agencies crank out official projections that not only use optimistic assumptions, but entirely ignore negative feedbacks. This isn't just a hypothetical question about the future. There's mounting evidence that negative feedbacks are already taking a toll. Over the last twenty-five years, as public debt has grown along with public retirement spending, the economic performance of the developed world has flagged. And in many of the countries where the tax burden has risen the highest, the economy has stopped generating new jobs in the formal (and taxable) sector. In Italy, for example, a mere 52 percent of the adult population is formally employed (compared with 74 percent in the United States); the rest are either disabled, retired, officially unemployed, voluntarily inactive, or working in the gray market. Many economists believe that part of the fiscal problem facing Italy—and other high-tax European countries—is the declining rate of formal employment among the *nonelderly.*

Meanwhile demographers are debating the adverse birth dynamic. Common sense suggests a link between the recent slowdown in real wage growth and the decline in developed-world birthrates. Surveys show that affordability ranks high among the reasons young people are now deferring marriage and choose to have fewer children.[25] It's no coincidence that the term "boomerang kids"—young adults returning home to live with their parents—was coined just as the average age of first marriage was rising to record heights in the late 1980s. President Clinton has warned that Social Security's future troubles could make this problem even worse. "I am the oldest of the baby boomers," he said. "I can tell you, all my friends at home . . . are worried about, number one, will they have a retirement? And number two, if they have one, will it be so costly to our children that their ability to raise our grandchildren will be compromised?"

The question of timing leads to a sobering conclusion: To meet the fiscal challenges of an aging society, the developed world must begin to undertake serious reform measures *right away—and these measures must include policies that generate substantial near-term economic savings, both less government dissaving (that is, lower deficits) and more private saving.*

We have little time left to choose and build a new paradigm before some catastrophe thrusts a new paradigm—not of our choosing—painfully upon us. The politics of procrastination, which would be a problem in any case, are being exacerbated in today's English-speaking world by the middle-aging of the post-World War II baby boom. In America, our current era has been called "a demographic Indian Summer"—which affords us a false sense of economic abundance and fiscal plenty before winter. Let America be forewarned: Sooner or later, the fiscal challenge of demographic aging will pose the same hard choices in every developed country.

6

Asking the Right Questions

"In the future, everybody will have fifteen minutes of health-care coverage."

ON HER DEATHBED, GERTRUDE STEIN IS SAID TO HAVE ASKED her old friend Alice B. Toklas, "What is the answer?" When Miss Toklas did not respond, Gertrude then asked, "In that case, what is the question?" I don't profess to know all the questions, much less the answers. It is one thing to say with some certainty that global aging will pose many profound demographic and fiscal challenges. It is another to say that these challenges can be summarized by quantitative projections. Of course, they can't. To understand the full consequences of global aging, we must not stop where the quantitative trail ends, but examine a broad array of economic, political, social, cultural, business, and family issues, even though they are less strictly projectable. In short, we must pose questions that cut across disciplines and require a more qualitative approach.

How will the coming demographic transformation restructure the economy? How will it reshuffle the ethics of life and death—as medical progress is forced to acknowledge limited resources? How will it reshape family life and redefine work and retirement? How will global aging change the relationship between young and old? How will it reconfigure political parties, platforms, and ideological debates? How will it transform the culture—as youth becomes a less conspicuous phase of life? How will it alter attitudes toward innovation, toward progress, toward posterity? How will it influence the foreign policies of the great powers? How will it affect national security and efforts to establish a New World Order? Even if I lack the answers to these questions—and I freely admit I do—I would be remiss if I did not put them on the table and try to stimulate reflection on the totality of what's at stake.

HOW WILL GLOBAL AGING TRANSFORM THE STRUCTURE OF OUR ECONOMIES?

The eighteenth-century luminaries who invented the formal study of economics (or "political economy," as Adam Smith called it) were keenly interested in the role of youth and age in determining "the wealth of nations." Living in an era of plentiful children and expanding populations, they wanted to know how demographic growth altered wages, savings, and output, which classes benefited, and whether a larger population was a long-term blessing or burden. Two centuries later, we would do well to return to this original emphasis on demography. Only this time, our questions must focus on the reverse phenomenon: What happens to the structure, size, and dynamism of the developed world's economies as they adjust to a new plenitude of elders, a new dearth of young workers, and stagnating (indeed, in most cases declining) total populations?

As a society ages, its economy inexorably shifts from sowing to reaping. Over the next few decades, the economies of the developed world will shift in just this direction. To begin with, consumers will demand less of whatever young households buy (from orthodontics and youth clothing[1] to kitchen appliances and starter homes) and more of whatever elder households buy (from cardiology and eyewear to leisure travel and reverse mortgages). Many industries, from higher education to cosmetics to sporting goods, will hire creative minds to repackage their youth products for the older consumer. In the United States, the retail economy is currently changing its focus from young adulthood to middle age. As the massive baby boom moves along its lifecycle trajectory, the most hyped products and pastimes are aging with them. In the 1980s, the hot new vehicle was the economy minivan; in the 1990s, it's the luxury RV. Back then, the recreation of choice was tennis; now it's golf. Not long from now, the retail economy will be trying to follow boomer tastes through yet another transition, this time from middle age to elderhood.

Though the most rapid growth of the elderly population has yet to happen, the steadily rising profile of the elder consumer is already visible to most retail shoppers—with hair dye outselling baby formula, with diapers for all age groups stocked in drugstores, and with senior-cruise brochures replacing the ads for kids' summer camps. "Golden demographics," the American marketers' idiom for young buyers, is now struggling against the allure of "golden oldie" customers, whose relative affluence is rising along with their relative numbers.

To the extent these new consumption trends run toward publicly subsidized items—health care, for example—they will, of course, push up government spending (even if retirement benefit programs are reformed). But there may be other important effects that have as yet received little attention. Growing consumption by elders is likely to favor personal services over manufactured goods. On the plus side, this could lighten inventories and mitigate the severity of the old stop-and-go business cycle. On the minus side, by accelerating the ongoing global trend toward services—where gains in output per worker are more difficult to achieve or even measure—it could act as a further brake on the developed world's already slowing productivity growth trend. On this score, we haven't yet started to ask the right questions about what twenty-first century governments can do to help raise productivity, and thus living standards, in an era when the economy will depend more on deploying at-home nurses than stamping out auto bodies.

Household surveys suggest that people become financially less equal as they grow older. As a result, we may also see more luxury goods and niche marketing—along with a more visible stratification of consumers by income group. The rising and worrisome disparity of incomes within the developed world's large middle-age population is not about to reverse itself as that population ages another twenty years. On the other hand, a long-term boom in personal services (with more people living longer lives, needing everything from maids to nursing-home attendants) may give an extra boost to jobs for low-skilled workers. Whether these jobs will get the respect and pay they deserve and whether they create jobs for native-born youth or become new magnets accelerating the immigrant flow to affluent nations remain open questions. Today's Philippine strategy—large poor families "exporting" their daughters to do the caring and cleaning for aging societies abroad—may yet become a profitable if controversial model emulated by a number of younger, developing countries.

That we will consume *differently* seems relatively certain. But will we consume *more*? There are two answers to this question. To the extent that consumption is limited by production, consumption per capita will surely grow more slowly than it has in recent decades—perhaps in part because the productivity trend may fall, but in any case because of the falling ratio of producers to consumers in an aging society. On the other hand, consumption as share of national product will surely rise. This will happen not only in America, which has long set the pace in inventing new ways to consume, but also in today's high-savings societies in Europe and Asia. An aging economy, say the experts, is likely to experience a declining rate of private-sector savings. Earlier in life, most people are net savers, whereas after retirement they become net dissavers. So as the latter group becomes relatively larger, all households (together with the private pension plans they belong to and businesses they own) will tend to save less of their aggregate income. How much less? No one really knows. What we do know is that if the decline is significant—and is accompanied by large fiscal deficits—the result could give rise to a global capital shortage, compounded by dangerously fluctuating interest rates and cross-border investment flows.

WHAT WILL IT MEAN IF GDP DOES THE UNTHINKABLE—AND STEADILY SHRINKS?

In preparing for this book and beginning to think about the possibility that many developed countries will soon see sustained declines in population for the first time in modern history, I asked leading economists and think-tank experts whether anyone has examined the impact on the economies of these countries. Everyone I spoke with agreed that workforce shrinkage was a significant and provocative question, though one that academics have hardly begun to explore.

One need not be a Nobel Laureate in economics to understand that a country's GDP growth is the product of workforce growth and productivity growth. If work forces are shrinking significantly, GDP may shrink as well, unless productivity rises fast enough to make up for the loss of workers. By the 2020s, at the latest, the working-age population in Japan and Europe (western and eastern) could be shrinking at a rate of well over 1 percent per year. Even assuming reasonable productivity growth, this means that at least some of these nations are likely to experience a *chronic decline* in total production of goods and services—that is, in their real GDPs—from one year to the next. In the United States, where the labor force is fueled by somewhat higher rates of fertility and immigration than other developed countries, the possibility of chronic GDP decline is more remote. But even here, the magnitude of the coming slowdown is worth considering. From the 1940s through the 1990s, Americans have grown accustomed to seeing the real size of their economy double every two decades. By the 2020s and beyond, they may have to wait *six decades or more* to see such growth.

The developed countries have yet to prepare for this about-face in workforce and GDP growth—or even consider how it may overturn their settled habits of economic thinking. For at least half a century, legislators and business managers have used expressions like "fiscal dividend" and "market growth" to refer to the natural tendency of tax revenues and sales to rise in a normal year. What happens, in this new environment, when everyone expects them to *decline* in a normal year? Economists define "recession" as two or more quarters of negative GDP growth. What would be the word for an economy that as a whole finds itself in an *endless* "recession," quarter after quarter?

Provocative as they are, these questions may not impress economists, who usually focus on real GDP *per capita* as the bottom-line indicator of a society's living standard. Why, many of them would ask, is there anything wrong with a smaller GDP as long as real per-capita income continues to rise? After all, the principal goal of economics is not to swell the aggregate wealth of nations (the title of Adam Smith's masterpiece notwithstanding), but rather to elevate the wealth of each person or worker or family within a nation. Still, a nation's economy is more than simply the sum of its parts, which is why I believe that the trend in total GDP does matter. This is easiest to see when we think of the aggregate resources that a nation can make available for collective endowments: everything from the breadth of its infrastructure and the depth of its basic research to the strength of its national security and the weight of its position in the world. But an historic change (or even reversal) in the GDP growth trend raises many other questions worth asking. How will it affect the composition of goods and services? Or the need to expand capacity? Or the pace of technological innovation?

WHERE WILL AGING MAKE THE DEEPEST ECONOMIC IMPACT?

To get a feel for the economics of a rapidly aging developed world, let's look at how the transition to a static or declining GDP might play out in a number of specific sectors of the economy—and let's start with sectors where we can expect significant problems:

- *Real Estate: A Troubled Long-Term Investment?* In the fastest-aging developed countries where populations will soon be shrinking, the long-term demand in the next century for new housing, new office space, and new production facilities may erode substantially. Think about what happened to downtowns all over America in the 1960s and 1970s as populations moved to the suburbs—and think in particular about what happened to major snowbelt cities as populations left for the newly air-conditioned sunbelt. These cities ended up with huge numbers of empty and rapidly depreciating buildings in once proud and prosperous downtown locations. A few desperate landlords even turned to arson in the hope that insurance money would make up for falling rent rolls.

    In New York State, the Buffalo metropolitan area is a case in point. Buffalo's population has fallen by 11 percent since 1960, while its elderly population has increased by 57 percent. The share of young working-age adults (aged 20 to 44) in Buffalo's population is among the lowest of any major U.S. metropolitan area.

The number of new home building permits per 100,000 residents is only about 36 percent of the U.S. average. From 1990 to 1997, during a strong housing market, the price of existing Buffalo area homes fell every year—from 81 percent to 66 percent of the U.S. median.[2]

On balance, falling populations—combined with the growing integration of information technology with daily life (more people "telecommuting" and shopping from home)—will probably mean a reduced aggregate demand for office and retail space in many major cities of the developed world. New technology will still be driving the construction of new "smart buildings." But with lots of office space available at low prices, the technology will have to offer more than incremental advantages to get investors to see the value in new construction. One expert speaks of real estate as likely to suffer a near-perpetual recession through the early decades of the next century in those developed countries whose population is declining significantly.

While the overall outlook for real estate in those countries may be negative, there will surely be offsets and counter-currents. For example, the year 2010 may be a bad time to build trade-up homes on spec for growing families, but it may be a great time to build senior citizens' group living communities and nursing homes, or to convert elementary schools into senior centers. New office buildings for middle management in cold northern cities may be a poor investment, but the availability of affordable senior citizen housing in warmer climates could create retirement building booms in unexpected places—from small ranch towns in the U.S. Southwest to the Black Sea resorts of Eastern Europe. And if land gets cheaper, because there are fewer people around to buy it, those who do buy may be able to build bigger and more expensive homes. This is especially true in countries like Japan where decent housing is now hard to come by even for middle-class families.

- *Physical Infrastructure: The End of Keynesianism?*
Falling populations and shrinking GDPs can also be
expected to discourage investment in additions to the
developed world's physical infrastructure—such as new
schools, roads, bridges, dams, and harbors. Obviously,
there will always be a need to maintain and upgrade
existing facilities. And there will be some conversion to
technology-intensive systems (such as "smart" high-
ways). But the developed countries have already invested
heavily in physical infrastructure in recent years. With a
declining population and tax base, together with the
need to devote new revenues to paying for retirement
benefits, the congresses, assemblies, diets, and parlia-
ments of the 2020s won't be able to reach into the pork
barrel in their accustomed fashion. For the last five
decades, most developed countries have regarded public works as an integral tool of Keynesian demand management. With the numbers of young workers in these
countries shrinking, however, there will be less reason
to engage in such spending to alleviate unemployment
and to prime the economic pump. Obviously, the construction industry will be profoundly affected by the
double hit in both real estate and public works—which
is one of the reasons the large global construction companies are so eager to expand their reach into China
and other emerging markets.

- *National Security: Will Governments Be Able to Maintain Their Global Commitments?* Anything with a *fixed
cost* becomes a problem for governments when that
cost has to be spread over a smaller population and
funded out of shrinking revenues. National defense is
the classic example. When it comes to threats to national
security, what matters is total size, not per-capita size.

    If I had to identify another great challenge to the
developed world alongside demographic aging, it would
be the increasingly complex security threat posed by

rogue states or even individuals with biological and chemical weapons, terrorists capable of hacking into vulnerable computer systems, and the continuing problem of nuclear weapons proliferation. None of these external threats will shrink along with domestic population or GDP.

In the early twenty-first century, therefore, there will be many compelling reasons for the leading developed countries to spend as much as or more on defense investment than they do today. But the age wave will put immense pressure on governments to cut back. The reality is that the countries where populations are still exploding rank high on any list of potential trouble spots, whereas the countries most likely to lose population—and to see a weakening of their commitment to expensive defense programs—are the staunchest friends of liberal democracy.

As economist Gary Hufbauer has observed, "Political power in the world has always gone hand-in-hand with economic power, which means that the power shift to demographically younger nations is almost inevitable."[3] Because younger economies can accumulate capital at a higher rate and can expand their capacity faster, they have the dynamics of growth on their side. We can hope that this power shift will unfold peacefully, but if defense commitments weaken in the developed world, the result could be destabilizing and dangerous.

Falling birthrates, together with a rising labor-market demand for young workers, will inevitably mean *smaller armies*. With fewer soldiers, total capability will be maintained by large increases in the technology and weaponry at the disposal of each soldier. But boosting military productivity returns us to a Catch-22 worthy of Private Yosarian: How will governments get the budget resources to pay for high-tech weaponry if the senior-weighted electorate is demanding appropriations for high-tech medicine? In any case, there will be a premium on military equipment and tactics that require fewer personnel and on weaponry that minimizes the risk of casualties.[4] Military "capital" will be substituted for military "labor." Under such circumstances, women may be more actively recruited and even accepted in combat roles. And like the Roman Empire in its late stages of demographic decline, some countries may expressly invite immigrants who are willing to serve in the military as one of the obligations of citizenship. Such pragmatic expedients will of course generate controversy.

One possible danger of depopulation is that the developed nations may perceive that they have only two extreme (and relatively inexpensive) choices at their disposal to deal with security threats—a low-level response, consisting of anti-terrorist strikes and cruise-missile diplomacy, and a high-level response with strategic weapons. According to one expert, the developed countries "are moving toward militaries that can fight either a nuclear war or a war in Chad."[5]

- *Will There Be Anything Left for "Discretionary Spending"?* For all the talk about reforming and improving educational systems to meet the needs of the twenty-first century, the melancholy fact is that in North America (and increasingly even in Europe) school funding is being voted down. Senior citizen lobbies are often more concerned about today's tax costs than tomorrow's payoff from investments in human capital. This trend may continue. At the same time, the "education industry" may shift some of its focus away from the public education of children and toward private opportunities in corporate retraining and "lifelong learning" for older workers and retirees. Aside from education, virtually every area of discretionary public spending where costs are relatively fixed will face unremitting pressure: from post offices to national parks, from public health to the weather service.

Demographic aging, of course, is not all bad news for business. In a market economy, a new problem in one sector typically creates a new opportunity in another. And indeed, there are many market niches where aging will give rise to new profit opportunities. Here are some of the sectors that I would identify as potentially attractive:

- *Asset Management: A Sure Thing in an Unpredictable Future?* Because today's pay-as-you-go retirement systems are unsustainable—and will increasingly be perceived as such—I believe that there will be a rising household demand for precautionary savings throughout most of the world. I also believe that we will see growing public support for mandatory funded pension plans—following the models already being pioneered in Britain, Australia, Chile, and Singapore. Given popular cynicism about government in general—and considering the growing frustration among working-age citizens as they come to understand that their payroll taxes have not been held in "trust"—I believe that mandatory plans will increasingly take the form of portable, personally owned, and privately managed accounts.

  If this popular groundswell does indeed result in the founding of new funded retirement systems in the major developed countries, the collection and investment of the savings—asset management, in other words—will be an enormous growth sector within the financial services industry. Indeed, at least one reason for the wave of mega-mergers in banking and other financial service firms is the widespread anticipation that asset management may soon become a much larger business than it is today. Naturally, the major global companies will want to be in on the collection as well as on the investment side.

Not all will be rosy for the assets under management, of course. Whether or not retirement systems are reformed, there is likely to be a significant "dissavings" trend by the 2020s as a very large generation of elders (especially in the English-speaking countries) moves fully into retirement and spends whatever personal nest-egg capital they have accumulated. During that same decade, as boomers all try to cash out their savings simultaneously, asset prices could enter a long and steep bear market: Just imagine the bull market of the 1990s on total rewind. Despite these challenges, or even to some degree because of them, financial services—and not just asset management, but annuities, life insurance, long-term care insurance, and reverse mortgages—will be in great demand by households at all ages and income levels. Governments will need to adopt regulatory policies to prevent private-sector fraud and abuse, and to encourage financial services to be competitive on price while serving a burgeoning market. But the sheer magnitude of the investment flows suggests that these will be profitable lines of business for well-run, competitive, and prudent financial service firms.

- *Health Care: The Great Boom Ahead.* Even in countries where health-care budgets are stretched to the limit, most sectors of the health-care industry are likely to remain very profitable, especially those less reliant on public funding. These include special geriatric services and surgeries (cataracts, for example, are predominately a senior citizen phenomenon), pharmaceuticals, including so-called functional medicines, and specialty manufacturers of everything from prosthetics and vision aids and hearing implants to insulin pumps and artificial joints and other miracle products still on the drawing board. At one end of the spectrum, high-end private clinics (on- or off-shore) for those who can afford to pay out of pocket will do very well—as will exotic new anti-aging therapies (such as Human Growth Hormone, a treatment that currently costs $10,000 to $20,000 a year). At the other, do-it-yourself home diagnostics and therapies will become a standard recourse for middle-class patients.

- **Professions with Expertise Related to the Elderly.** Beyond health care and finance, there is sure to be a rising demand for professionals who specialize in a number of other areas, from family counseling to real-estate advice to legal services ("elder law," including trusts, estates, and age discrimination) to gerontology (in academia).

- **"Fountain of Youth" Products.** Cosmetics, hair dyes, plastic surgery, and specialized exercise training and equipment will all be likely growth bets.

At the same time, many businesses will be able to profitably redefine the experience of daily living around the tastes, schedules, and physical limitations of older people:

- **Retirement Lifestyle: A New Mainstream Market.** As the senior population grows, expect a wide variety of "lifestyle" industries to target older age brackets. Sporting resorts and equipment retailers will move toward gentler activities—from tai chi and low-impact aerobics to golf, hiking, and gardening. We can expect the entertainment business to focus more on hassle-free modes of remote viewing—including new satellite and cable options and high-tech electronic devices for aging couch potatoes. Cruise lines and other travel services will thrive, as will businesses that build, sell, or manage mobile homes, second homes on golf courses and in mountain resorts, downsized, all-amenities condos near major cultural centers, and, of course, assisted living and nursing-home communities.

- *Personal Transportation.* There will be a large new market in luxury automobiles that feature comfort, convenience, driver visibility, and ease of entry and exit. New kinds of motor carts able to navigate across retirement villages and even along wilderness trails will be increasingly popular.

- *Food.* Successful food producers and retailers will shift their focus toward lines that are considered healthy (with special vitamins and nutritional supplements), easy to eat and digest (such as soups, whose per-capita consumption is today twice as high among Americans over 50 as among younger people), very easy to prepare (for the disabled elder), or very challenging to prepare (for the retired connoisseur). If the over-50 set, now twice as likely to eat at a restaurant as younger people, retains its penchant for eating out, we can expect a proliferation of restaurant concepts and chains to suit senior tastes.

- *Home Repair and Personal Services.* Large-scale personal-service businesses of all kinds—from grocery shopping to home maintenance—will mushroom. Because seniors will spend more time in their homes, those who can afford it will want to upgrade them to make them more comfortable (installing central air conditioning, for example). With more free time, some seniors may head for Home Depot to drive a new do-it-yourself boom, but more may prefer to call up a brand-name repair service. Home alarms and the home security business should also do well.

- *Grandparenting.* The changing relationship between generations within the extended family will also create new opportunities. Gift-giving from old to young will continue to grow, not just from grandparent to parent, but from grandparent to grandchild—inspiring entirely new types of recreation (like "grandtravel"), of mail-order shopping (there is already at least one company publishing a grandparent gift-giving catalog), and of financial assistance (like trust funds set up for the grandchild's college tuition). The exploding number of grandparents and great-grandparents, together with greater mobility among working-age families, may revive the long-distance phone industry and inspire a whole range of new ways to communicate with family and friends, from electronic greeting cards to video e-mail.

- *Ethnic Markets.* The ethnic mix in the United States and many other countries will also be changing as their populations age, especially as young immigrants arrive to fill shortages created by shrinking domestic work-forces. Not only products but services targeted to burgeoning ethnic niche markets are likely to experience above-average growth. For example, if immigration grows, international communications will also grow.

- *Death Care.* Even with people living longer, there will be record numbers of deaths per year. This will drive an expansion in cemeteries, funeral homes, and other death care products and services, not to mention a variety of exotic niche businesses that are already developing, from cryogenics to outer-space burial.

On balance, demographic aging will present businesses with more challenges than opportunities. Profits will be there for the firm that positions itself well and gets the timing right. Any good entrepreneur, manager, or investor, however, will have to look closely to identify the silver linings in the gray clouds ahead.

IS POPULATION DECLINE ECONOMICALLY GOOD OR BAD?

Beyond the wrenching transition, it's worth taking a look at the ultimate steady-state the developed world will reach once the transition is complete. In the very long run, what will zero or negative aggregate growth mean for our personal and social well-being? The benefits and costs of a static (or even shrinking) economy have been much debated within the social science academy. Here we can contrast two opposing schools of thought, each with a long pedigree.

On the one hand, there is the "small-earth" school, which emphasizes *decreasing returns to scale*. Its basic argument is that, since nature's bounty is finite, more growth hurts and less growth helps. The most obvious examples are natural resources and the environment: Per unit of output, it's cheaper to grow less food with the same available land, to pump less oil from the same reservoir, or to emit less pollution into the same air and water. Humanity's number and appetites can grow without limit; but the earth's carrying capacity cannot. That is why, as economist E.F. Schumacher famously put it, "Small is Beautiful." Still another fixed resource is a nation's past accumulation of physical capital—its infrastructure, plant, and equipment. In order to maintain the same stock of capital per worker, a growing economy must invest enough to equip each new worker with new productive tools. A static economy doesn't have this burden. Since it need only worry about replacing the existing capital stock as it depreciates or becomes obsolete, the economy can let its investment rate drop with no decline in the ratio of capital per worker—nor, say some economists, in the productivity growth. (In a shrinking economy, just think of all the warehouses and shopping malls we could simply "use up" without having to build new ones.) As a result of lower investment, significant resources would become available for other purposes.[6]

Although this case for no-growth or slow-growth may have some merit, it must be qualified with serious caveats. To begin with, many of the natural resource arguments only make sense from a global perspective. From the point of view of any single nation, the size of its own economy won't have much effect on the cost of food or the likelihood of global warming, since these are determined internationally. Indeed, an economy's slower growth may do nothing to save on resources if other economies grow faster as a result—for example, if lower energy prices caused by slower growth in Europe encourage Asia to grow faster with less regard for the environment.

As for the notion that slower growth allows us to save less without any penalty in living standards, this too is open to question. True, a slower-growing, lower-saving economy might not suffer from any loss in capital-per-worker—and classical economic theory says that output per hour depends solely on this ratio of capital to labor, all other things being equal. But will all other things remain equal? According to many economists, productivity breakthroughs depend upon the "learning by doing" that happens when producers are constantly trying to expand capacity and overcome new bottlenecks. More broadly, it may be that a society that no longer *has* to invest for the sake of capacity expansion may also no longer *care or bother* much about investing for productivity improvement. In other words, without a demographic spur to growth, many types of investments may become less attractive. This view, sometimes called the "secular stagnation" thesis, was originally inspired by the experience of the Depression 1930s—an era of low birthrates, low investment rates, and shrinking employment.

Now let's turn to the "pro-growth" school, which emphasizes *increasing returns to scale*. Its basic argument is that many large-scale economic activities become more efficient as the size of the activity increases along with the size of the society.[7] Thus, more growth helps and less growth hurts. To take some U.S. examples, consider what a large corporation like AT&T, a large public agency like the National Weather Service, and a large engineering project like Hoover Dam all have in common. In every case, the operating cost per unit of output (or per citizen) declines dramatically as the scale of the enterprise grows larger. A static economy or population would put an end to these cost savings, and a shrinking economy or population would throw them into reverse. Another pro-growth argument is that aggregate economic size is all that matters when the aggregate cost of a social challenge is externally determined—by nature (putting a man on the moon) or by foreign powers (victory in war). When it comes to national defense, as I've already mentioned, sheer size often determines the outcome. It is fair to observe that, historically, most government efforts to boost population growth have been triggered by worries about war. This has been true for states and empires since at least the time of Thucydides—and it may yet be true for some time to come in our global future.

Again, my primary purpose is to start asking the right questions, not to insist on the answers. As I have indicated, I believe global aging is a predictable certainty, yet we seldom acknowledge that it is the most *economically consequential* of all predictions we can now make about the next century. It will change everything from fiscal policy and household finances to consumer demand and industrial structure. But what overall positive or negative impact will it have on the living standards and social welfare of the developed world? We don't yet know. On the debate over decreasing versus increasing returns to scale, the jury is still out. The most extreme episode of sudden depopulation in the civilized world was the Black Death—which killed roughly one of every three Europeans between 1348 and 1351. Even here, the economic results were mixed. On the one hand, the plague made possible a large gain in average real wages once marginal farmland was taken out of production. On the other hand, this gain occurred after a wrenching generation of transition—and it pushed Europe into a century-long era of commercial contraction along with violent political and social upheavals.

My own prognosis is this: The aging of the developed world will be accompanied by far-reaching economic changes. Among these changes will be a rapid deceleration in aggregate economic growth and, for some countries, a chronic decline in the national output of goods and services. The transition to slower growth could usher in traumatic changes in many sectors of the economy. Moreover, these hardships will surely be exacerbated by the relentless fiscal pressure of ballooning retirement programs. Remember that this pressure could trigger an economic or demographic vicious cycle that could slow economic growth much more than any of the projections now indicate. If reform efforts fail and retirement policy is left on autopilot, the developed countries will also experience an unprecedented squeeze on what are often called "public discretionary" activities—most fatefully, on national defense—which are often the same activities most likely to suffer from declining economies of scale.

IS HEALTH CARE A MAXIMUM RIGHT?

Nowhere, I suspect, will the developed world face more daunting challenges than in the health-care arena. Developed societies have long debated government's role in providing health care. Is health care a right of citizenship to which every person must be guaranteed equal and unlimited access—what my friend Dan Yankelovich calls a "maximum right"? Or is it something more like food or housing or pensions, for which government simply establishes a guaranteed floor of protection? As global aging puts relentless pressure on public health-care budgets, the second view is sure to gain more support. The optimist in me believes that developed-country governments—even those now in denial about the magnitude of the challenge to come—must eventually recognize that at some point it's less important to spend another dollar on high-tech medicine than to spend another dollar educating children, investing in infrastructure, or cleaning up the environment. But at what point precisely will the limit be drawn—and who will draw it? How will society define the "care" or "cure" that it covers? Should age or cost or probability of survival matter? What about "bad" genes or risky lifestyles? In short, who lives? Who dies? And who decides? How these profound ethical questions will be resolved I do not know. What I do know is that they will gain new urgency as already out-sized health-care budgets devour even more GDP.

Societies will differ in how they set limits on health care. Europe and Japan, where patients are accustomed to deferring to their doctors and complying with government health-care standards, may require less public debate. Most likely, the limits will be implicit, shrouded in "a deliberate fog" (as one British physician puts it) as providers try to allocate scarce resources within overall health budgets fixed in advance. In a more rights-oriented society like the United States, such an approach would surely provoke controversy. Some believe that only explicit guidelines—such as the list of covered illnesses and treatments recently established by the state of Oregon for its Medicaid program—will satisfy Americans' traditional sense of fair play. Others believe that the answer is to give public beneficiaries a fixed-dollar voucher to purchase private insurance—and then let patients and providers work out the trade-offs for themselves.

A wise man once told me that there are two kinds of health-care economists: the standing-up kind and the lying-down kind. The standing-up economist says yes, we'll have to submit all treatments to a cost-benefit analysis. And then there's the lying-down economist, who looks up from his bed and says, "Doc, are you sure you've tried everything you can?"

It's much easier, in short, to accept the inevitability of limits in the abstract than to follow through in practice. In the United States, where a third of all Medicare spending goes to patients in their last year of life, nine in ten adults say they approve of living wills—but only one in ten actually has one. Most chronically ill elders, according to one recent poll, would prefer three months of extra life (no matter what the cost or discomfort) to a healthier life that is three months shorter. Meanwhile, as new medical technologies are introduced, the public worries that wealthy people will soon be able to purchase effective but costly treatments which the average person will be denied. Widespread patient complaints about HMO cost-cutting are already leading to a serious political backlash.[8] No research has yet shown that the quality of care in HMOs is worse than in the most lavish fee-for-service plan. But what happens if and when such research appears? It is far from clear how all of these dilemmas will be resolved. One thing, however, is certain: No aging society can forever avoid the dread "R-word"—rationing. Implicitly or explicitly, with or without ethical debate, and with or without government regulation, *access to publicly funded health-care benefits in aging societies is going to be rationed.* There is simply no way to pay for the unlimited consumption of all the health care that an aging society may desire.

This is true even if we accept the official projections—though, as I have explained, these projections may be overly optimistic. In particular, they may vastly underestimate future gains in life expectancy. (This would be *pessimism* for most of us—but it's *optimism* for budgetary accountants.) What if the furious pace of today's biomedical research, new genetic testing techniques, and bioengineered pharmaceuticals pays off? What if medicine really does find cures for most types of cancer, heart disease, and other leading killers? What if the World Health Organization is right and a significant percentage of people born in the late years of the twentieth century do live into the twenty-second century? What if the more radical school of gerontologists is right and it turns out that there is no knowable limit to human longevity? What if we start finding large numbers of ordinary people (not just the fabled yogurt-eaters of Georgia) living to be 130 or 140?

Obviously, since we are not prepared to provide for even the number of people now projected to reach age 85, such a revolution in longevity could be fiscally ruinous. Let's just imagine that, by 2010, new therapies extend longevity for five years more than is now projected. As the CEO of a major pharmaceutical company reminds me, many of these new biotech regimens for longer life will be extraordinarily expensive for many years after their introduction. Will society simply spend everything it can to extend everyone's life? Or will society repeal a "maximum right" ethic that now makes even Viagra a basic human entitlement[9]—and find some way to rein costs in? Maybe we can imagine a day when the state will stamp "no payment" on sex-enhancement therapies. But it will surely be much more difficult for the state to tell people who might live years longer that it can't afford to help them do so. However you look at it, the new longevity revolution will pose sobering ethical questions. Indeed, when we contemplate the whole mix of fiscal, social, psychological, and ultimately political issues at stake, it's clear that controlling the costs of public health-care spending on the elderly presents an even more daunting and divisive task than controlling the costs of public pensions.

Just how unready most Americans are to support reforms that would produce major cost savings in public health-care programs is evident in a survey conducted on behalf of the Kaiser Family Foundation and the Harvard School of Public Health during August and September of 1998:[10]

- 84 percent oppose requiring seniors to pay a larger share of Medicare costs out-of-pocket (13 percent support it).
- 69 percent oppose a defined-contribution approach that would limit Medicare contributions for an individual to a fixed annual amount (26 percent support it).
- 64 percent oppose increasing worker payroll taxes (31 percent support it).
- 63 percent oppose raising the age of eligibility to 67 (34 percent support it).
- 56 percent oppose encouraging seniors in traditional Medicare to move to managed care (38 percent support it).

As Drew Altman, President of the Kaiser Family Foundation, observed in commenting on the prospects of the

National Bipartisan Commission on the Future of Medicare: "This process could end in a train wreck when the debate turns to specific proposals and their consequences if the public is not more informed about the problems facing Medicare and the options for reform."[11]

WHAT HAPPENS TO FAMILIES?

Aging is also sure to bring big changes to the family—society's basic social unit. In the future, as I have explained, families in the developed world will be much smaller but span more generational tiers than they do now. It's easy to imagine how this might make it harder for family members to raise children, care for the old, and support each other in times of trouble—sealing the much-predicted demise of the family as a functional institution. If families fail, or if we continue to allow the traditional functions of the family to be off-loaded to government, we will only compound the demands on scarce public resources.

We still need families to care for the old. In the developed world, for every elder now in a nursing home, it's estimated that there are *two other elders* receiving equivalent care from their families. For every elder now cared for by paid at-home nurses, *ten other elders* receive equivalent care from their families. And we certainly need families to raise the young. Since affordable fiscal projections presuppose a growing economy, an aging society counts on families that are strong enough to nurture and prepare the workers whose productivity will raise living standards in the next century. To the extent that families aren't up to this task, governments will have to step in—once again, at enormous cost and with inferior results.[12]

Can public policies and a public dialogue be fashioned that help shore up the family, especially in its role as an extended-care network for dependents of all ages? I certainly hope so, though the track record in most countries is not encouraging—and, with the share of nonmarried and childless households increasing, many voters may not perceive that this would make much difference in their own lives. One major U.S. opinion survey indicates, for example, that non-married and childless households of all ages vote by a big margin for candidates who promise to expand government programs that substitute for family care. Married households with children, on the other hand, vote by an equal margin for candidates who promise to oppose such expansion.[13] In an age when government budgets are dominated by transfers to the elderly (and not to children), this emerging "family gap" may have profound implications for fiscal policy. Does this new divide reflect contrasting attitudes toward public retirement benefits—with the first group either more dependent on them or expecting to be more dependent when they grow older, and the second group feeling personally closer to the children who (as adults) will ultimately bear their cost? Can the divide be bridged? Or is it destined to widen along with the rising number of childless households?

THE POLITICS OF OLD VERSUS YOUNG: DOES INTERGENERATIONAL WARFARE LIE AHEAD?

Though we often talk hopefully about our "common future," it is no longer apparent, in an era of proliferating interest groups, just what we all have in common. Some of us may feel we have a less direct and personal interest in the future than others do. And, in fact, we have recently witnessed the emergence of vast membership lobbies that appeal explicitly to the one group whose future is mostly behind it—namely, the retired elderly. In peaceful and propertied societies, the old have always had disproportionate political influence. Compared to younger adults, they are more likely to be better informed about public affairs, vote more often, and exercise more direct control over family property and social institutions. The rising power of senior organizations has tilted the political balance further in their favor—in part by encouraging elders to take an even more active role as voters and advocates. Together with their customary public influence and newfound lobbying clout, the rapidly growing number of elders has created a juggernaut that threatens to overwhelm the public claims of all other age groups.

In the early postwar years, the developed world regarded elder benefits as merely one part of a growing welfare state—and hardly the most consequential part. Today, they are regarded as the only part that really matters. During his quixotic effort in 1964 to derail U.S. President Lyndon Johnson's "Great Society," Senator Barry Goldwater strongly hinted that, if elected, he would curtail Social Security retirement benefits and (perhaps) replace them with "private insurance." Goldwater wasn't much concerned about what the elderly themselves might think of his proposal, nor did Johnson make a big issue of it: Elderly voters back then were small in number and disconnected from politics. They were also known to be hostile to "big government"—and, as it turned out, in the November election Goldwater won a larger share of votes from the elderly than from any younger age bracket. Much has changed from that era to our own, in which the political power of organized seniors is routinely described with such colorful phrases as "steamroller," "800-pound gorilla," and "third rail (touch it and you die!)." In a typical congressional election during the mid-1960s—around the time Goldwater ran for President—voters aged 65 and over were only *one third* as numerous as voters under age 45. Today, they are *half* as numerous. By the late 2030s, assuming current voting rates by age don't change, elderly voters will actually have a *slight numerical edge*

Backed by some of the largest and most strident interest groups on earth, U.S. elders have learned to make effective use of these rising numbers. There's the American Association of Retired Persons (AARP),[14] with 33 million members, 1,700 paid employees, ten times as many trained volunteers, and an annual budget (including subsidized "member services") of $5.5 billion. And then there's the National Council of Senior Citizens, Save Our Security, and Families USA—

The balance of electoral power will continue to shift toward the elderly.

Voters in U.S. congressional elections, as a % of all voters

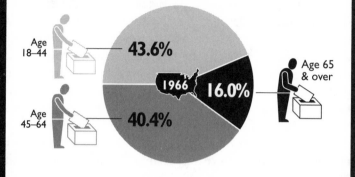

Age 18–44: 43.6% — 1966 — Age 65 & over: 16.0% — Age 45–64: 40.4%

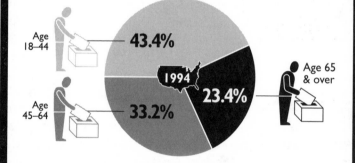

Age 18–44: 43.4% — 1994 — Age 65 & over: 23.4% — Age 45–64: 33.2%

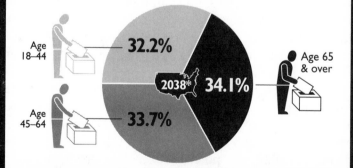

Age 18–44: 32.2% — 2038* — Age 65 & over: 34.1% — Age 45–64: 33.7%

* Projection of voters is based on age-specific voting rates in 1994

SOURCE: Census (various years); author's calculations

which can mobilize millions of voters with a single inflamma-
tory mass mailing—not to mention dozens of other more specialized groups, from the National Retired Teachers
Association to the National Association of Federal Employees. At the national level, these groups are consulted on practically every legislative decision affecting senior benefits and,
when thwarted, have the means (as demonstrated by the
"Mediscare" campaign of 1996) to blast their opponents off
the playing field. At the local level, organized elders use grass
roots tactics to procure everything from huge tax breaks (especially on state income and home property taxes) to generously
funded community services for people their age. In many communities, they have grown increasingly militant about voting
down school bond issues and other youth-oriented investment. Until recently, organized efforts to shield the old from
local school taxes or to champion spending on nursing homes
over infrastructure were limited to "retirement states" like
California, Florida, and Arizona. Now, these efforts are showing up in counties and towns across the nation.

Senior power is also on the rise in Europe—where it is
manifested not so much through independent senior organizations, as through labor unions and (often union-affiliated)
political parties that formally adopt pro-retiree platforms. In
Europe, unlike in America, most retired workers remain
active members of unions and continue to identify with them
politically and socially. (In the United States, big labor is also
a militant defender of the Social Security status quo, but its
political clout is not as strong.) Because Europe is older and
because workers retire earlier, pensioners make up an even
larger share of the electorate than in the United States.
Already, roughly one-third of voters in France and Germany
are retired. In addition, because the vast majority of retirees
depend so completely on public benefits, they are even more
motivated to vote their pocketbook.

Elder opinion looms large in the politics of every European country—from the German CDU's choice of *Sicher in
die Zukunft* (Secure in the Future) as its campaign motto to

the French Socialists' identification of retirement security with *la solidarité sociale*. Most European heads of state would not contemplate even a minor benefit reform without first lining up the support of the unions and parties who speak for pensioners. Despite all this attention and respect, polls show that three-quarters of European pensioners think their governments don't do enough for older people and that one-quarter would join a separate political party formed to further their interests.

Could age-based political parties be the wave of the future? The notion may seem incredible, but in the Netherlands such a "Pension Party" has actually formed. And in Russia, though the Communist resurgence is usually ascribed to nationalism and political nostalgia, a not-so-subtle demographic bias is at work as well. Market reforms are a young person's game, as exemplified by Russian Prime Minister Sergei Kiriyenko, who at 35 was one of the world's youngest national leaders. The Communists, meanwhile, have for all intents and purposes rehabilitated themselves as the party of and for elder retirees, who are aggrieved by how runaway inflation has slashed the real value of their pensions. In the 1995 Duma elections, over half of those aged 55 and older voted Communist—versus only 10 percent of those under age 40.

Thirty years ago, the retired elderly possessed little political clout. Today, in every developed country with the notable exception of Japan, they have become an organized colossus. Is it mere coincidence that those same thirty years have witnessed a redirection of public spending from children to elders, an expansion in the public debt burden, and a growing paralysis in government's ability to make choices on behalf of the future?

I think not. Yes, everyone claims to be in favor of children and posterity. But let's be realistic: In an era when most elders no longer live with their own grown children or depend on them financially, there's bound to be some deterioration in the natural bonds uniting the political interests of young and old. Posterity is a noble ideal—but to act on its behalf, most people have to identify it with their own future. Abraham Lincoln once observed: "Posterity has done nothing for us; and, theorize on it as we may, practically we shall do very little for it unless we are made to think we are, at the same time, doing something for ourselves." Renowned U.S. demographer Samuel Preston, who in 1984 delivered a seminal address on generational equity, summed up the new political calculus in similar terms: "Children don't vote; and adults don't vote on behalf of their own childhood, which is water over the dam. I daresay that if we passed through life backwards, adults would insist that conditions in childhood be made far more appealing."[15]

Yet senior power is not the only side of the political equation that has been changing. Over the past three decades, even as the elderly have become far more assertive and effective on their own behalf, youths have lost their once-vaunted ability to shake the establishment. Indeed, they show a growing cynicism and apathy about public life. With upbeat names like "senior citizen," elders have gained a reputation for civic competence; with cipher-names like "X" or "Bof" Generation (as in French for "who cares?"), youths have gained a reputation for civic withdrawal. Thanks to government efforts, most retired elders are used to seeing their economic hopes fulfilled or even surpassed. With government standing by, most young adults are used to seeing their economic hopes dashed—or, when they do get ahead, they typically regard themselves as lucky exceptions. In the United States, the age divergence in income paths over the last quarter century has been stunning: According to the U.S. Census Bureau, the real median income of all households aged 65 and over has grown nearly 30 percent, while that of all households under age 45 has actually *declined* (and that's before taxes!). In Europe, where youth's big concern is finding jobs, governments make it plain that guaranteeing pensions is a higher priority than guaranteeing employment.

A self-reinforcing dynamic may be at work, with each benefit check and each after-tax wage stub reconfirming both age groups in their attitudes. Even popular slogans can convey a different message depending on how old you are. "The era of big government is over," declared U.S. President Clinton in 1994. True, government is running dry for younger Americans—but it's still gushing like Old Faithful for their retired parents and grandparents. Not surprisingly, the voter participation gap between old and young continues to widen almost everywhere. Even in Japan, renowned for its habits of consensus across generations, the young are withdrawing from civic involvement. Kenichi Ohmae, prolific author and social critic, points with alarm to statistics showing that in Japan only one-quarter of all 25-year-olds vote, compared with two-thirds of all 60-year-olds.

Where is all this leading? Will global aging enthrone organized elders as an invincible political titan? The worst-case scenario—leading to the "intergenerational war" the late U.S. Senator Paul Tsongas often warned of—should not be ruled out anywhere in the developed world. Imagine a snapshot of America early in the next century. Picture retiring boomers, with inflated economic expectations and inadequate nest eggs, voting down school budgets, cannibalizing the nation's infrastructure, and demanding ever-steeper hikes in payroll taxes. Then picture their middle-aged "buster" children, struggling to make ends meet and withdrawing entirely from politics—until, at some future date, their bitterness over the diminished legacy and crushing tax burden being passed on to their own children boils over and throws the republic into civil turmoil. When I recently described this scenario to Singapore's Senior Minister Lee Kuan Yew, he told me simply, "I believe the young would probably either revolt or emigrate."

Some eminent commentators say an open conflict between generations could never happen. They argue that organized interest groups remain effective only when they are small enough not to provoke a taxpayer revolt. This is why Milton Friedman and others believe that the U.S. senior lobby's success cannot last much longer. They predict that it will wield no more influence in the twenty-first century, when seniors dominate the population, than rural populists did in the nineteenth century, when farmers comprised well over half of all workers.

I think this analysis is too sanguine. Although it is safe to predict that resource transfers from young to old cannot indefinitely grow faster than the economy, no one can say what political trauma may be required to stop this trend. Over the past thirty years, the typical retiree has made large economic gains relative to the typical young worker—without, however, making the young more politically assertive. The AARP's flagship magazine *Modern Maturity* now lures advertisers by documenting the affluence of its typical reader (net worth: over $150,000), but this doesn't undermine the efforts of AARP's lobbying arm to portray its constituency as largely poor and vulnerable.

Commenting on how the old seem to trump the young at every turn, Lee Kuan Yew once proposed that each taxpaying worker be given two votes to balance the extra lobbying clout of each retired elder. No nation, not even Singapore, is likely to enact Lee's suggestion. But the question must be asked: With a growing share of voters cashing out their civic contributions—and a declining share raising children in their own households—can anything motivate political leaders to act on behalf of posterity?

Perhaps something can. Even if numbers do not automatically undermine the senior lobby's success, the passage of time may. Perhaps it is wrong to assume that the attitudes of old and young are self-perpetuating. Instead, they could simply reflect the collective personalities of the generations that now happen to be passing through these age brackets.

Today's elders were shaped young by the uplifting experience of pulling together to rebuild the world in the aftermath of the global depression and war they all lived through. The "we generation" is accustomed to public reward and is comfortable with large one-size-fits-all government programs.

Throughout the developed world, voters of all ages tend to agree that these "senior citizens" are uniquely deserving. Adults today under age 50, on the other hand, were shaped by the disillusioning experience of turning inward in the aftermath of cultural turmoil and economic stagflation. The "me generation," possessing weaker civic instincts, is less inclined to rely on other taxpayers; their Holy Grail has always been the right to opt out of mainstream institutions. As today's elders pass away entirely, the members of this postwar generation, including America's boomers, may bring a very different self-image and reputation with them into retirement. Elder Aquarians may then feel less collectively entitled—and (a much safer prediction) younger generations may be inclined to agree. If so, "intergenerational war" may not be so likely after all.

Whatever happens, let's not make the mistake of assuming that the attitudes we now associate with different age groups will always keep changing in exactly the same direction. Generations never work like that; neither does history.

To help push attitudes in a future-oriented direction, leaders and citizens in the developed world must engage in a more open and candid dialogue about the aging of their societies. Leaders must do a much better job of educating the public. On this score, I must say that Bill Clinton's track record has been uneven. He has told me personally that he understands fully the pay-as-you-go "chain-letter" structure of Social Security. He knows that what really matters are not the "trust funds," but the annual operating balances, which will turn to deficits in 2013. But when political pressure heats up, what he knows so well in private is not what he says in public. Shortly after my conversation with him, the President declared to the nation: "Now here's the bottom line. The Social Security trust fund is sufficient to pay all the obligations of Social Security—both retirement and disability—until 2032, after which it will no longer cover those obligations." On the other hand, Clinton took a laudable step in 1998 by launching an unprecedented national conversation on the future of Social Security, consisting of four televised town meetings in which the nation's top leaders came face to face with ordinary Americans. The meetings were jointly sponsored by the AARP and The Concord Coalition, an organization (that I co-founded) devoted to the cause of fiscal responsibility. Watching these two opposing groups make their respective cases has given voters a good opportunity to sort out the facts. But while we are still a very long way from taking effective action, I grow increasingly confident that President Clinton, ever more aware of his domestic legacy, will make Social Security reform his priority imperative in 1999.

For their part, citizens will have to enable leaders to speak the truth without imperiling their political careers. In the United States, it still takes great courage to advocate serious entitlement reform. But with change in the wind and so many public figures now speaking out—including Senators Bob Kerrey, Pat Moynihan, Judd Gregg, and Rick Santorum—citizens at last may be making it safer for leaders to do the right thing.

Much will be at stake over the next decade. Will younger voters re-engage in the debate over their future as they become more aware of what global aging and current fiscal policy could do to their life hopes? Will fledgling youth organizations devoted to generational equity (like Third Millennium, FIRST, Economic Security 2000, and Vox Futuri in the United States) grow stronger? Will boomer-age politicians make radical fiscal reform on behalf of today's children the same sort of idealistic crusade that once mobilized their generation over Vietnam? Will a leader of Al Gore's generation try to educate and rally the country as Gore himself did on the environment? Will seniors who believe in fiscal fairness for their children and grandchildren become an effective antidote to the mainstream "we first" senior lobby? All age groups have a role to play, but I believe the senior lobbies will maintain their advantage unless and until the young find their own political voice. After all, it's their future.

I have a hunch that someone who is today in college will figure out how to translate the aging challenge in the United States into a central campaign issue that will define the politics of the next decade and beyond. I think—or at least hope—that person will ride the issue all the way to the presidency of the United States. Maybe this will happen in 2016 or 2020, when the fiscal, economic, and cultural repercussions of an aging society come bursting into the everyday life of Americans. Perhaps we will see similar movements in other developed countries, with like-minded young leaders emerging to represent their increasingly disenfranchised younger generation.

DOES AN AGING SOCIETY
MEAN AN AGING CULTURE?

In *Gulliver's Travels,* Jonathan Swift imagines a society which includes a special caste of biological freaks called Struldbrugs. What makes the Struldbrugs special is that they never die—though Swift observes that with advancing age they grow ever feebler, both physically and mentally. Among their many dreadful attributes, these immortals have "no remembrance of anything" but what they learned early in life and have "not the least curiosity" to learn new things. Regarding them as a mere economic burden, the society at large gains nothing from their learning or wisdom—indeed, can no longer even understand the archaic dialect in which they speak. Swift's satire points to perhaps the most searching question the developed world will have to ask itself: How will demographic aging affect a society's cultural vitality, its power to innovate and re-imagine the future, and indeed the energy with which it pursues economic and social progress?

As the culture ages, the social temperament will grow more conservative and less flexible. Will this be a good or bad thing? Yes, the crime rate will fall, but so may the taste for innovation and risk. Looking ahead two or three decades, one wonders: Will tomorrow's managers and workers maintain today's enthusiasm about the global cyber-age, which is often described as an endless era of questing, experimenting, and market flux? Will tomorrow's leaders and citizens maintain a willingness to sacrifice their near-term comfort, even their lives, to make the world more secure for their posterity?

I hope so. But with the number and influence of youth gradually receding, it might be harder than we imagine. Especially in America, the developed world's obsession with newness, progress, and the future has always derived its energy from the numerical heft of each new rising generation. As recently as 1970, when a new "youth culture" redefined the American Dream, the U.S. median age was only 28—not much higher than the median (about age 18 to 20) of the typical premodern society. Today, with the U.S. median age hitting an unprecedented 35, the American public hears a lot less about the ideals of youth than about the worries of the middle-aged and old. And this is just the beginning: By the year 2030, the median age will reach at least 40 in the United States and at least the late forties in much of Europe. Back when America's boomers were warning each other, "Don't trust anyone over thirty," Americans over thirty were *in the minority*. Over the foreseeable future, they are certain to remain a solid majority. By the year 2030, over one-half of all adults will be aged 50 and over—and thus eligible to join the American Association of Retired Persons. While this fifty-and-over crowd will outnumber all younger adults in the United States it will outnumber all younger adults *and children* in some countries in Europe.

What do these numbers mean for our culture? Clearly, they mean a much greater focus on the interests and activities of the old over those of the young. For decades, the mass media in the United States and around the world—TV, movies, popular music, and radio—have aggressively courted the all important under-fifty "demo" (demographic). How will the business, as well as the substance, of popular culture change as it becomes evident that the elderly represent the fastest-growing component of the total population and youth the fastest-shrinking one? We should not be surprised to see pension issues eclipsing college issues on the front pages of newspapers. Yet the numbers may have a deeper influence. Along with experience and wisdom, it has long been observed that old age brings with it an aversion to risk and change. Cicero put it this way: "Young men for action, old men for counsel." As people age, moreover, the formative era that shaped their education and outlook becomes ever more remote in time—making them seem, in a changing world, increasingly "out of date" from the perspective of youth. As the entire population of the developed world grows older, the attributes of personal aging may come to define the tone and pace of the culture at large.[16]

The shrinking size of the average family may reinforce this trend. In a world of steadily falling fertility, a growing share of the population will consist of only and first-born children—who, many social scientists say, are typically more conservative in their social outlook than later-born siblings. According to historian Frank Holloway, "First-borns . . . are less open to innovation; they tend to be more conforming, more traditional, and more closely allied with their parents."[17] Another possibility is that smaller families may make society less willing to put its young at risk in national emergencies such as war. In past generations, families who lost a son in battle could usually take some solace in the survival of his brother, and indeed governments have sometimes exempted only-sons from wartime service. At a fertility rate of 1.5—about the average for the developed world today—less than 15 percent of families will have two or more sons. In the coming decades, will developed societies be willing to place their scarce youth in harm's way to defend vital national interests? Or will they defer and appease, no matter what the long-term cost, to avoid confrontation with younger and more risk-prone societies?

"Few men know how to be old," the French aphorist La Rochefoucauld once observed. We may soon learn that few societies do either. Beyond the structure of their economies, aging promises to transform social life in the developed countries, bringing potentially profound changes to everything from retirement and health care to the family and the culture. What will these changes mean for the future shape and vitality of society? Will aging be a scourge? Or can the developed world learn to adapt gracefully?

Much will depend on whether aging societies move successfully beyond the traditional three-box lifecycle of education, work, and retirement and begin to reintegrate the elderly into the mainstream of productive life. It won't be easy. With the average retirement age in the developed world falling for half a century—and with today's mid-life adults saying they want to retire even earlier than their parents—how can public policies help workers face up to the new realities? Will businesses be able to adapt to a labor market in which so many new jobs must be filled with retrained older workers instead of newly trained young ones? Can society help older workers keep up with the demands of the emerging information-age economy through "lifelong learning" policies, or is this phrase destined to remain just a trendy cliché? All of these challenges will be easier to overcome if workers have maximum flexibility to move from employment to leisure or training and then back again. This is one more reason I believe that aging societies must replace today's one-size-fits-all public pensions with personally owned retirement accounts.

In short, are the developed countries fated to move toward a world in which newness is shunned, markets are restrained, and risks are feared? Will they become what the French demographer Alfred Sauvy, commenting on the future of the West, describes as a "society of old people, living in old houses, ruminating about old ideas"?[18] Or can our aging societies find some way to replace the energy and daring that biology naturally bestows upon the young, while retaining the wisdom and experience of the old? That may be the greatest challenge of all.

WILL GLOBAL AGING OVERWHELM
CAPITAL MARKETS?

An aging world is certain to launch different societies on very different fiscal and savings trajectories. As I have explained, most developed nations are now on track to incur massive fiscal deficits, and thus massive savings deficits, unless they undertake decisive reform of their public retirement systems. Inevitably, some nations will do little to change course while others may even succeed in *boosting* their national savings rate, at least for a while, through a combination of fiscal restraint and greater household thrift. Meanwhile, many of the developing countries that are just starting to set up capital markets are opting for fully-funded pension plans right from the start. The result could be a volatile disequilibrium between the supply and demand for global capital among the various regions and nations of the world. In my view, nothing more urgently demands international attention than the prospect of large and unpredictable shifts in cross-border capital flows.

Over the postwar era, the older and more affluent developed countries have generated most of the world's excess savings, much of which has been exported (through official loans and grants, bank loans, and regional stock markets) to developing countries. In the long run, one overriding trend seems clear. As the developed world grows much older, its aggregate rate of savings will decline and its net capital exports will shrink. What can't be predicted, until we know the developed world's response, is the timing of this trend: When will it start? How rapidly will it progress? How far will it go? Nor can we predict its effect on the total supply and demand of global savings, and thus on global interest rates, without knowing whether the developing world will start generating more savings to make up some of the difference. Although the global savings equation is complex indeed, it isn't hard to point out bellwether indicators of which way the long-term trend is heading.[19] The United States, the largest developed economy, is also the world's largest debtor, with total liabilities to foreigners now exceeding $5 trillion. China, the largest developing economy, has recently become a major capital exporter, with a capital surplus reaching $63 billion in 1997.[20] Much of this is invested in bonds issued or backed by the U.S. government (such as Fannie Maes), which means that China now helps finance the U.S. federal budget and indirectly helps fund the mortgages for middle-class American homeowners.

Any large-scale failure to respond to the aging challenge could destabilize the global economy—and strain financial and political institutions around the world. Consider Japan, which today runs a large current-account surplus—accounting for well over half the capital exports of all the surplus nations of the world. Then, imagine a scenario in which Japan leaves its retirement programs and fiscal policies untouched. Thirty years from now, under this scenario, Japan would have to become a massive capital *importer* (and thus run a large trade deficit) to keep its domestic economy from collapsing—the same transition the United States underwent in the 1980s. This would require a huge reversal in global capital flows. To get some idea of the potential volatility, note that Japan's pension deficit swing over just the next decade is projected to be roughly *three times larger* than Japan's current (and massive) capital exports to the United States; from now to 2030, the swing is projected to be *fifteen times larger*. Before long, wildly fluctuating interest and exchange rates might short-circuit financial institutions and trigger a serious market crash.

Some might argue that creditors would look ahead, anticipate the danger, and pull back in advance. But in my experience, financial traders seldom take the long-range view—at least when it comes to anticipating sudden future changes in the overall economic environment. They are expert at calibrating and comparing the distant rewards of specific investment projects. But financial traders rarely look "outside the box," and their political and economic time horizon is typically a matter of months, not years. Query most money managers today about the impact of a possible retirement crisis on global interest rates, and they will ask you to repeat the question. To the financial markets, global aging lies off in a far distant and, one might even say, largely irrelevant future.

To the extent that they anticipate these dangers, some national leaders may advocate tightening capital controls (reversing the deregulatory trend of the last two decades) as a way to restrict capital exports. Like ordering the tides to recede, such efforts will be to little avail. Even in authoritarian, state-controlled economies, capital controls are notoriously hard to enforce. (One fascinating bit of evidence: According to the IMF, all the nations of the world together report that they import over $100 billion more in capital annually than they export!)

Even more important, most capital controls would run directly against the economic interests of both savers and borrowers in an aging world. Older societies that succeed in maintaining high savings rates will be anxious to avoid declining profits on an excess of domestic investment and will be eager to seek out higher returns abroad. High-investing younger societies will be just as eager to borrow abroad and boost the productivity and wages of their growing workforces. And as the insecurity of pay-as-you-go public benefits becomes better known, workers everywhere will pay increasing attention to the return on their personally owned assets and will insist that it be competitive with the return on globally traded assets. From Beijing and Tokyo to Paris and Rome, citizens are in rebellion against policies that suppress the available return on household savings and funded pensions in order to keep capital at home and offer "discount" interest rates to favored domestic corporations. (This complaint is especially justified in Japan.) In short, the trend today is strongly in the direction of further *de*regulation of global capital flows—at least for economies not immediately threatened by financial crisis.

Fundamental questions have yet to be asked—much less answered—about the behavior of global capital markets over the next few decades. Will the markets slowly assimilate new fiscal information and respond with a gradual rise in long-term interest rates? Or will they fail to focus on such issues until they are panicked by some palpable event? If so, what would the event be? Might it be, for example, a Japanese decision to launch an unprecedentedly large yen-bond offering to finance its pay-as-you-go pension deficit? Might Japan, at the same time, decide to stop buying (or even sell off) U.S. Treasury bonds? If so, how might that affect American and world capital markets? What would be the impact on exchange rates if Japanese interest rates were to rise in response to these developments? Would a resulting sharp hike in home mortgage rates finally wake up political leaders who simply can't be bothered with fiscal projections? Will the kind of "beggar thy neighbor" policies we have historically associated with trade flows now move to capital flows? Is it too extreme to imagine a financial crisis of the type Asia has experienced since 1997 unfolding throughout the world as financial markets come to understand the fiscal implications of global aging?

Because these questions are largely unexamined and because they could have such significant financial and economic effects, I have proposed that a group of leading global financial traders, those who work and live in these markets, be convened. First, I would suggest that this group be fully informed about the magnitude and timing of the fiscal challenge facing the developed economies. Then, given this understanding, I would ask them to lay out the likely scenarios. Hopefully, the new Agency on Global Aging that I propose in the following chapter could use these insights to design preventive policies that would alert markets to emerging financial disequilibria and defuse financial panics before they spread.

WILL THE EMU RUN AGROUND ON
DEMOGRAPHICS?

The leaders of the European Union (EU) have known from the outset that they will have their hands full trying to manage the differences among member nations in their new Economic and Monetary Union (or EMU)—from the timing of their business cycles to the diversity of their credit institutions and political cultures. For this reason, the EU has established official public debt and deficit criteria (3 percent of GDP) for membership to prevent one or more maverick nations from placing undue economic burdens on the others. But the EU, which is already celebrating its plans to mint a new "Euro" currency, has yet to face up to what is perhaps the biggest challenge to its future viability: *the likelihood of varying national responses to the fiscal pressures of demographic aging.* Indeed, the EU does not even include unfunded pension liabilities in the official EMU debt and deficit criteria— which is like measuring icebergs without looking beneath the waterline. When these liabilities come due and move from "off the books" to "on the books," the EU would, under current constraints, be required to penalize EMU members. A recent IMF report concludes, "Over time . . . it will become increasingly difficult for most countries to continue to meet the deficit ceiling . . . without comprehensive social security reform."[21] The EU could, of course, retain members by easing the deficit ceiling. But once the floodgates are opened, the resulting differences in fiscal policy from one nation to the next might lead to a bidding war over who could rush fiscally backwards the fastest.

The brute fact of the matter is that, historically, Europeans have relied on exchange rate flexibility to compensate for wide divergences between national economies. The United States, by contrast, relies on labor mobility and fiscal transfers among the fifty states to equilibrate diverging trends in regional economies. (There was, for example, a net outflow of two million Californians to other states during the last recession.) While Europeans in the new EMU are becoming somewhat more mobile, it is hard to imagine them moving nearly as easily in large numbers from Italy to Sweden as Californians move to Arizona or Washington. So what will Europeans do when their exchange rates are permanently "fixed" through a single currency?

Consider the example of Italy, which has come to epitomize all the problems of an aging society—with its huge unfunded liabilities, low birthrates, large numbers of retirees, strong unions, limited private pension options, long tradition of impassioned leftism, and unique (and splendid) national culture and character that make Italians, let's just say, very different from Germans. Now let's imagine a scenario in which Italy, faced with huge fiscal troubles a few years from now, decides that rather than cut benefits or increase taxes it will try to "finance its way out" of trouble through massive public borrowing. And let's assume the very Teutonic European central bank tells the Italians they can't do this because they are going to bust the EMU deficit ceiling. This European central bank starts to be seen as Italy's "oppressor"—and a foreign oppressor at that, just as some in Indonesia view the IMF after the Asia crisis. The left and the unions suddenly begin to portray what is happening as "foreign" German bankers telling a sovereign Italian state how much it can pay in retirement benefits to Italian workers.

Under this scenario, Italy might try to opt out of EMU. But what if, by this time, its economy is so interlocked with the rest of Europe that Italy's departure would become the economic equivalent of the U.S. Civil War—a test of whether nations can secede from an increasingly frontierless Europe? Would Italy go ahead anyway? And if it does, would other countries eventually follow? We should not discount the possibility that demographic pressure could unravel the EMU and even the European Union itself. According to one witty observer, America did it right: First it had its civil war, then its greenback became the nation's only currency. Hopefully, an aging Europe will not undergo this process in the reverse order.

WILL TRADE AND IMMIGRATION BECOME POLITICAL FLASHPOINTS IN AN AGING WORLD?

Surveys indicate that public opinion in the developed world—with the possible and unsettling exception of the 1920s—has never been more sharply divided than it is today on the issue of global economic integration. Economists and corporate policymakers, who stress the upside (efficiency and profits), tend to look favorably on "globalizing" trends. Voters at large, who focus more on the downside (layoffs, community dislocation, destabilizing exchange rate volatility, and loss of national sovereignty), tend to be suspicious and distrustful. As the world grows older, globalization may turn in unexpected new directions and push this division of opinion past its flashpoint, igniting open political conflict. Entirely apart from its impact on capital flows and financial markets, global aging will give rise to wrenching changes in the worldwide trade of goods and services, in the migration of labor, and in foreign relations among countries.

As I have explained, most developed economies in the 2020s will be experiencing a secular stagnation (in some cases, even a decline) in real GDP and an accelerated shift from the production of goods to services. Goods like manufactures and raw materials are tradable across borders, while many personal services are not—which means that the value-added of the typical export-oriented industry or firm may be steadily shrinking from one year to the next. Historically, expanding markets (both at home and exports abroad) have helped to make trade liberalization politically popular as a national goal. Contracting markets, on the other hand, have often given renewed appeal to calls for protectionism and "beggar-thy-neighbor" policies.[22] This will be especially likely in aging societies that are running large current account and trade deficits—and which have large, unionized, and politically well-connected manufacturing industries.

Consider as well that in developed countries that don't succeed in reducing the fiscal cost of their retirement programs, firms and workers may be subject to repeated tax hikes—and these could further undermine the competitiveness of their exports in world markets. It is estimated that in Europe, for example, the hikes in payroll tax rates needed to cover the rising cost of pensions would add, by the mid-2020s, a cumulative $5 per hour (in today's dollars) to manufacturing costs. In theory, this extra tax burden could be shifted onto workers in the form of lower wages, but in practice such adjustment may prove to be politically impossible. The resulting economic crosswinds could give rise to a variety of mutual antagonisms—between the manufacturing sector and the service sector (where tax evasion is easier) or between nations that face rising fiscal costs and those that don't. The ideal of open borders is likely to come under serious attack. Will an aging world continue to espouse the liberalization of trade? Or will it retreat behind the tariff walls of yesteryear?

Meanwhile, certain service industries will be looking for new ways to sell their "products" across borders. As services comprise an ever-greater share of the developed world's economic output, we are likely to witness a whole range of export innovations, especially in harnessing cyber-networks to market, sell, and deliver any information-related product around the world at minimal cost. This trend will spread far beyond such obvious candidate industries as the media and financial services. Think about health care, which will remain a surefire boom industry in our aging world for decades to come. Already, firms are designing diagnostic software to bring the very best medical expertise to doctors' offices and operating rooms in the furthest corners of the world. Already, elite hospitals (like the Mayo Clinic) "export" their quality of care by routinely flying in patients from abroad. Why couldn't cardiac experts at Massachusetts General Hospital start live advice hotlines to doctors in Calcutta? If such innovation continues, some of today's major service industries may become tomorrow's major export industries, brightening what might otherwise be a troubled outlook for international trade.

Goods and services aren't the only things that can move across borders. So can labor, which may make immigration the most contentious issue in the policy debate over economic integration. Early in the next century, workers—especially young and low-skilled service workers—will be highly sought after in the oldest and most affluent countries. There will be great incentives in the developed world to procure them, and great incentives in the developing world to supply them. Wherever possible, businesses will seek out ways to hire bargain labor without the cost and trouble (for either party) of relocation and assimilation. Indeed, this is already happening. U.S. clerical firms now deliver office records on-line to foreign keyboarders for processing. Japanese, Turkish, and Korean construction companies now transport all-foreign crews to building sites, board them in isolation, and transport them back when the job is done. Many European resorts are issued seasonal visas so that foreign maids can take up the slack during peak-demand months. Even so, many businesses will require permanent immigrants. As the developed world's demand for foreign labor grows, it is bound to be accompanied by huge new pressures (from both those who hire and those who get hired) to expand the allowable inflow of newcomers. As I explained earlier, the question of how the developed world responds to this new immigration pressure will be a major global agenda item, as well as a hotly debated political issue in many individual countries.

WILL YOUNG/OLD BECOME THE NEXT NORTH/SOUTH FAULTLINE IN GLOBAL POLITICS?

It has often been observed that diverging demographic trends usually lead, with a lag, to dramatic changes in the balance of power between societies. As political scientist Samuel Huntington recently put it, "The juxtaposition of a rapidly growing people of one culture and a slowly growing or stagnant people of another culture generates pressure for economic and/or political adjustments in both societies."[23] The developed countries will have to ask themselves how their aging may change their relationship with the rest of the world— that is, how it will reshape the geopolitical contours of tomorrow's global order. Developing countries, though also aging rapidly, will remain much younger for decades to come. Accompanying this age gap may be a profound divergence in social temperament, political stability, and attitudes toward the future.

What are the strategic dimensions of this divergence? On one side of the equation, there are some sobering facts to keep in mind about the developing world. In many parts of it, the total fertility rate remains very high (7.3 in the Gaza Strip versus 2.7 in Israel), most people are very young (49 percent under age 15 in Uganda), and the population is growing very rapidly (doubling every 26 years in Iran). These parts also tend to be the poorest, the most rapidly urbanizing, the most institutionally unstable—and the most likely to fall under the sway of rogue leadership. They are, in short, the very kinds of societies that have spawned most of the military strongmen and terrorist enclaves which have bedeviled the United States and Europe in recent decades.

Long-term planners at the U.S. Pentagon are currently assuming that outbreaks of regional anarchy will occur more frequently early in the next century. To pinpoint when and where, they are tracking the appearance of what they call demographic "youth bulges" in the world's poorest urban centers. So far, the planners are expecting "asymmetrical conflicts" in which the disturbance can be localized and the developed world can wield overwhelming military superiority. But are these expectations valid? In time, could rising strife in these demographically volatile regions draw in other nations and trigger more serious threats to the geopolitical order?

Then, on the other side, we have to ask how the aging of the developed nations will affect their role in world affairs and their likely response to crises beyond their borders. Will fiscal pressure, as it limits the foreign policy options of the great powers, itself pose a danger to world peace? Will the metastasizing costs of retirement benefits crowd out public spending on international affairs and, in particular, on

By 2050, the twelve most populous nations will include only one of today's developed countries: the United States.

Largest countries ranked according to population

	1950	1998	2050
1	CHINA	CHINA	INDIA
2	INDIA	INDIA	CHINA
3	U.S. *	U.S.	U.S.
4	RUSSIAN FED.	INDONESIA	PAKISTAN
5	JAPAN	BRAZIL	INDONESIA
6	INDONESIA	PAKISTAN	NIGERIA
7	GERMANY	RUSSIAN FED.	BRAZIL
8	BRAZIL	JAPAN	BANGLADESH
9	U.K.	BANGLADESH	ETHIOPIA
10	ITALY	NIGERIA	CONGO
11	FRANCE	MEXICO	MEXICO
12	BANGLADESH	GERMANY	PHILIPPINES

SOURCE: UN (1998)   * Gray boxes indicate "first" or "second" world countries

defense? As the populations and GDPs of the G-7 nations shrink as a share of the world total, the human and economic resources available to pursue geopolitical goals may be further constrained by the changing temperament of ever-older electorates—including an unwillingness to sacrifice current consumption, a complacency about the "old order," and an aversion to risk. Will parents of ever-smaller families allow their only child to join the army and go off to war? How will these constraints affect regional security arrangements like NATO and the prospects for world peace and stability?

The developed world's role in world affairs could also be constrained by a reversal in the identity of creditors and debtors. If some of today's largest low-income societies—most notably, China—set up fully funded retirement systems to prepare for their own future aging, will they produce ever-larger capital surpluses? More to the point, will today's great powers someday depend on these surpluses to keep themselves financially afloat—and look to the demographically growing developing countries as the world's new economic engine? If so, how can we expect these new suppliers of capital to use their newly acquired leverage? Will they call for wholesale changes in the priorities of global financial institutions? Will they turn the tables in international diplomacy? For example, will the Chinese someday demand that the United States shore up its Medicare system the way it once demanded the Chinese change their human rights policies as a condition of lending?

Historically the richest industrial powers (consider Britain during most of the nineteenth century and America during most of the twentieth) have been demographically growing, capital exporting, globally philanthropic giants that projected their power and mores around the world. In the future, the richest industrial powers may be none of the above. They may be demographically imploding, capital importing, fiscally starving neutrals who twist and turn to avoid expensive international entanglements. How will this change the relationship between the developed and developing worlds? Today, their respective identities are described in terms of rich versus poor.

A quarter-century from now, will they be better described in terms of growth versus decline, surplus versus deficit, expansion versus retreat, future versus past? By then, in short, will the contrast between North and South be transformed into a global division between Old and Young?

Let me return to where I began: Is demography destiny, after all? Is the rapidly aging developed world fated to decline? Must it cede its leadership role to younger and faster-growing societies? If history is to record that the answer is no, the developed world will have to redefine that role around a new mission. What better mission than to show those younger yet more tradition-bound societies, which will soon be aging in their turn, how a world dominated by the old can still make room for youth?

7

Toward Global Solutions to a Global Problem: An Open Letter

To:	To the Leaders of the G-22[1] countries: Argentina, Australia, Brazil, Canada, China, France, Germany, Hong Kong SAR, India, Indonesia, Italy, Japan, Korea, Malaysia, Mexico, Poland, Russia, Singapore, South Africa, Thailand, United Kingdom and the United States.
From:	Peter G. Peterson
Re:	The Time to Act on the Challenge of Global Aging Is Now!

I KNOW THAT MOST OF YOU ARE FAMILIAR WITH THE CAUSES and dimensions of the global aging challenge and with the unsustainable burden that today's public retirement promises in the developed countries threaten to impose on their own economies—and ultimately on the global economy—early in the next century. I also know that most of you have not hesitated to speak out and take principled stands on many issues critical to the world's long-term future, from promoting world peace to protecting the environment. Yet on the aging issue, nearly all of you have hesitated to act. Why?

Is it too vast? Do those of you in the leading developed world economies find the unfunded liabilities of pension and health-care programs so overwhelming that it's easier to deny this impending reality? Do you feel like Dante entering hell—"Abandon all hope, ye who enter here"? Do you believe that the extreme sensitivities of powerful interest groups—from senior lobbies to labor unions—make it too politically toxic to handle? Is it too long term? Are you inclined to agree with Margaret Thatcher, when she observed that most leaders would simply rather duck an issue that will hit on somebody else's watch ten to twenty years from now? Do those of you from comparatively younger and still developing economies think this is not your problem?

I would like to hope that each of you, with your portfolio of political and leadership skills and with your concern for your nations' youth and their future, are anxious to face up to what you already understand: that overcoming the challenges described in this book is central to nearly every country's prosperity and security in the next century—and indeed, to the well-being of the entire world. Surely you must agree that the time to begin acting on these challenges is now.

The first steps won't be easy, of course. To prepare the way, perhaps what you need is some international framework for voter education, collective burden-sharing, and global leadership. Once national constituencies begin to grasp the magnitude of the global aging challenge, they will be more inclined to take reform seriously. Once governments are in the habit of cooperating on what in fact is a global challenge—due to sweep over all the developed countries at roughly the same time and rock the developing world as it does so—none of you need incur the economic and political risks of acting alone. And if even just a few of you take the lead, the example will be set for others to follow.

This multilateral approach should sound familiar. It is, after all, an approach that many of you have recently and successfully employed—in rallying disparate nations to join the EMU, in reconfiguring NATO for the post-Cold War era, in strengthening the roles of regional groups from ASEAN to APEC, and in forging a new international consensus on a host of trade, business, security, and environmental concerns, from NAFTA to Bosnia, from non-tariff barriers to intellectual property and telecommunications.

So the means are available. But the choice remains yours. You can find reasons to delay preparing for the seismic consequences of what will be one of the most fateful transformations in the history of civilization. Or you can help assemble the community of nations in an arduous but positive-sum global enterprise in which everyone, in the long term, wins by working together.

History teaches that the economic crises of great powers can quickly metastasize throughout the world, changing the course of human events. Think back over the most dramatic instances of national insolvency: Spain in the sixteenth century (overspending on the Armada while banking hopelessly on El Dorado), France in the eighteenth (*"aprés nous, le déluge"*), or Britain in the early twentieth (on whose overextended empire the sun finally set). In each case, the crisis helped push the world into an era of commercial and political chaos that ultimately changed the geopolitical order.

Also in each case, as historian Paul Kennedy has pointed out, the crisis was touched off when an overly ambitious government agenda eventually collapsed due to insufficient economic resources. Early in the coming century, we may witness this old story play itself out once again but with a new twist: Instead of yesterday's "imperial over-stretch" that pushed the military hegemony of so many great powers beyond endurance, what may break today's developed countries will be "domestic over-stretch"—excessive commitments to an entitlements empire, consisting of unsustainable public retirement promises.

Each country's situation is unique, and to some extent each will face the aging challenge on its own terms. In the long run, the impact of a nation's policy response—on savings, on tax rates, on fiscal balance, on productivity—will redound largely to the benefit of its own citizens. Nonetheless, the developed and developing countries do have a genuine *collective* interest in the success or failure of individual actors in today's global economy. Success in one country makes the world safer, while failure in one country can be contagious.

Left to their own devices, countries will respond to the aging challenge with widely divergent policies. A major objective of international dialogue would be to reconcile the demands of national sovereignty with every country's common interest in growth and an open global economy. Without concerted effort, global aging could jeopardize that common interest. Indeed, it could create highly destructive divisions between economic winners and losers, and open up whole new ideological fault lines in the post-Cold War era.

As I have tried to illustrate throughout this book, we are confronting demographic changes so substantive that they could redefine economic and political systems in the developed countries over the next generation. Inevitably, this transformation will have profound effects on the developing countries as well. If the developed world can no longer invest in emerging markets because of acute capital shortages at home, for example—or conversely, if mature developed countries become dependent on borrowing from young emerging economies—major new issues of international relations will arise. Similarly, if we begin to see much larger flows of young worker immigrants, or if developed countries no longer believe themselves able to bear the cost of global security arrangements, the shape of the twenty-first century world order will be deeply affected, whether viewed from Beijing or Berlin. Even the developing countries that today have youthful populations and few institutionalized retirement arrangements to pay for will find that their own benign demographics will change. In time, they will need to cope with a rapid increase in their number of elderly and a steady rise in their median age. Aside from the indirect impact of the developed world's entitlement folly, developing countries will ultimately have to come to grips with the direct effects of their own aging as well.

Clearly, all countries would be well served by some means of collective deliberation over the choices that lie ahead. For that reason *I propose a major summit on global aging* at which national leaders would define the problem, debate the issues, and discuss their different strategies. Few venues are as well covered by the media as a global summit. You have been willing to convene summits of this type to discuss global *warming.* Why not global *aging,* which will hit us sooner and surer? By calling attention to what's at stake, a global aging summit could shift the public educational process into fast forward. That alone would be a major contribution. In addition, this summit should launch a new multilateral initiative whose function would be to lend the global aging agenda a visible institutional presence. This *Agency on Global Aging* could set up a small secretariat utilizing staff resources at existing multilateral organizations (such as the OECD, IMF, and World Bank). It could share information, publish research, develop best-practice policy guidelines, and encourage civic leaders (in or out of politics) to mount the bully pulpit and speak out.

The Agency on Global Aging will have to engage a whole range of questions that affect how developed countries should reform their retirement systems and how developing countries should set them up right the first time. Perhaps the most basic question is how fiscal policy should weigh the interests and well-being of one generation against the next's. Then there's the issue of defining the safety-net standard of "social adequacy." Is there a minimum level of retirement income that should be the right of every citizen—and if so, what should it be? To what extent should retirees at higher income levels receive a public subsidy? These questions, in turn, raise the role of personal and family responsibility. Should retirement security be left largely to people's own resources, that is, to how successful or fortunate they've been with their health, wealth, and families? If not, when should government pick up the pieces—and how can it do so without discouraging responsible and far-sighted behavior? Or should government compel people in advance to make better life choices, say, by enacting a mandatory savings program?

There are also a great many complex practical questions surrounding each of the major reform strategies. Which specific policies are most effective in encouraging later retirement, enlarging the workforce, encouraging higher fertility, investing in the productivity of future workers, strengthening generational bonds within families, targeting dependent elders who are most in need, and prefunding society's retirement liabilities? Nor is effectiveness the only issue. How much do these strategies cost? How can we minimize any side effects that are perceived as undesirable—for example, the side effects of more immigration or higher fertility? And how long do these strategies take to work?

One critical early task for the Agency on Global Aging would be to assemble (and if necessary commission) research on the aging challenge that integrates everything we need to know about its timing, magnitude, and location. How would today's official fiscal projections change if they were run on assumptions that are both globally consistent and—when it comes to longevity, fertility, and health-care costs—more realistic than those now in use? Do they now understate the future problem in some countries and (perhaps) overstate it in others? How big are total unfunded liabilities on a global basis—not just for pensions, but also for all forms of health care? Where are the weakest links in the global chain? Which countries will be hit earliest and hardest? What might happen to interest rates, exchange rates, and cross-border capital flows under various political and fiscal scenarios? What will be the direct and indirect effects of this developed world crisis on developing countries?

The agency I propose could also publish a high-visibility annual report that would update these calculations, continue to build global awareness, and give coherent voice to the need for timely policy reform around the world. This report might highlight and hold up as models whatever major steps had been taken in the prior year to reduce unfunded liabilities, establish funded benefit programs, and promote generational equity. The Agency on Global Aging could also establish a collective early-warning system to allay fears that excessive pension debt in one country might ignite a conflagration in regional or global financial markets. And it could brief other summits convened by developed and developing countries, which should make ample room on their agendas for the global aging challenge.

The agency could set up a clearinghouse for exchanging information on demographic trends, actuarial assumptions, and pension management practices. It could help publicize efforts to promote longer work lives and to fight ageism in the workplace. On these and many other issues, we all have much to learn from each other—just as those who favor mandatory funded pension plans have been able to learn from the examples of Chile, Britain, Australia, or Singapore. (Since Britain, Singapore, and Australia are members of the G-22, they are in a unique position to give other countries the benefit of their experience.) The agency could become a vital resource for fast-aging developing countries which wish to learn from the successes—and avoid the costly mistakes—of the developed world. It could also investigate how to turn the asymmetrical impact of global aging into an opportunity for cooperation among "young" and "old" nations rather than a potential breeding ground of hostility.

In conjunction with existing multilateral organizations, the Agency on Global Aging could set up special financial arrangements similar to the "rain forest bonds" that have been issued to reward certain developing countries for sound environmental management policies. This retirement backstop would provide capital at reasonable rates to help restructure bankrupt national pension systems—in developed and developing nations alike—*provided that* the indebted nations act swiftly to reduce their unfunded liabilities and put their systems on a sustainable footing. Since some of the developing countries may have to provide some of the funding to resolve the financing problems of the major developed countries, it strikes me as entirely reasonable that they should participate in the deliberations over the terms and conditions of any such restructuring programs.

Most of you have been advocates for political democracy and freer markets. Today, we are experiencing what President Clinton has rightly called "the worst economic crisis in half a century." In too many places in the world, this crisis threatens the growing openness of the world economy. But it pales in comparison with the challenge of global aging—which in time could entirely unravel the world economy, and even threaten democracy itself. By making tough choices now, you, the world's leaders would demonstrate that you genuinely care about the future, that you understand this is a unique opportunity for young and old nations to work together, and that you know freedom is not free and history cannot be fooled.

I am certain that your place in history will be much enhanced by your willingness to implement the critical reform program so urgently needed. *As the new century arrives, I urge you to take the first steps: Convene a global summit and establish an Agency on Global Aging.* An unprecedented gray dawn is approaching. It is high time to establish institutions that can help us manage the transition to a much older world.

Acknowledgements

TAKING ON AN ISSUE AS BIG AS GLOBAL AGING—WITH ITS
worldwide reach and multi-trillion dollar unfunded liabilities—is a huge effort. A number of people deserve special
recognition for their contributions to this book.

First, I must thank Random House and Times Books for
all they have done not only to publish this book but also to
do it under intense pressure in a very short space of time. My
friend Jason Epstein, America's greatest living editor—the
kind they often say doesn't exist anymore—helped sharpen
the argument, hone the prose, and shepherd the book
through the many complexities of today's publishing world.
Many other heroes of Random House/Times Books rapid
deployment force were enormously helpful as well, including
Scott Moyers, another talented editor at Random House,
and Peter Bernstein (publisher) and Luke Mitchell (editor) at
Times Books.

Neil Howe, a gifted economist and economic historian,
with a great command of budgetary and fiscal policy details,
worked on every aspect of this effort, ably assisted by Richard
Jackson. Between the two of them, Neil and Richard comprise
one of the country's leading think tanks on the issues that are
at the heart of this book, and I am very grateful to have benefited from so much of their research and knowledge.

Dan Burstein, a colleague of mine at The Blackstone
Group, convinced me to undertake this book in the first place,
helped define the concept, and in general kept the many
moving pieces of this project flowing to fruition.

A number of economists, demographers, and other
experts shared their work with me and some of them even
critiqued mine as the manuscript developed. I am especially

grateful to: Fred Bergsten, Nicholas Eberstadt, Andrew Hacker, Gary Hufbauer, Nicholas Lardy, Stephen Rosen, Sylvester Shieber, John Shoven, Michael Teitelbaum, and Ben Wattenberg.

Peggy Noonan, one of my favorite people and writers, tried to teach me how to say what I wanted to say so someone else might actually want to read it.

My colleagues at The Concord Coalition have been deeply supportive of my research and have been in the forefront of those taking up the cause of entitlement reform. My thanks go out to Warren Rudman, Sam Nunn, the family of the late Paul Tsongas, and Martha Phillips.

Many friends have offered valuable input, important advice, and badly needed moral support. There are far too many to mention, so let me say a collective thanks to everyone.

Nigel Holmes, a gifted designer with a good grasp of the underlying issues, did the design work on the charts.

My assistants in my office put in hundreds of hours at the word processor, through numerous rounds of revisions of every chapter. I believe they now know the material well enough to recite it by heart, although I doubt they will ever want to hear about it again. My deep thanks to Patricia Selden McQueen, Laurie Carlson, and Christine Hadlow. And every author should be so lucky as to have someone like Frank Pena to remember where everything is, find it, copy it, fax it, and organize it at all hours of the day and night.

My five children and five grandchildren have been my inspiration throughout this project, as they have been for my prior books, because it is, after all, their world that I am most concerned about.

Finally, none of this would be possible without the patient and loving support of my wife, Joan Ganz Cooney, stoic throughout the sacrifices of nights, weekends, and holidays that a book of this type requires, and always there with a brilliant insight, clever turn of phrase, or wise judgment about the right thing to say or do.

Notes on Sources

"THE MARK OF A CIVILIZED MAN," WROTE GEORGE BERNARD Shaw, "is the capacity to be deeply moved by a statistic." It is also, he might have added, the desire to ensure that the statistic in question is correct. Throughout *Gray Dawn*, I've exercised considerable care in selecting demographic and fiscal numbers. Because it's impossible to cite and comment on all the sources for these numbers in the text, allow me to explain my basic approach here. Let's start with historical and projected demographic statistics (including total population, population by age bracket, total fertility rates, and longevity).

For statistics describing the entire world, the developing countries, or regions including any developing countries, I generally rely on the United Nation's *World Population Prospects: The 1998 Revision.*[1] By general consensus, this is the most comprehensive and up-to-date global data set. It provides historical numbers since 1950, and several projection scenarios through 2050. Unless otherwise indicated, all of my projection numbers are drawn from the "medium variant" UN scenario.[2] Since the year of the latest historical number varies by country, my references to today's value are typically drawn from the UN projection for the average value from 1995 to 2000.

For statistics describing only the developed countries as a group, or individual developed countries, I rely (unless otherwise indicated) on recent publications of the Organization for

---

[1] United Nations (Department of Economic and Social Affairs, Population Division), *World Population Prospects: The 1998 Revision* (1998).
[2] I discuss the UN's "low variant" scenario in Chapter 3; elsewhere I sometimes allude to it when using conditional words like "may" or "could" to indicate the full range of demographic outcomes. Otherwise, however, all references are to the UN's "medium variant" scenario.

Economic Cooperation and Development (OECD), especially *Ageing in OECD Countries* and the OECD's new *Ageing Working Papers.*[3] The OECD's demographic statistics
(both historical and projections) are very similar to the UN's
historical and "medium variant" numbers, assuring a high
degree of consistency. And since they contain more detail
than the UN numbers and are perfectly integrated with the
fiscal projections I use (see below), they offer obvious advantages. The United States is sometimes an exception. When
the United States is included in or compared with other
developed countries, I stick with the OECD sources. But
when the special findings of U.S. official sources, such as the
Census Bureau or the Social Security Administration's
(SSA's) Office of the Actuary, are of particular interest,[4] I
draw from them as well.

Also appearing frequently in this book are government
fiscal numbers (current, historical, and projected; outlays,
revenues, indebtedness, and unfunded liabilities; total, by
level of government, by spending function, and by program;
public pension coverage and payroll tax rates). Figures for
governments in the developing countries are drawn either
from the excellent appendix to *Averting the Old Age Crisis,*
published by the World Bank,[5] or from specialized articles and
monographs. Most figures for governments in the developed

---

[3] Organization for Economic Cooperation and Development, *Ageing in OECD
Countries: A Critical Policy Challenge* (Social Policy Studies No. 20, 1996), and
*Ageing Working Papers: The OECD Horizontal Project on the Policy Implications of
Ageing* (OECD web site, 1998). See also from the OECD, *Maintaining Prosperity in
an Ageing Society* (1998), *Caring for Frail Elderly People: Policies in Evolution*
(Social Policy Studies No. 19, 1996), and *New Orientations for Social Policy* (Social
Policy Studies No. 12, 1994).

[4] See U.S. Census Bureau, *Population Projections of the United States by Age, Sex,
Race, and Hispanic Origin: 1995 to 2050* (Current Population Report P25–1130;
February 1996); and the Social Security Administration's Office of the Actuary,
Social Security Area Population Projections: 1996 (Actuarial Study No. 110; August
1996) and unpublished demographic data and lifetables.

[5] World Bank, *Averting the Old Age Crisis* (1994).

countries are drawn from OECD sources.[6] Only where OECD figures are unavailable (for example, the current and projected ratios of taxpaying workers to pension recipients) do I draw from other official sources (in this case, studies of the International Monetary Fund or IMF).[7] Again, the United States is sometimes an exception. When the United States is not being grouped with or compared to other developed countries, I sometimes draw on figures from the U.S. SSA and Health Care Financing Administration (HCFA).[8]

Naturally, in a book of this scope I have cited facts and figures from numerous other sources as well—from academic monographs and policy journals, from official government reports and commissions, from conference proceedings and trade and industry studies, and from the general and financial news media. My absorbing interest in this subject (some might say an obsession!) also led me to speak and correspond directly with several of the world's leading demographers, economists, and social scientists. Some of the more important or provocative findings from these sources are cited in footnotes to the text. The interested reader may also want to consult the bibliographies included in many of the footnoted sources. The useful literature is expanding rapidly as the magnitude of the global aging challenge becomes better known. Increasingly, the greatest obstacle to an effective response is not our lack of information—but our inability to acknowledge and act on the abundance of information at our disposal.

---

[6] For all of the major pension and health spending projections, see OECD, *Ageing in OECD Countries* (cited above). For calculations of unfunded public pension liabilities in the major developed countries, see OECD, *Pension Liabilities in the Seven Major Economies* (Economics Department Working Paper No. 142 by Paul Van den Noord and Richard Herd, 1993). See also OECD, *Future Global Capital Shortages: Real Threat or Pure Fiction* (1996); and *Public Pensions and Public Policy* (Social Policy Studies No. 9, 1992).

[7] See International Monetary Fund, *Aging Populations and Public Pension Schemes* (Occasional Paper 147 by Sheetal K. Chand and Albert Jaeger; December 1996).

[8] See especially *1998 Annual Reports of the Social Security and Medicare Trustees* (prepared by the Social Security Administration's Office of the Actuary and the Health Care Financing Administration, 1998).

Notes

2. IS DEMOGRAPHY DESTINY?

1. Allan Pfifer and Lydia Bronte (Eds.), *Our Aging Society* (1986).
2. The developed world in this book refers to the countries of Western Europe (Austria, Belgium, Denmark, Finland, France, Germany, Iceland, Ireland, Italy, Luxembourg, Netherlands, Norway, Portugal, Spain, Sweden, Switzerland, and the United Kingdom) plus Greece, the United States, Canada, Australia, New Zealand, and Japan. These 23 countries comprised the membership of the Organization of Economic Cooperation and Development (OECD) from 1973 to 1993—and are often referred to collectively and in a number of data sources as "the developed world."
3. Throughout this book, *elderly* refers to persons aged 65 and over. For the developed countries as a whole, following OECD practice, *working age* refers to persons aged 15–64, and *children* to persons aged 14 and under. For the United States, childhood is defined differently—as either persons under age 18 or under age 20. The 65-and-over definition of *elderly* does not, of course, imply that such people never work or should not work (nor that "working age" people always do work). To the contrary, I believe that the expectation of "work life" should be extended well beyond the age of 64 for most people (see Chapter 5)— and if this requires pushing up the age definition of the word "elderly," I'm all in favor of it. To isolate the impact of demographic aging on the rising fiscal cost of pensions, however, it's necessary to adopt age-bracket definitions that are fixed over time. That is the only reason I have adopted them here.
4. Note that today's average age (64) overestimates the actual average age of retirement, since 62 is the earliest age at which people can receive a Social Security retirement pension even though many people now retire well before age 62 (often on private pensions).
5. A *pay-as-you-go* pension system is one that raises funds from current (worker) contributions and pays these out more or less directly to current (retired) beneficiaries. In the developed world, nearly all nationwide public pension systems are pay-as-you-go. Officially, most of

these systems do accumulate trust-fund assets—either very minor ("reserve" or "contingency") amounts to handle temporary economic downturns or more substantial amounts in accordance with a "partial prefunding" strategy (followed, for example, by the U.S. Social Security system since 1983). In practice, however, these trust-fund surpluses are used to offset deficits elsewhere in government and thus do not constitute genuine economic funding. This is why most economists refer to all of these public systems as de facto pay-as-you-go. The opposite of a pay-as-you-go system is a *fully funded* system (the norm for most private pensions), in which sufficient external assets are accumulated to pay of the claims of all contributing workers to date. See further discussion in Chapters 4 and 5.

6. In the typical developed country, at least three-quarters of retired households depend on public pensions for at least half of their income. In every major developed country, at least half of retired households depend mainly on public pensions.

7. Gunhild Hagestad, "The Family: Women and Grandparents as Kin-Keepers," in Allan Pfifer and Lydia Bronte (Eds.), *Our Aging Society* (1986).

8. The 1935 figure refers to males alone, since the typical career worker was a man. (The average life expectancy of both sexes at age 65 in 1935 was 12.6) The 2040 figure refers to males and females combined. Thus, about 10 percent of the increase in retiree longevity at age 65 has been due to the changing sex composition of career workers.

9. Some do not agree. Leon Kass has written thoughtfully and passionately on the other side of the argument. "It is probably no accident that it is a generation whose intelligentsia proclaim the meaninglessness of life that embarks on its indefinite prolongation and that seeks to cure the emptiness of life by extending it. For the desire to prolong youthfulness is not only a childish desire to eat one's life and keep it, it is also an expression of a childish and narcissistic wish incompatible with devotion to posterity. It seeks an endless present isolated from anything truly eternal and severed from any true continuity with past and future. It is in principal hostile to children because children, those who come after, are those who will take one's place: they are life's answer to mortality and their presence in one's house is a constant reminder that one no longer belongs to the frontier generation. One cannot pursue youthfulness for oneself and remain faithful to the spirit and meaning of perpetuation." (See Leon Kass, *Toward a More Natural Science,* 1985.)

10. Nicholas Eberstadt (correspondence with the author).

11. Robert W. Fogel, "Can We Afford Longevity?" (annual address to alumni, Graduate School of Business, University of Chicago; 1998).

12. And the elderly as a whole, of course, already consume much more health care per capita than young adults. In 1995, the typical U.S. male age 80 and over consumed $16,256 in health care, thirteen times more than the typical U.S. male age 20–24 ($1,284). See Watson Wyatt Worldwide, *Providing Health Care for an Aging Population* (1996).

13. See American Council of Life Insurance, *Who Will Pay for the Baby Boomers' Long-Term Care Needs?* (1998).

14. The *total fertility rate* equals the number of children that a woman would bear if, over her lifetime, she bore them at every age at the same rate as all women currently do at every age. Demographers usually prefer it to the simple birth rate (children born per 1,000 persons or women), which can in any given year be pushed up or down by the age-distribution of women—for example, by a large cohort of women suddenly moving into or out of the prime child-bearing age bracket. The total fertility rate, because it is unaffected by the age-distribution, is considered a better indicator of underlying child-bearing behavior.

15. In the developing world, this acceptance was fostered by the dedicated efforts of many multilateral organizations. In the developed world, it has spread through nearly all social classes and religious faiths. In the United States, for example, the contraceptive behavior of American Roman Catholics was markedly transformed over this period: By 1975, with the exception of sterilization and abortion, it was no longer possible to distinguish between Catholic and non-Catholic birth control practices.

16. According to Michael S. Teitelbaum and Jay M. Winter, "fertility levels were also affected by a nearly universal trend toward liberalization of abortion laws in Western countries, beginning in the 1960s and accelerating in the 1970s. By the end of that decade, abortion was substantially legal in virtually every country in Western Europe and North America, and in 1978 abortion was legalized even in Italy despite the strenuous opposition of the Vatican." See Teitelbaum and Winter, *The Fear of Population Decline* (1985).

17. Demographers traditionally regard 2.1 as the *replacement rate* because, at this fertility rate, every 1,000 women will eventually give birth to 2,100 children. Of these children, the biology of human reproduction dictates that roughly 1020 will be born female. About 20 are needed (in modern societies) to replace those who don't survive through their childbearing years, which effectively leaves 1,000 women in the next generation to replace the 1,000 women in the original generation.

18. Many demographers believe the officially reported fertility rate for China is probably understated. The harsh penalties for violating government-imposed birth limits may lead to falsification and evasion.

19. As Jean Claude Chesnais, Director of Research at France's National Institute of the Study of Democracy recently lamented, "You cannot have a successful world without children in it."

20. More precisely, the U.S. total fertility rate fell from 3.7 in 1957 all the way to 1.7 in 1976, before rising back up to a steady 2.0 during the 1990s. The large dip and partial rebound do not entirely reflect changes in women's preference for lifetime births. They also reflect a new preference (mainly through later marriages among Boomer women) for bearing children at older ages. This showed up as a *temporary* downturn in the total fertility rate.

21. Antonio Golini, quoted by Ben Watternberg in "Beware the 'Bambino Bust,'" *USA Today* (April 17, 1997).

22. Japanese Ministry of Health and Welfare, "On the Basic Viewpoint Regarding the Trend Towards Fewer Children: A Society of Decreasing Population, Responsibilities and Choices for the Future" (1998).

23. See Wolfgang Lutz, Warren Sanderson, and Sergei Scherbov, "Doubling of World Population Unlikely," *Nature,* vol. 387 (June 19, 1997).

24. Sociologist Jack Goldstone reports that immigrants are most likely to maintain the family practices of their native culture when large surges of immigrants form self-contained communities within the host countries. These practices wane when immigration falls and the communities break up.

25. Of course, some childbearing by women past their late 30s will slightly reduce the ultimate fraction of boomer women who are childless.

26. Lutz, Sanderson, and Scherbov, *op. cit.*

27. The Census estimates are the mid-range (18 million) and high-range (31 million) Census projections published in February, 1996. The views of demographers Ronald Lee (21 million), James Vaupel (39 million), and Kenneth Manton (49 million) are discussed in the Report of the *1994–1995 Advisory Council on Social Security,* vol. 2 (1996).

28. See, however, Marvin Cetron and Owen Davies, *Cheating Death: The Promise and the Future Impact of Trying to Live Forever* (1998).

29. Nicholas Eberstadt, "World Population Implosion?" *The Public Interest* (Fall, 1997).

30. Stephen Rosen, professor of strategic studies, suggests that one cultural trend that might mitigate the long-term fertility decline is the growth of religious groups which encourage large families (notably, evangelical Christians, Mormons, Orthodox Jews, and Moslems). (Correspondence with the author.)

31. See Jay Olshansky, quoted in *USA Today* (July 23, 1992).

3. FISCAL REALITIES

1. To simplify the methodology, the OECD does *not* include many minor, regional, and sector-specific public pensions in its overall public-pension projections. Thus, the figures shown here understate the total fiscal burden, both today and tomorrow, and may therefore differ from official national figures reported elsewhere in this book. The OECD, for example, shows Italy's public pension spending at 13.3 percent of GDP in 1995; yet the official Italian figures show spending above 15 percent of GDP in every year since 1993.

2. The G-7 nations are the United States, Canada, Japan, United Kingdom, France, Germany, and Italy.

3. The Employee Retirement Income Security Act (ERISA), enacted in 1974, established the basic framework of federal regulations governing private pension plans in the United States. Under ERISA, employers are required to follow certain accounting standards in reporting the financial status of their defined benefit pension plans. Among these standards is the requirement that any unfunded benefit liability be amortized over 30 years—that is, written off as equal dollar losses against earnings over the next 30 years so that the present value of all the losses exactly offsets the liability.

4. David Hale, "Has America's Equity Market Boom Just Begun, or How the Rise of Pension Funds Will Change the Global Economy of the 21st Century" (condensed version appeared in *The Financial Times;* April 22, 1998).

5. This movement was in part a reaction against Japan's dictatorial efforts to increase its population during the 1930s and World War II. In one postwar survey, 80 percent of Japanese women opposed having the government orchestrate pronatalist programs.

6. Masahiro Yamada, quoted in "Japan's Baby Bust," *U.S. News & World Reports* (October 5, 1998).

7. Michiko Mukuno, Japanese Ministry of Health and Welfare, "A Society of Decreasing Population: Responsibilities and Choices for the Future" (1997).

8. It's not just that more Italian mothers are employed, but—as journalist Michael Specter points out—Italian husbands still expect their working spouses to make dinner in the evening and take complete charge of the family. "Women have responded by realizing that with only 24 hours in each day, something has to give. Children have become that something." See "Population Implosion Worries a Graying Europe," *New York Times* (July 10, 1998).

9. Massimo Liv-Bacci, quoted in "Population Implosion Worries a Graying Europe," *New York Times* (July 10, 1998).

10. Some economists now argue that dramatically rising equity prices mean that investors believe that business capital is becoming dramatically more productive. It could mean that. But it could also mean that investors believe any number of other things—for instance, that other investments are less desirable or that real interest rates are falling or that tax rates on investment income will soon be cut. And then again, investors could be wrong on all counts. It is worth noting that the 90s-era surge in U.S. equity prices has been accompanied by little if any acceleration in real GDP per work hour.

11. Victor Fuchs, quoted in "It's Not Just Social Security," *Business Week* (October 26, 1998).

12. According to the United Nations, the life expectancy today in the twenty-nine sub-Saharan African countries most affected by AIDS is seven years less (47.5 versus 54.1) than it would be without AIDS.

13. Middle-aged Russian males have shown the highest increase in mortality. According to a recent UNICEF report, about half of this increase is due to "an epidemic of heart and circulatory diseases." Most of the rest is due to "external causes," which include murder, suicide, accidental deaths, and environmental poisoning.

14. See "For One-Child Policy, China Rethinks Iron Hand" (*New York Times;* November 1, 1998). While mainly focusing on how the Chinese are trying to enforce this one-child policy more humanely, the article also notes, "In 1997, only 39 percent of women who underwent tubal ligation had counseling before surgery, according to the Family Planning Commission."

15. Nicholas Eberstadt, "China's Population Prospects: Problems Ahead" (forthcoming, 1998).

16. Lin Ying, "The Aging of the Population: A Severe Challenge," *Guangming Ribao* (April 6, 1996).

17. It is true that the official one-child policy makes an exception for (mainly rural) ethnic minorities and for rural parents whose first child is a daughter. It is unclear, however, how often this exception is allowed.

18. Even so, by the year 2025, at least one-quarter of China's elderly will have no living sons. According to Eberstadt, these elders "could find themselves in the unenviable position of depending on the largesse of their son-in-law's household—or even worse, competing for family resources against their son-in-law's own blood parents." Eberstadt (1998), *op. cit.*

19. *Ibid.*

4. NO EASY CHOICES

1. It's worth noting that, like raising the fertility rate, boosting immigration permanently reduces the future retirement burden only if the higher immigration rate is also permanent. A one-time immigration surge will reduce the burden in the near term—but increase it in the long term when today's extra workers become tomorrow's extra retirees.

2. The transition cost is also known as an "unfunded liability." For Social Security alone, it amounts to about $8 trillion. According to the Federal Accounting Standards Advisory Board, a program's unfunded liability is a "rough estimate of the maximum transition cost of the program if it were to move from the present pay-as-you-go system to one that, like most pensions plans, sets aside resources during workers' careers to finance the benefits they will receive after they retire."

3. According to the Pension Benefit Guaranty Corporation, the total unfunded liability of underfunded U.S. private pension plans was $63.7 billion at the beginning of 1996.

4. For an interesting discussion of the issues raised by government investment in the stock market, see Carolyn L. Weaver, *How Not to Reform Social Security* (American Enterprise Institute; August 1998).

5. Some might object that this isn't true for small nations whose debt is widely purchased and traded in global financial markets. For such nations, they say, many or most of the bond-owning losers will be foreigners while all of the stock-owning winners will be native citizens. But here again there's a fatal catch. These are also the nations that will pay the biggest penalty for financial wizardry, such as issuing bonds backed by stocks, that injures their global reputation for fiscal prudence. That penalty will take the form of a hike in the interest rate (again, a risk premium) exacted by savvy global investors.

6. Fred Bergsten, Director of the Institute for International Economics, makes another (half ironical) suggestion: "If governments really get serious about maximizing yields on their own investments to pay aging costs, perhaps one serious step is to sell all their gold reserves. The United States is holding a huge stock (about $100 billion at current market prices) that earns nothing." (Correspondence with the author.)

7. Victor Fuchs, "Provide, Provide: The Economics of Aging," in Thomas R. Saving and Andrew Rattenmaier (Eds.), *Medicare Reform: Issues and Answers* (forthcoming).

8. William Schwartz, cited in Hilary Stout, "Delicate Decisions: Clinton's Health Plan Must Face Huge Costs of a Person's Last Days," *The Wall Street Journal* (April 22, 1993). This is not to deny, of course, that some future technologies (e.g., an AIDS vaccine) may reduce costs.

Historically, however, technologies have usually raised costs—by vastly increasing the capital and skilled labor that can be effectively used in treating any condition, especially when the treatment does not effect a cure, and by keeping alive costly "marginal survivors" who earlier would have died.

9. Even so, HCFA estimates that Medicare costs will rise from 2.7 percent of GDP today to 5.9 percent of GDP by 2030. Compare this to projections run by researchers at the employee-benefits firm of Watson Wyatt Worldwide, who assume that future per-capita cost growth will be closer to historical experience. These projections show Medicare costs rising to just over 14 percent of GDP by 2030. See Watson Wyatt Worldwide, *op. cit.*

10. John Shoven (correspondence with the author).

11. Richard Leone, "Don't Worry, Generation X," *Washington Post* (April 30, 1996).

12. Economist Richard Posner, in *Aging and Old Age* (1996), takes this argument a step further by including all nonemployed persons as "dependents." Calculated this way, the decline in the total dependency ratio since 1960 has been even more dramatic, due to the massive shift of women from homemaking into paid employment. But Posner's view is based on an obviously questionable assumption—that you have to be paid in the marketplace to be a full social and economic contributor.

13. International Monetary Funds, "World Public Debt and Real Interest Rates" (IMF Working Paper by R. Ford and D. Laxton, 1995).

14. Organization for Economic Cooperation and Development, "Globalization and Linkages" (Economics Department, Working Paper No. 181, edited by Pete Richardson, 1997).

15. This is true for all nationwide systems. For public systems covering special groups of workers, there are exceptions. U.S. state and local pension plans, for example are mostly funded. They hold over $3 trillion in trust-fund assets and are typically forbidden to invest in debt issued by the same governments that manage them.

16. There are actually two kinds of double-counting, both of them fallacious. The first is to count all surplus revenue into the trust fund as an addition to trust-fund assets, and then, after the general budget borrows it, to count it again as unborrowed income to the general budget (because it is not borrowed from the public). The second is to count interest income into the trust fund as an addition to trust-fund assets—since, although the general budget pays this interest, it again borrows the money back and spends it for other purposes.

17. John Hambor, "Economic Policy, Intergenerational Equity, and the Social Security Trust Fund Build-Up," *Social Security Bulletin* (October, 1987).

18. The 30 to 60 percent range refers to the payroll tax rate on wages *excluding* employer contributions. This "net wage" method of computing tax rates is often used by government agencies, including the U.S. Social Security Administration. Alternatively, payroll tax rates can be measured as a percent of wages *including* employer contributions. This "gross wage" method generates a lower figure—much lower in the case of some countries (such as France) where employer contributions exceed one-quarter of the total or "gross" wage bill.

19. Such large hikes may come as a surprise to some U.S. readers who have seen news reports that a payroll tax hike of a "mere" 2.2 percent would "balance" Social Security for the next 75 years. This figure is highly misleading, however, since it assumes that trust-fund "assets" accumulated in past years (plus interest-earning cash "surpluses" expected in the near-term future) will offset widening operating deficits after the age wave hits in earnest. In 1998, although Social Security is projected to start running an operating deficit in 2013, its accumulated assets are projected to keep the system solvent for 19 more years—until 2032. If a 2.2 percent tax hike were immediately enacted, the operating deficit date would be delayed only 9 years (until 2021), but the insolvency date would be postponed for over 40 more years—to just beyond 2073, which currently marks the time horizon of the system's official definition of "actuarial balance."

There is, unfortunately, no basis to the fantastic notion that Social Security will be able to run widening cash deficits for nearly half a century without putting any burden on the federal budget or the U.S. economy. As I've already explained, trust-fund assets cannot be redeemed without either issuing public debt, cutting other spending, or raising taxes. The proper measure of Social Security's future burden is its projected annual operating balance—that is, tax revenues minus outlays—which by 2035 is expected to reach 5.0 percent of payroll under official "intermediate" assumptions and 8.7 percent of payroll under an alternative "high-cost" scenario (which more faithfully reflects recent economic and demographic trends). And this leaves out health care, which in the United States constitutes most of the cost challenge. Add in the projected cost growth in both parts of Medicare, and the total *extra* cost burden for 2035 climbs to 12.9 or 29.8 percent of payroll, respectively.

Beyond its reliance on trust-fund accounting, the 2.2 percent actuarial balance measure has two other flaws as well. First, it is meaningful only if we can imagine that the payroll tax could be hiked by the full amount beginning in 1998—something that obviously cannot happen. To the extent the hike is delayed, the total savings needed to keep Social Security technically solvent will rise. Second, assuming that the actuaries' official projection period remains 75 years, the 2.2 percent hike would only be a temporary solution. We would have to raise taxes by an additional slice of payroll in each future year as yet another distant deficit creeps within the actuaries' time horizon.

20. Leaders are also reluctant to raise payroll taxes for obvious political reasons. In the United States, to choose an illustrative example, roughly three-quarters of all workers pay more in combined (employer and employee) payroll taxes than in total personal income taxes. Payroll tax hikes will thus fall most heavily on middle class voters—the same voters who are repeatedly told by leaders that they deserve a tax cut.

21. Economists Larry Kotlikoff and Willi Leibfritz summarize their recent findings as follows: "Leaving current Americans untouched and maintaining the current projected time-path of government purchases will leave future Americans collectively facing roughly 50 percent higher net tax rates over their lifetimes than those confronting a newborn American based on current U.S. tax-transfer policy. For future Germans, the imbalance, if not rectified, means they would face lifetime net tax rates that are roughly twice as high as those now in place. And for future Japanese, policy inaction means lifetime net tax rates that are more than 2.5 times as high as current values." See Laurence J. Kotlikoff and Willi Leibfritz, "An International Comparison of Generational Accounts" (NBER Working Paper 6447; March 1998).

22. Craig Karpel, *The Retirement Myth* (1995)

5. NEW STRATEGIES

1. See Jonathan Gruber and David Wise, "Social Security Programs and Retirement around the World" (American Enterprise Institute; May 1988).

2. When one looks only at the actuarial adjustment to annual benefits, some countries, including Japan and the United States, appear to impose no penalty on later-retiring workers. When one includes lifetime payroll taxes in the calculation, however, even these countries offer a considerable incentive to early retirement. U.S. Social Security expert Eugene Steuerle explains: "The current OASI system does indeed tend to treat people better the earlier they retire. This is generally true regardless of income level or gender. Incentives for retiring early (or penalties for delaying retirement) are particularly strong for men with average or high lifetime wages." See Steuerle, *Retooling Social Security for the 21st Century* (1994).

3. One recent analysis of fifteen countries across several decades finds a very strong statistical correlation between the rising generosity of

"non-employment" public benefits to males aged 55 to 64 and the declining labor force participation of that age group. See Sveinbjörn Bindel and Stefano Scarpetta, "The Retirement Decision in OECD Countries" (OECD Aging Working Paper 1.4, 1998).

4. Sylvester Schieber (correspondence with the author).

5. Medicare's "secondary payor" provision for workers aged 65 and over saved the U.S. government an estimated $1.5 billion in 1995—but at the cost (which cannot be estimated) of making elder workers considerably less employable.

6. Studies show that, in most developed countries, health problems rarely rank very high in the reasons why some workers retire earlier than others. In the United States, among workers who retired in 1993 and 1994, workers retiring at age 62 (the minimum age for collecting a Social Security pension) were no more likely than later retirees to be in "poor health." Also, they were just as wealthy and much more likely to be eligible for a private employer pension. Only one-quarter reported *any* health condition that affected their ability to work.

7. Specifically, I have proposed raising the U.S. retirement age 3 months per year for 20 years until it reaches age 70. No country has yet indexed the retirement age to longevity. In its 1998 pension reform, Sweden did introduce a longevity index in order to stabilize long-term pension costs as a share of its economy. This longevity index, however, is not used to adjust the future retirement age, but rather to "actuarially adjust" future benefit levels.

8. As Michael Teitelbaum observes, "Immigration of a magnitude sufficient to offset very low fertility rates seems unlikely to be politically viable in most settings, unless the immigrant streams are socially perceived as 'part of' or 'similar to' the indigenous population. Examples include the postwar migrations of East Germans to West Germany, of the *pieds noirs* to France, of oriental Jews to Israel, of Italians to Argentina, and of Angolan colonials to Portugal. More moderate levels of immigration, however, do appear to be sustainable; the resulting pace of demographic change is slower, and can be accompanied by gradual changes in the relevant social definitions that facilitate public acceptance of immigration." See "Consequences of Sustained Below-Replacement Fertility," paper presented at Expert Group Meeting on Below-Replacement Fertility (November 1997).

9. No one can be certain, of course, how long this higher level of fertility will last. Sweden's fertility rate, for example, rose from 1.68 to 2.14 during the 1980s—but since 1992 it has been falling rapidly. In 1996, the last year for we have official data, it was 1.61, and many experts today believe it has since fallen to somewhere between 1.5 and 1.6. If this decline continues for another few years, Sweden's

margin will disappear. It is worth noting, however, that this recent decline has coincided with cuts in child-benefit levels due to fiscal austerity and with rapidly rising unemployment among young adults (who lose both their primary source of income and their access to employer-related child benefits). Parental leave benefits, which were pegged at 90 percent of earnings in the early 1990s, were cut to 80 percent in 1995 and to 75 percent in 1996.

10. This is an especially troubling issue in societies in which there are relatively large social divisions along racial or class lines—or (as is now common in the developed world) the young are much more ethnically diverse than the old. Such societies may be less likely to acknowledge a common purpose in raising the next generation or to perceive that "other kids" are really our kids too.

11. Burggraf explains the rationale behind her "parental dividend" proposal by imagining the following newspaper ad: "WANTED: Parents willing to bear, rear, and educate children for the next generation of Social Security taxpayers and to carry on the modern culture of learning and progress. Quality parenting preferred. Large commitments of time and money required. At least one parent must be willing to work a double shift and/or sacrifice tenure and upward mobility in the labor market. Salary: 0. Pension benefits: 0. Profits and dividends: 0." See Shirley P. Burggraf, *The Feminine Economy and Economic Man* (1997).

12. In 1990, according to the Congressional Budget Office, among households receiving retirement-related benefits (Social Security, Medicare, Medicaid, veterans benefits, and federal pensions), those in the over-$150,000 bracket received $15,738 in annual federal benefits—while those in the under-$10,000 bracket received just $6,027. Even averaged over all U.S. households (whether receiving benefits or not), there was no noticeable tilt toward the poor. All households with incomes under $10,000 received an average of $4,100 in retirement-related benefits, while all households with incomes over $75,000 received an average of $4,300 in these benefits.

13. World Bank, *Averting the Old Age Crisis* (1994).

14. Congressional Budget Office, *Reducing Entitlement Spending* (September, 1994).

15. Today, provident funds are used in some twenty countries (mostly former British colonies). Workers make mandatory payroll contributions into personally owned accounts, which are managed as a group by central government authorities. Provident funds offer workers the security of ownership, but typically pay back much less than the market return. Administrative costs are often high, and investment choices are often politically motivated. (In the wake of the Asian financial

crisis, for example, many provident funds are being pressured to bail out bankrupt firms.) Indeed, in many countries where funds are invested largely or exclusively in state-owned enterprises, real returns have been sharply negative.

16. This public pension reform, enacted in 1998, will replace Sweden's old basic and supplemental pension programs with a new benefit package consisting of a pay-as-you-go "notional account" (costing 16 percent of worker payroll) plus a mandatory 2.5 percent funded personal account. The notional account is a defined-contribution pension in which the benefit payout is strictly determined by the total accumulation of worker and employer contributions plus interest. Since it is unfunded, however, the applicable interest rate is not the market rate of return to capital—but rather an index that reflects average income growth in the economy.

17. To be fair, a comparison of pension reform in Britain and the United States must take institutional differences into account. The wage-related SERPS program, which was founded in 1975 and began operating in 1978 (just a year before Thatcher became Prime Minister), constituted a recent addition to Britain's welfare state. As such, it had not yet acquired the deep-rooted political and popular constituency enjoyed by Britain's Basic State Pension (whose origins go back to 1908). In the United States, which has no equivalent to SERPS, wage-related benefits and low-income subsidies have always been included in the same (Social Security) program.

18. José Pinera, architect of the Chilean system and Labor Minister at the time, made a special contribution to its acceptance by speaking directly to workers through regular television broadcasts. He stressed that the extra savings and investment generated by this system would lead to more growth in the economy, higher wages, and greater job security.

19. Paul Samuelson, in *Newsweek* (February 13, 1967).

20. "Security in Retirement," in *Road to the Manifesto* (London: Labor Party, 1996), cited in Louis Enoff and Robert Moffit, *Social Security Privatization in Britain: Key Lessons for America's Reformers* (Heritage Foundation; August 1997).

21. Cited in "UK Private Pensions Form Cautionary Tale About People's Choice," *The Wall Street Journal* (August 11, 1998).

22. It is particularly important to keep administrative costs and management fees to a minimum. This can be facilitated by having the government offer several "default" investment funds to all workers who are either unable or unwilling to deal with a private financial manager. These funds, consisting of large and efficient indexed portfolios administered by an independent oversight board, would have very low administrative costs and thus be very competitive with any private fund.

23. See Jeremy J. Siegel, *Stocks for the Long Run* (1994).

24. Personal ownership does pose a challenging design issue: How would a system of personal accounts prevent people from taking "their" money and investing it as they wish and spending it when they please—even long before retirement? The legal problem can be surmounted through regulation and (in English-speaking countries) by such common-law devices as trusteeship. The political problem is more troublesome, starting with families who face "exceptional" emergencies and want access to the money they "own." As such exceptions multiply, they could unravel the system. This issue doesn't arise in pay-as-you-go systems offering defined benefits, in which citizens understand that they have no claim of ownership over the contributions they have paid in—and that their promised benefits are always subject to legislative modification.

25. Affordability refers not just to the minimum cost of raising children, but also to the rising cost that society expects parents to incur on behalf of their children—together with the rising "opportunity cost" of full-time motherhood for women (who now receive 55 percent of college BAs awarded annually in the United States) in terms of the income they forego in the labor market. Demographer Andrew Hacker has pointed out to me that the rising level of education and earnings of women relative to men is a major reason for the rapid decline in fertility (and rapid rise in "spinsterhood") among African-Americans.

6. ASKING THE RIGHT QUESTIONS

1. On September 30, 1998, Levi Strauss announced plans to close four factories in Europe. *The Financial Times* reported that "Levi Strauss said European demand had been hit by a declining European youth population—set to fall 5 percent by 2005."

2. I am grateful to Gary D. Keith, Vice President of the Manufacturers and Traders Trust Company of Buffalo, New York, who alerted me to these numbers.

3. Gary Hufbauer (correspondence with the author).

4. The U.S. Navy, for example, is now designing a new class of destroyers that require crews only one-quarter of their current size. Its decision to mothball old battleships, which require very large crews, was largely based on the imperative to save on personnel.

5. Stephen Rosen (correspondence with the author).

6. Many leading economists in fact predict that rapid demographic aging in the developed countries, while reducing their household savings, will reduce their need for investment even more—where need is defined as the investment necessary to maintain an unchanged growth

in the capital-to-labor ratio. Thus, an aging society can get by with a lower private-sector savings rate. All this assumes, heroically, that the public-sector balance does not worsen. See, for example, David M. Cutler, James M. Poterba, Louise M. Sheiner, and Lawrence Summers, "An Aging Society: Opportunity or Challenge?" (*Brookings Papers on Economic Activity*, 1990:1).

7. This by no means applies to all or even most activities. The optimal scale of a firm is often smaller than the limits placed on it by the size of its relevant market—which, in today's global economy, is itself often not limited to a single nation. Nonetheless, there are many important (often quasi-public) undertakings whose optimal scale, for reasons of geography and politics, is the nation state.

8. The most dramatic evidence of such a backlash is the strenuous efforts of both U.S. political parties in 1998 to fashion legislation ensuring "quality care" in HMOs. Interestingly, the backlash is much less conspicuous in opinion polls, which show (as of late 1997) that 88 percent of HMO patients are "satisfied with quality"—versus 92 percent of traditional plan patients. This slim margin in favor of traditional plans is dwarfed by the HMO advantage in cost: The same polls show that 79 percent of HMO patients are "satisfied with costs"—versus 65 percent of traditional plan patients.

9. The U.S. experience may be a leading indicator. On July 3, 1998, the U.S. Health Care Financing Administration issued a directive instructing that Viagra must be included as a covered prescription drug under the joint federal-state Medicaid program.

10. Kaiser Family Foundation and Harvard School of Public Health, *The Kaiser/Harvard National Survey on Medicare: The Next Big Health Policy Debate* (October 20, 1998).

11. Drew Altman, quoted in press release to *ibid.*

12. According to Sylvester Schieber, "Ironically, thirty years from now it will be these grown children who will be burdened not only with caring for their own parents, but financing the care for the self-centered childless elderly who will continue to demand that they get their fair share in old-age." (Correspondence with the author.)

13. See Wirthlin Worldwide, "Ending the Season: Lessons from 1996," The Wirthlin Quorum (December, 1996).

14. AARP has the most powerful reputation. But like any large national organization serving a diverse constituency, AARP's official positions do not of course reflect the views of many members. Recently, I questioned a large group of AARP members about their reasons for membership. Very few mentioned any specific political agenda. Virtually all mentioned a number of cost-saving perquisites (such as discounts on travel, drugs, and insurance).

15. Samuel H. Preston, "Children and the Elderly: Divergent Paths for America's Dependents" (Presidential Address at the Annual Meeting of the Population Association of America; published in *Demography;* November 1984).

16. Part of this tone may be a general slowing down of the pace of social life. As Andrew Hacker observes, "Have you noticed how much longer it takes New York City buses to get going, since elderly passengers take so much longer boarding and leaving? Or the wait at your bank and post office, when the aged person at the window doesn't understand what she's being told? Plus having more seventy- and eighty-something drivers on our streets and roads." (Correspondence with the author.)

17. Frank Holloway, *Born to Rebel: Radical Thinking in Science and Social Thought* (1997).

18. Alfred Sauvy, cited in Ben J. Wattenberg, *The Birth Dearth* (1987).

19. Many economists suggest that the recent Asian crisis, by suddenly cutting short a large capital inflow to the developing world, may in retrospect mark a historic turning point. When the emerging economies of Southeast Asia start growing again, they may do so as net capital exporters to the developed world—a status they may retain for decades thereafter. Indeed, much of today's "excess global imports" (as reflected in the IMF's negative grand total for all of the world's current accounts) is probably generated by these economies. In this respect, some argue that the current crisis, over the long term, might be a helpful development since it may discourage a number of developing countries from relying on private capital inflows and thus may reduce their use of the developed world's increasingly limited savings.

20. The *capital surplus,* which equals the current account surplus plus foreign direct investment, represents the funds available for the net acquisition of foreign securities.

21. International Monetary Fund, "Are Europe's Social Security Finances Compatible with EMU?" (IMF Paper on Policy Analysis and Assessment, by George Kopitis; February 1997).

22. Beggar-thy-neighbor policies, when they trigger political retaliation, can lead to their own vicious cycle of imploding world trade—as they did between early 1929 and early 1933, when global trade fell (in U.S. dollar terms) by two-thirds.

23. Samuel P. Huntington, *The Clash of Civilizations and the Remaking of the World Order* (1996).

7. TOWARD GLOBAL SOLUTIONS TO A GLOBAL PROBLEM: AN OPEN LETTER

1. This group of developed and developing nations was convened on April 16, 1998 at the suggestion of U.S. Treasury Secretary Robert Rubin, who serves as Chairman of the group. At its first meeting, it examined issues related to "the stability of the international financial system and effective functioning of global capital markets." This group has met on several occasions since its first meeting, most recently at the end of July of 1998.

Index